Language in the Academy

LANGUAGES FOR INTERCULTURAL COMMUNICATION AND EDUCATION

Series Editor: Michael Byram, *University of Durham, UK* and Alison Phipps, *University of Glasgow, UK*

The overall aim of this series is to publish books which will ultimately inform learning and teaching, but whose primary focus is on the analysis of intercultural relationships, whether in textual form or in people's experience. There will also be books which deal directly with pedagogy, with the relationships between language learning and cultural learning, between processes inside the classroom and beyond. They will all have in common a concern with the relationship between language and culture, and the development of intercultural communicative competence.

Full details of all the books in this series and of all our other publications can be found on http://www.multilingual-matters.com, or by writing to Multilingual Matters, St Nicholas House, 31-34 High Street, Bristol BS1 2AW, UK.

LANGUAGES FOR INTERCULTURAL COMMUNICATION AND EDUCATION
Series Editor: Michael Byram, University of Durham, UK
and Alison Phipps, University of Glasgow, UK

Language in the Academy
Cultural Reflexivity and Intercultural Dynamics

Joan Turner

MULTILINGUAL MATTERS
Bristol • Buffalo • Toronto

Library of Congress Cataloging in Publication Data
A catalog record for this book is available from the Library of Congress.
Turner, Joan
Language in the Academy: Cultural Reflexivity and Intercultural Dynamics/
Joan Turner.
Languages for Intercultural Communication and Education: 20
Includes bibliographical references.
1. English language--Rhetoric--Study and teaching--Great Britain. 2. Academic
writing--Study and teaching--Great Britain. 3. College students--Great Britain--Social
conditions. 4. College students--Great Britain--Language. I. Title.
PE1405.G7T87 2010
808′.042071141--dc22   2010041288

British Library Cataloguing in Publication Data
A catalogue entry for this book is available from the British Library.

ISBN-13: 978-1-84769-322-8 (hbk)
ISBN-13: 978-1-84769-321-1 (pbk)

Multilingual Matters
UK: St Nicholas House, 31–34 High Street, Bristol, BS1 2AW, UK.
USA: UTP, 2250 Military Road, Tonawanda, NY 14150, USA.
Canada: UTP, 5201 Dufferin Street, North York, Ontario, M3H 5T8, Canada.

The policy of Multilingual Matters/Channel View Publications is to use papers
that are natural, renewable and recyclable products, made from wood grown in
sustainable forests. In the manufacturing process of our books, and to further
support our policy, preference is given to printers that have FSC and PEFC Chain
of Custody certification. The FSC and/or PEFC logos will appear on those books
where full certification has been granted to the printer concerned.

Typeset by Techset Composition Ltd., Salisbury, UK.
Printed and bound in Great Britain by Short Run Press Ltd.

Contents

Chapter 1
General Overview

Introduction

This book foregrounds language as a central rather than a peripheral player in the work of higher education. The empirical reality of language, its materiality, its uses in academic performance, its importance in intercultural communication and the cultural values associated with it, and performance in it, all play an important role in contemporary higher education in the United Kingdom. As such institutions have become increasingly international in recent years, the experiential reality of intercultural communication has reached larger numbers of students and staff. This has not always, however, been accompanied by richer ways of interpreting what is actually going on in many of the varied kinds of intercultural encounters that occur. It is one of the aims of the book to illustrate some of that variation and make the interpretative possibilities more widely available. This includes analyses of intercultural encounters between tutors and students, of student perceptions of those encounters, as well as the cultural background values that have motivated the linguistic behaviour or subject positions of those involved, along with discussion of frequently foregrounded topics of intercultural concern such as silence, being critical, individualist opinion giving or speaking in relation to group orientation. The empirical reality of intercultural communication, given its increasing presence in contemporary higher education is also seen as an important driver of change, even if unplanned, in the pedagogic practices of higher education.

A further important aim of the book is to frame language in the contemporary academy as an object of cultural theory. This is to some extent a counterfoil to the perception of language as a superficial practical concern. While the relentlessly practical nature of language work is not denied, and indeed seen in need of more positive evaluation, the fact that its issues circulate predominantly within a deficit discourse is subjected to critique. Reasons for the ready availability of this discourse are sought in intellectual cultural history, in particular in relation to how attitudes to knowledge developed through the scientific revolution and the European Enlightenment effectively made language invisible. This invisibilising process is theorised in Chapter 5 through what I have called 'occidentalist inscription'. The rhetorical values which have been formed in relation to this inscription, the rhetorical norms which have been set up, the evaluative metalanguage which corresponds to the rhetorical norms in the assessment of student writing and the rhetorical subject positions which academic writers are normatively obliged to take up are the focus of Chapters 5 and 6. The rhetorical norms are seen as part of wider cultural practices and the effects of social and political power, rather than as an independent codification of rules which must be adhered to.

Addressing the Institutional Interface between Language and Higher Education

From a pedagogical perspective, as those of us who work as language teachers of one sort or another in higher education will know, the empirical reality of language and intercultural communication lends a relentless practicality to the issues that need addressing. It is, however, also the case that such practical issues affecting pedagogy and curriculum in the different contexts of teaching and learning language or languages have already been prolifically identified and addressed in a wide range of publications, Byram (2004), Byram and Grundy (2003), Celce-Murcia (2001), Kramsch (1993), Nunan (1998) and Tudor (2001), to name but a few, as well as in journals too numerous to mention. While those practical and pedagogic issues of language, language teaching and learning have developed their own professional spaces, the institutional interface between language and higher education remains a neglected area. It is a major aim of this book then to address, and redress, this neglect.

Furthermore, while the ways students are expected to perform through language in higher education has been the focus of pedagogy and curriculum design in English for Academic Purposes (EAP), the cultural values inscribed in those expectations have themselves received little attention. For example, the question of why we evaluate academic writing in the way that we do is not often asked. The focus is rather on teaching its pedagogical genres and their rhetorical norms as if given. This is another unexplored topic, which the book takes on. It does this with historical reflexivity, locating specific sites in intellectual cultural history where conceptualisations of language were generated, which continue to hold sway, if only implicitly, in the institutional context of contemporary higher education. Furthermore, the preferred ways in which language is used in pedagogic academic contexts are seen as linguistic and rhetorical inscriptions of cultural values that have gained power, at specific moments, or over the course of intellectual history.

In putting the interface between language and higher education in the frame for cultural-theoretical research, the book constitutes an intellectual effort to make the workings of western academic culture, as it relates to how language is used and evaluated in higher education pedagogy and assessment, available to critical reflection and transformation. This is in marked contrast to the prevailing institutional discourse, whereby discussion of language issues circulates in a deficit discourse, and language work is marginalised.

Re-configuring Marginalisation

The teaching of EAP, or academic writing/academic literacy, as well as that of modern foreign languages, is routinely sidelined in the institutional discourse of higher education. All such pedagogic practices, whilst they have their own strong professional backgrounds, are, in institutional terms, seen as less important 'services' rather than as being of substantive academic merit in their own right. To foreground them at all then becomes a matter of institutional politics. In a small way, it disrupts the language/content dichotomy that has grown up around language and languages. As has been shown in post-structuralist theorising, notably in Derridean deconstruction, dichotomies privilege one pole over the other (Culler, 1982; Derrida, 1974, 1978; Norris, 1982). In the case of the language/content dichotomy, it is invariably language that is less privileged. As Carter and Nash have put it in relation to courses in literature and media studies, they 'look *past* language' (Carter & Nash, 1990: 24) in order to focus on what is considered more 'important', namely ideas or content. This same privileging of literature over language, in relation to how its teaching is perceived, is also referred to by Kramsch, who states:

> Teaching language is consistently viewed as a less sophisticated, hence less difficult, task than teaching literature. (Kramsch, 1993: 7)

The position of language at the negative pole of the dichotomy with 'content' is manifested also in the relentlessly remedial representation of language issues in the institutional discourse of higher education, as discussed further in the following chapter. The book therefore aims to refigure this representation, to critique the widely circulating deficit discourse for language, along with the dominant representations and conceptualisations of language that have promoted it.

A major argument is that the role of language, and the concomitant performances of languaging, along with what I call the languaging pedagogies, are underestimated, undervalued and marginalised in the institutional discourse of higher education, and this marginalisation needs to be conceptually and discursively rewritten. It is my hope that this book will make a contribution to that rewriting.

In re-focusing the role of language in higher education as a central player, the book mirrors conceptually a major focus of post-colonial studies, that is, making what has been peripheral, central. It is therefore an important aim of the book to rewrite this ancillary position of language in relation to knowledge, to re-inscribe language into the complex process of knowledge production and reproduction, to recognise the constitutive nature of language, and to acknowledge the integral role of language in academic performance. Language plays a role in every discipline, not only in their textualisations but also in how they are taught and assessed. It is imbricated in epistemological shifts and theoretical frameworks. It plays a role as carrier of the past and mediator of future discourses.

Ultimately, not only language-related pedagogies but also the pedagogic practices of higher education itself, such as the seminar and the lecture, alongside assessment tasks such as the essay and other genres of academic writing are quintessentially language or languaging practices. They can all be seen through the lens of language.

The Conceptual Construction of Language in Western Intellectual Cultural History

In focusing on language in the academy, the book is informed by dual perspectives. One looks backwards, considering how we have got to where we are now, and the other looks at the transformative potential of the contemporary context, and assumes a forward-moving dynamic whose future is unpredictable. In the first case, it is seen as important not only to critique the marginalisation of language and the ubiquity of its association with remediation but also to explore why such marginalising discourses for the role of language are so readily available. The question is addressed to 'western' intellectual cultural history, the ground on which conceptualisations of language in the contemporary academy were grown, and where contemporary attitudes towards language, and representations of language issues were formed. It is also the ground on which the rhetorical roots of ways of using language in the academy, especially in an Anglophone, 'western', institutional context, were planted. Conceptualisations of language which have taken hold socially and culturally, and therefore circulate widely, along with preferred ways of using language, which continue to be maintained are seen as the effects of culturally embedded power.

Chapters 5 and 6 look at how in relation to what might be encapsulated as the European Enlightenment project of the search for truth and knowledge, language became subsidiary, indeed one could say, subservient to knowledge. What was considered to be culturally important was, on the one hand, the scientific method(s) by which knowledge was to be determined, and on the other, the means whereby knowledge was communicated. The correct exercise of reason and the careful transmission of knowledge were the sociopolitical and intellectual–cultural watchwords of the scientists or natural philosophers who were vying with each other to find out how things worked or to come up with better means of doing so. A flavour of this scientific and social ethos in the 17th and early 18th centuries can be absorbed in the 17th century documentation of the transactions of the Royal Society (Sprat, 1958 [1667]) or in Jardine's more recent account of the times in *Ingenious Pursuits* (Jardine, 1999).

While the use of language was necessarily implicated in those scientific and knowledge-producing activities, it was focused on more as an obstacle that was to be overcome, or a medium that was to be moulded into a particular shape. What was primarily at stake was the communication of knowledge or the manifestation of correct reasoning. Locke's (1975 [1689]) conduit metaphor for language and Bishop Wilkins' 1668 (1968 [1668]) notion of a *Real Character and a Philosophical Language*, as well as the German philosopher Leibniz's vision of a *characteristica universalis* or universal character were conceived of as different ways of keeping the channels of communication clear. One meant fashioning language in a scientific manner without the distortions of how language was used in everyday interaction, and the other meant eschewing language altogether in favour of an artificial notation, based on mathematics.

Making Language Invisible in the Visibilising Economy of Rationality and Knowledge

What constituted knowledge had to be 'clear and distinct' to use a well-known Cartesian trope, although as with philosophical rationalism generally, it was in the mind's eye that analytical or conceptual categories, not to mention the steps of logical deduction were to be 'clear and distinct'. Empirical science, on the other hand, as promoted particularly in England at this period, through the auspices of the Royal Society, encouraged direct observation and experimentation that made processes visible. Both of these modes of working, one theoretical and the other empirical, may be seen as visibilising procedures. They were concerned to make knowledge visible.

What is particularly striking about this visibilising economy of rationality and knowledge, however, is the paradox it creates whereby language itself is made invisible. It was important that the means of communicating should not itself tarnish the object of communication. Such a construal of invisibility for language persists and complicates, or even obscures, ways of promoting a more positive discussion around language issues in the academy. Language use is only marked when it is perceived as being faulty, and unmarked when the message is apparently clearly delivered (Turner, 1999a, 1999b, 1999c). In this way the deficit discourse is maintained.

The Rhetorical Values of Academic Writing as an Effect of Power/Knowledge

A major emphasis throughout the book is the point that preferred ways of using language are interrelated with wider cultural processes. The social and cultural power accruing to scientific rationality in the wake of its success in the European political, cultural and economic ethos of the time meant that its scientists' preferred ways of using language, in effect the inscription of the values of their scientific culture, became rhetorical values. Those values are now the taken-for-granted rhetorical norms deemed appropriate for academic writing.

In other words, the values of clarity, the making visible of things or ideas and logic, where its steps are clearly marked, are interlinked with epistemology and cultural politics at the time when European scientific rationality was being established. Its success and power had wider social, political and, as is foregrounded here, rhetorical effects. These rhetorical effects were not the result of a mechanical operation, but may be seen rather as the workings of what Foucault called 'power/knowledge' (Foucault, 1980). This is the process, whereby power and knowledge are disseminated, but it is at the points of their dissemination, that their values are maintained and perpetuated, thereby also embodying and enacting the effects of power. The idea of Jeremy Bentham's panopticon, which Foucault draws on in his account of the social history of punishment and prison, is a good exemplification of this process. The panopticon idea works well because within its structure prisoners are at all times subject to possible surveillance. Internalising this possible surveillance at any time, those who are subjected to imprisonment, or indeed any other means of control, begin to police themselves, and behave as it is expected they ought to behave (Foucault, 1977).

In a conceptual analogy then with the techniques of surveillance that Foucault discusses with regard both to the treatment of prisoners and with the development of medical practice in the 18th and 19th centuries (Foucault, 1973c), I characterise the rhetorical practice of academic writing as policed by a visibilising economy of rationality, language and knowledge, in which language is 'disciplined' by the demands of the other two, as they were promoted throughout the period of the European Enlightenment. Such disciplining includes the rhetorical embodiment of clarity as well as the rhetorical projection of an observer/writer, one who is in the position of surveying and mapping the conceptual or thematic territory required by the task of writing.

In Chapter 5, for example, I look at Bazerman's (1988) analysis of Newton's efforts to get the rhetoric right for the communication of his scientific ideas and methodology, and the importance of conveying them with authority, and suggest that the position of the academic writer as a rhetorical map-maker as it were, continues to draw on the strategies that Newton successfully inscribed in scientific writing. Chapter 6 shows further how the concept of clarity has been important throughout western intellectual–cultural history, and continues to be highly prized, along with the related rhetorical values of concision and brevity. These values continue to be important, especially with regard to assessing academic writing. They also appear prominently in the kinds of feedback given to students, and are promoted in textbooks on academic writing.

The continuing promotion of the values of clarity and the mapping out of argumentation indeed make the institutional practice of academic writing itself a locus of power/knowledge, perpetuating European Enlightenment values and its visibilising economy. I call this specific cultural embodiment of values in rhetorical practice, occidentalist rhetoricity. This is to acknowledge the specific historical and cultural values in the western intellectual tradition, whose power has influenced the constitution of what continue to be the preferred ways of writing academically in English. The notion of occidentalism, and occidentalist inscription, is explored further in Chapter 5, but will be touched on briefly here.

Occidentalism and Occidentalist Reflexivity

The notion of occidentalism, foregrounded for example, in the work of Venn (2000), draws its critical force from Said's (2003) highly influential thesis of 'orientalism'. Orientalism signals the construction of the orient from a western perspective, and the negative positioning of the orient vis-à-vis a superior west. At the same time, the term is used to critique the colonial perspective in that move. The term 'occidentalism' assumes the west's legacy in this respect, acknowledges it and interrogates its effects, not only in relation to the west's others but also in relation to the west's own practices and systems of value. Specifically, 'occidentalism' is a reflexive construct. It reflects back on how the western intellectual and cultural tradition has constructed its sense of self, especially since the beginnings of the colonial period and the consolidation of its world view during the European Enlightenment. So what constitutes knowledge and how best to find or achieve it, and how language is conceived in this project is an occidentalist project. It has been constructed by the west, in the west and has become hegemonic.

Foregrounding Intercultural Communication

A substantial portion of the book foregrounds the vibrant and dynamic role of intercultural communication in our increasingly internationalised institutions of higher education (Chapters 7–13). In this context, the performance of intercultural communication is an increasingly widespread experience for all concerned. I would submit that nearly all students and all teachers in higher education, regardless of discipline, are also participating in intercultural communication, even if they do not always fully recognise it. Intercultural communication is happening live, *in situ*, between tutors and students, student and student, and as a result, taken-for-granted norms of rhetorical and social interaction are being put to the test. Sometimes, they are being skewed, at other times accommodated. At yet other times, the genre or mode of interaction is hybridised, for example, when practices from differing educational cultures are brought together into the one tutorial, as outlined in what I have called a 'discursive dance' in Chapter 13.

The experience of intercultural communication often poses an opportunity for individual language users to reflect back on their 'home' culture. At the institutional level, which is foregrounded here, the practice of intercultural communication provides an opportunity for dual modes of interrogation. One asks why 'we' do things this way, and the other what motivates 'them' in their ways of doing things. This need not necessarily result in a finely balanced comparative perspective, however. As the interactions analysed in this book take place in a UK university, in other words, an inner-circle, Anglo-centric, context, the balance is already weighted. The hegemonic assumptions that Kachru's phraseology of 'inner circle' brings with it (Kachru, 1985, 1992a), constitute the mediating ground for the performance of intercultural communication.

In data from one-to-one intercultural tutorials, I look at how the inter-action reveals what tends to be taken-for-granted in the kinds of utter-ances the British tutors make. Their interlocutors are Japanese students and their resistance to performing the appropriate pragmatic uptakes reveals the hidden nature of the British tutors' expectations. This is not at all to suggest that British students would inevitably provide the appropri-ate types of response to tutor speech acts. As has often been reported, for example, by Lea and Street (1997, 1998) and Haggis (2006), university tutors are not always explicit enough about what they want from their students. In all cases, whether of home students or international students whose first language is not English, it is recognised that it takes time to be inducted into disciplinary discourses specifically, and the expectations of academic culture at large. Indeed, retrospective interviews with those Japanese students one year later showed that by and large they had come to understand what was required of them. They were then able to act with a metapragmatic awareness of what was required of them in their tutori-als. Aspects of the tutorial data are discussed more widely in relation to the literature on communication styles and tutor–student interaction in the Confucian heritage, along with other studies of East Asian student behaviour in western institutions in Chapters 10–12.

Cultural Reflexivity

The point to be made here is not only a pedagogical one, whereby it is important to make students aware of socio-pragmatic expectations (Blum-Kulka *et al.*, 1989; Thomas, 1983), especially when working in another language, it is also an opportunity to be culturally reflexive. The question is why are the tutors making the kinds of utterances they do in the tuto-rial context? What are the intellectual cultural values inscribed in the genre, tutorial? I hear echoes of the Socratic dialogue in these interac-tions, and attribute this to the long-standing, and continuing, valorisa-tion of the dialogic, for example, in the widespread contemporary influence of the work of Bakhtin (1981) and Holquist (1990), in the intel-lectual genealogy of the west.

Given this reflexive stance then, interpreting intercultural communica-tion is not a question of locating 'the other' in the interplay as the exotic, to be named, explained and tamed, as Appadurai (1996) has put it, but of looking at how *one genealogical* other performs alongside *a different genea-logical* other. Such a stance helps to point up what is taken for granted, and therefore not in itself often subject to interpretation. This is especially the case in what might be seen as the 'host' institution for international education: in this case, western institutions. Thus, it is the rhetorical norms embedded in the British tutor's speech acts that are the focus of analysis. They in turn point to the cultural expectations of a student's uptakes. This reflexive approach to norms of tutor–student interaction in the western intellectual tradition is the focus of Chapters 8–10, where the power/ knowledge effects of the Socratic dialogue are looked at in terms of both cultural valorisation and the expectation of verbalisation as a major mode of learning.

Genealogical Inheritance

To signal the power of embedded cultural value, I speak in terms of 'genealogical inheritance' whereby the everyday notion of genealogy, tracing back one's blood relatives, is extended metaphorically to the notion of cultural or intellectual tradition. Just as one can discern the familial inheritance of physical traits, so can the workings of intellectual traits be recognised in specific cultural and social practices. This is the case with processes of cultural and social power and the establishment of rhetorical values in academic writing, as well as the processes of subjectification in relation to academic writers, which are discussed in Chapters 6 and 7. A similar process of power/knowledge and rhetorical regulation may be seen working in tutorial interaction in western institutions as an effect of the Socratic dialogue. The Socratic dialogue is so deeply embedded in the culture of the academy in the western tradition that it manifests itself in the subject position of the teacher in that context, who continues to deploy its rhetorical strategies. It also positions the student at a disadvantage when she/he lacks prior knowledge of the academic cultural context and its presuppositions.

Contrasting Cultural Genealogies on the Contemporary Higher Education Stage

The kinds of issues which arise in the intercultural data analysed here, as well as those referred to in other work, are intended to be representative, if indeed not comprehensive, of those that arise more widely in contemporary international education in an Anglophone context. The contrasting assumptions and expectations of the tutor and student roles are projected primarily through the lens, on the one hand of the Socratic dialogue as a valorised cultural institution, and on the other, through that of Confucian learning and teaching culture. This is the case even when the students demonstrating these alternative values are Japanese, and not Chinese, who might be deemed the more prototypical Confucian subjects. While individual Chinese, Japanese and Korean students of course differ, as do individual European, British or American students, the Confucian lens vis-à-vis the Socratic lens is intended to make broad contrasts, albeit with micro-level effects.

The focus is ultimately set at the genealogical level, at the level of deep-set cultural predispositions, which continue to manifest themselves. Indeed the manifestations are sharpened through being offset by the contrasting dispositions. It is unlikely that the interlocutors themselves are aware of the cultural values they are activating in their behaviour. That is the nature of cultural values. In this case, both the genealogical heritage of the Socratic dialogue and that of the Confucian mentor have created specific kinds of rhetorical subject. In the data presented here, the focus is on the tutor as a Socratic subject, while the focus on the student is as a Confucian subject.

The focus on Confucian values of learning and teaching is not to suggest that they are the only ones interacting with deeply embedded western norms, but the numbers of East Asian students in the United Kingdom and other western institutions of higher education are sizeable enough, and the contrasts in approaches to teaching and learning different enough, that they form a suitable counterpoint. Each perspective is different enough to highlight the other, and each is grounded in a rich and powerful intellectual cultural heritage.

The Intercultural Performative/Transformative

The interplay of intercultural communication on the ground of contemporary western institutions is also a dynamic source of change and differentiation in the languaging practices of higher education. I theorise this future-facing prospect through the concept of performativity, see especially Chapter 4. To borrow the metaphor of 'flow' from Appadurai (1996) as a way of characterising the process of intercultural communication in contemporary higher education, the cultural 'flows' are at minimum bi-directional, not always disjunctive or at cross purposes in a negative way, not always very visible, but in their subtlety often also transforming practice and performance.

Throughout the book, I have drawn particular attention to what I consider to be points of transformativity, whereby the normative performance of the British institutional context is re-shaped in some way by the intercultural dynamic. There were notably three such points of transfor-mativity. One might be seen as a space of resistance, which I have called in describing the data, 'reverse midwifery' (discussed in Chapter 10), whereby the roles of tutor and student are effectively reversed and the less powerful participant (both institutionally and linguistically) induces the more powerful into an explicating and self-reflexive mode. The other two are examples of intercultural hybridity, whereby an East Asian dynamic is at work. In the first case, a British tutor is in effect remoulded as a Japanese tutor, when he performs a demonstration of his own work, thereby acting as a model for the students, in conformity with their expectations of the tutor role (Chapter 12). In the other case, the kind of interpersonal mentor-ing relationship between a more senior and a junior student, quite common among East Asian students, is described and discussed in a vignette of a tutorial encounter with a British course convenor, whereby this East Asian practice is enfolded into the advisory session (Chapter 13).

What these points of transformativity show is that intercultural com-munication in the context of higher education is seldom only a case of adaptation to the 'home' institution or the 'target' culture. The intercultural works subversively, as some might see it, and thereby also transforma-tively, as well as adaptively. With the impact of intercultural communica-tion on our contemporary institutions of higher education come fissures, insertions and open-endedness. Higher education then, is in the process of becoming, as intercultural communication is happening live, as it were, on its international stage. The intercultural in effect disrupts the occidentalist hegemony of the academy and its languaging practices, and the ultimate trajectory is as yet unknown.

Interculturally Rewriting Language in the Academy

In summary, this book is a mix of analysis of current practice and domi-nant evaluations related to language and language use, and an interpre-tive, intellectual–cultural, exploration of how these practices have come to be as they are, and how they are subtly changing as our institutions of higher education become more international or possibly 'transnational' in their ways of doing things, not least with and through language.

The issues treated range from a critique of the dominant deficit dis-course in which language issues circulate in higher education, to a rewrit-ing of the representation of language, foregrounding the centrality of languaging in the process of higher education and signaling its dynamism in not only carrying pre-established intellectual and cultural values, but also constituting a major motor of change.

While the major jumping off point for pedagogical discussions is the kind of work that is, likely to be undertaken by academic literacy and EAP practitioners, the issues discussed are also relevant to modern foreign languages teachers/researchers, and those focusing on learning and teaching in higher education more generally. Intercultural communication in the academic context is an integral part of EAP and academic literacy work; it is also a routine experience for all concerned in the business of higher education, whether they acknowledge this or not. Academic staff in higher education in the English-speaking world increasingly need to take cognisance of the increasingly intercultural dynamic of their pedagogic interactions. The examples discussed in the book therefore provide a range of interpretive resources which can be drawn on to help understand what is going on in the performance of intercultural communication in academic settings.

As well as showing and analysing examples of intercultural communication in action, especially in tutorial interaction between tutors and students, the book emphasises its transformative potential for higher education practices. This is linked to the suggestion that intercultural communication has itself a performative dimension, whereby in being enacted, it inevitably and unpredictably changes expected or established formats or types of exchange. Such repeated or disruptive performances of intercultural communication then begin to constitute a transnational or global higher education, on its own stage.

Chapter 2

Language, Language Pedagogies and Intercultural Communication in Contemporary Higher Education

Introduction

This chapter focuses on the contemporary context of higher education where students are expected to use language in ways which may not be completely familiar to them. This is the case for many so-called 'home' students as well for international students, whose educational background cultures may be very different. In effect then, all students may be said, to a greater or lesser extent, to be participating in intercultural communication. On the one hand, this would be between the everyday culture of their social surroundings and the specific context of academic culture. On the other hand, it is more a case of interacting between two linguistically and culturally different academic cultures. The chapter also looks at the language-related pedagogies which have grown up in the wake of the internationalisation and diversification of the universities.

My aim here is to treat the various pedagogies and methodological approaches to language and literacy teaching in the academy in an inter-disciplinary fashion as languaging practices rather than opt into any one practical, traditional or theoretical model. I will inevitably reveal in my use of terminology or way of thinking what I have absorbed in my own experience and practice as a teacher and researcher, but ultimately it is the intercultural context of contemporary 'western', but particularly UK higher education, in which those pedagogic practices operate that forms the empirical backdrop to this chapter, rather than the pedagogical models themselves. They are already well catered for in numerous publications on English Language Teaching (ELT) pedagogy, writing pedagogy and intercultural communication pedagogy.

Foregrounding Language in the Academy

While for some, a focus on language may seem like a counter-current to the upsurge in attention to multimodality; see for example, Kress and van

Leeuwen (2001) in contemporary communication contexts, including class-room discourse, this book is not a counter-argument to multimodality. It rather foregrounds a context where the role of language has been neglected. While within the broader context of contemporary culture, the visual predominates, higher education is one place where language, and its uses, comes to the fore, not least in procedures of pedagogy, such as the lecture and the seminar, and processes of assessment such as the essay and other written genres. Here, language remains the primary, although not exclusive, semiotic resource. The point is that it is taken for granted rather than recognised for its importance.

Language Issues in Higher Education Policy Changes

With the shift from an elite to a mass conceptualisation of higher edu-cation (Barnett, 1985, 2000; Burgen, 1996; Scott, 1995, 2005), what is known as the 'home' student population in the United Kingdom is diversifying. Higher education policies such as 'widening participation' encourage increased numbers of students from a wide range of backgrounds, tradi-tionally unrepresented within the university, to go to university. Such students are generally first-generation university students, who may come from ethnic minority families, or white working-class families, or have come to study later in life rather than immediately from school.

Higher education policies such as 'widening participation' tend to be made in the interests of social engineering, assuming that getting a degree confers a degree of upward social mobility and economic success on hold-ers. Often left out of the planning, however, is the degree to which such students have to adjust to an academic culture with which they are unfa-miliar. In particular, such policies tend not to recognise the importance of the role language plays. Looking at the situation from the students' point of view, and particularly in the context of the demands of academic writ-ing, Lillis (1999: 127) identifies what they see as an 'institutional practice of mystery'.

While policy documents on higher education such as Dearing (1997) focus on key skills, there is no mention of the importance of language, other than by implication, through 'communication'. Communication skills, however, are seen largely as a by-product of academic study, some-thing that will enhance students' employability, rather than as something that may be addressed directly and intrinsically, as part of the study process. It is the contention here, however that language, and to a greater or lesser extent, intercultural communication, is at the core of students' engagement, whatever their backgrounds, in and with academic discourses and with processes of academic assessment. The specific issues of intercultural communication that arise from teaching international students from very different language and cultural backgrounds will be addressed more specifically in later chapters, through examples of intercultural communication with East Asian students studying in western institutions.

Language-Related Pedagogies in Higher Education

Despite the lack of planning for the intrinsic role that language plays in academic culture, the above-mentioned policies and their wider political and economic assumptions have in fact created a practical need for an increase in the kind of work which deals with language issues. More explicit practical measures have therefore had to be taken. In the United Kingdom, this work is variously titled study skills, academic literacy, academic skills and writing skills. These areas of work have effectively come into being, or increased, with the change in social purpose of higher education. They have surfaced with the need to induct new student populations from a variety of social and ethnic backgrounds into the academy, along with the need to keep them there. These, at any rate, are the reasons normally given for this kind of work.

Usually treated separately from such cohorts of 'non-traditional' home students, are 'international' students. Their separate treatment accrues predominantly from their economic status. Their fees are increasingly necessary to the financial well-being of the institutions at which they study. As 'international' tends to be associated with students whose first language is not English, although this is not necessarily the case, their language needs are institutionally recognised, and they are treated as a distinct category. As a result, English Language Units or Centres have sprung up to deal with those needs. The pedagogic practice of relevance here is known as EAP, and is discussed further below.

The development of this 'languaging' work in the academy has been piecemeal and therefore the relevant practitioners may not always be working together in the same department. Home students are likely to be segregated from international students, dyslexic students from others and so on. Language may be foregrounded in some contexts, learning in others. However, I would maintain that there is a fair degree of commonality to all those areas of practice, and that it is performance in use of language that is, key. The background assumptions invested in the relevant pedagogic practices is discussed briefly in the following section.

English for Academic Purposes

The pedagogic practices of ELT have developed a range of different names according to their contexts of operation, and the political priorities they respond to at local or institutional level. EAP is the one most commonly found in the context of higher education. In the United Kingdom, it is the predominant label for teaching academic English and inducting international students into British academic culture. It aims to develop language proficiency at the same time as it develops an understanding of the pedagogic practices of the academy such as the tutorial, the seminar presentation, the lecture, the essay, the PhD and so on. The term 'EAP' is used also in Hong Kong, Singapore, Australia, New Zealand and more recently, the United States. It is differentiated from more generalist terms used in teaching English to non-native speakers such as English as a Foreign Language (EFL), English as a Second Language (ESL), English as an Additional Language (EAL) or English for Speakers of Other Languages (ESOL). These pedagogic practices of ELT have developed the range of different names according to their contexts of operation, and the political priorities they respond to at local or institutional level. Only EAP is elaborated on further, here.

EAP has been around since the 1960s and gained currency under projects funded by the British Overseas Development Agency, predominantly in support of the teaching of science and technology to developing countries. Historical overviews are available in, for example, Swales (1985), Dudley-Evans and St. John (1998) and Benesch (2001) and its research perspectives explored in Flowerdew and Peacock (2001). This context of emergence associates it with the discourses of economic and technological development, which have set up a hierarchical relationship between the developed and developing world or the first world and the third world. As Jack (2004: 127) points out, this discourse 'assumes that industrialisation should be the goal of all nations'. He further notes, citing Westwood (2004: 70), the teleological mode of thought, which assumes a convergence 'towards managerial and industrial structures and practices and a common societal model'. The assumption behind this teleological model is also that it is the right thing to happen.

A similar convergence model lies implicitly behind the teaching of EAP, which has now moved beyond its association with teaching English for Science and Technology only (EST), as the market for international students (and their fees) has widened. So although the education of international students in the United Kingdom as well as in other national institutions of higher education is no longer associated predominantly with 'development' in a third world – first world direction, the fact that through processes of globalisation, English has become the dominant language of international education, not to mention academic publishing, means that a similar dynamic is at work. The flow of students and staff is not the same as at the outset of EAP. The source of financing has changed, the students usually have to be rich enough to pay for themselves, but the assumption that international students will simply accommodate to (converge with) the expected norms of academic performance in English works within a similar 'convergence' mould.

English and Globalisation

It is acknowledged here that English in the context of globalisation is not a simple concept. While many practitioners and researchers are beginning to question the simplicity of 'convergence' as discussed above, notably in reaction to the effects of globalisation on English, this is not the case within the institutional discourse of higher education. While the spread of Englishes and the use of English as a Lingua Franca have created new research fields in their own right, see, for example, the work of House (2006), Kachru (1988, 1992b), Y. Kachru (1997), Jenkins (2006), Mauranen (1993) and Seidlhofer (2002), among others, the assumptions and expectations which prevail in Anglophone institutions concerning the use of English, and language generally, remain rooted within the predominantly technicist discourse, which assumes that language is easily dealt with, and easily fixed when this is required. These issues are further developed in the following two chapters.

Academic Literacy/ies

Whereas EAP is used predominantly for teaching high-fee paying international students, a more recent label has emerged, namely 'academic literacy' or 'literacies', which has a more inclusive application to student groups across the spectrum of higher education. This term has quickly proliferated in different national academic contexts such as the United States, for example, Johns (1997); Zamel and Spack (1998); South Africa, for example, Carter (1998, 2000); and the United Kingdom, for example, Jones *et al.* (1999); Lea and Street (1998); Lea (2004); Lillis (2001); Lillis and Scott (2007). It situates the teaching and learning of reading and writing in the context of higher education, within a social practice perspective. This perspective emphasises people and what they do/are expected to do in specific social contexts rather than the language skills which EAP foregrounds. However, unlike EAP, which is a fairly stable term and embedded in a pedagogic tradition, academic literacy remains a contested term, notably with its plural form 'academic literacies'. In their book titled *Negotiating Academic Literacies*, the editors Zamel and Spack state:

> it is no longer possible to assume that there is one type of literacy in the academy. Academic literacy, which once denoted simply the ability to read and write college-level texts, now must embrace multiple approaches to knowledge. Hence our use of the term academic literacies. (Zamel & Spack, 1998: ix)

A similar epistemological positioning, namely social constructionism, which goes along with seeing disciplines as social practices which are inevitably undergoing change, can be seen in the work of many others, such as Bartholomae (1985), Belcher and Braine (1995), Berkenkotter and Huckin (1995), Carson *et al.* (1992), Lave and Wenger (1991) and Johns (1997).

While also coming broadly from a social practice perspective, Lea and Street (1999) use the term 'academic literacies' somewhat differently. For them it is a theoretical term, linked to the new literacy studies, for example, Street (1984), Gee (1990, 2000). They apply it to their tripartite model of different approaches to inducting students into their academic disciplines. This term is intended to subsume the other two approaches they outline while essentially critiquing them. The other two approaches namely 'study skills' and 'academic socialisation' models are seen as limited, with a tendency to pathologise the student by suggesting a 'quick fix' model of help.

Another analytical perspective can be discerned in the use of the term by applied linguists such as for example, Candlin and Hyland (1999) and Hyland (2000), whereby they refer to linguistic and rhetorical analyses of differing disciplines. In this way, it is similar to the notion of academic discourses, whereby certain linguistic features can be highlighted as germane to specific disciplines, and such features can then be emphasised in teaching students of those disciplines. This kind of research is particularly amenable to the methodology of corpus linguistics, scanning numerous texts from the same discipline. Here, the distinctive ways in which specific discourse communities construct their knowledge and make convincing arguments can be crystallised in different ways by corpus analysis of published articles, and homing in on specific linguistic features, the occurrence of 'may', for example, Thompson (1999); or the detailed analysis of 'hedges' in specific disciplines, as in Hyland (1994, 2000); or the occurrence of first person pronouns (Harwood & Hadley, 2004). These analyses can have useful pedagogic applications, not least in the context of EAP, and some EAP practitioners work in this way.

I theorise the concept of academic literacy differently, although ultimately also viewed within a social practice perspective. My focus is not on specific disciplines and their uses of language, but rather on the power/knowledge effects of a unified notion of how language should be used, based on European Enlightenment assumptions of knowledge and its communication. Basically, language in this tradition should be clear and concise, and not get in the way of the message. This conceptualisation of language has become naturalised, such that it circulates unproblematically in the institutional discourse of higher education and beyond. As such, expectations of how language should be used cut across disciplines. This is what Johns also found in her interviews with academic faculty across disciplines. She put it thus:

> There may be some general academic discourses, language, values, and concepts that most academics share. Thus faculty often identify themselves with a college or university and its language and values, as well as with the more specialised areas of interest for which they have been prepared. (Johns, 1997: 56)

While acknowledging the difficulties this widespread attitude poses for academic literacy practitioners, who are geared up to help students write within the demands of their specific disciplines, Johns reiterates this generalist position, illustrating the strength of its cross-disciplinarity. She states:

> Faculty have their own discipline-specific allegiances (to biology, chemistry, sociology, engineering); nonetheless, many believe that there are basic, generalisable, linguistic, textual, and rhetorical rules for the entire academic community that can apply. (Johns, 1997: 57–58)

Thaiss and Zawacki (2002) also found discipline-specific academics with similar attitudes, although many others felt that good writing in their discipline was related to the specific genres students were asked to write in, and not generic. The following is quoted from an anthropologist they interviewed:

> If undergraduates can write clearly, logically and reasonably, I'm happy. I'd rather awaken in them a sense of how to essay an experience logically in a little five-page paper than to have them execute an ethnographic study. (Thaiss & Zawacki, 2002: 68)

My position is that such generalised attitudes to language have been formed by power/knowledge effects in intellectual culture, and continue to promote them. They are evidenced also in the evaluative metalanguage used to give feedback to students' academic literacy performances. Examples of this metalanguage, around structure, clarity and concision, are discussed at greater length in Chapter 6. In the meantime, examples of how students struggle to write within this evaluative discourse are presented and discussed in the next section.

The 'Elite' Pedagogy of Osmosis

The values associated with academic language use have formed over time and are reproduced in assessment norms and ways of speaking and writing that constitute doing things academically. Often these norms and ways of doing language are not explicit, and certainly not transparent for students, while for their tutors they are taken for granted. Tutors therefore do not feel the need for more detailed and exemplified explanations, as, for example, shown in research by Lea and Street (1998). In this research into lecturers' perspectives on what constitutes good academic writing, Lea and Street found that lecturers foregrounded notions of 'argument' and 'structure' as key elements, but were unable to specify exactly what they meant by those terms. Similar findings are documented also in the work by Hounsell (1987) and Norton (1990). As it is unlikely that such lecturers would be unable to give more detail regarding an analytical term germane to their own discipline, their failure to do so with regard to 'argument' and 'structure' suggests that they are taken-for-granted terms in the value system constituting 'good' academic writing. This suggests that the taken-for-grantedness of what notions such as 'argument' and 'structure' mean in academic writing may be seen as an example of what Polanyi (1966) has called 'tacit knowledge', that is, acted upon by expert practitioners but not explicated, or possibly deemed inexplicable. The fact that little need is perceived to explicate something that plays an important role in the assessment procedures of higher education, however, demonstrates a general lack of critical awareness of what languaging in academic writing means for many students in contemporary higher education. Indeed, it shows a reliance on students having the same degree of tacit knowledge as themselves. At the same time, it reveals the traditional academic pedagogy, or rather non-pedagogy, of osmosis. The assumption of osmosis is predicated on sameness. The same kinds of people enter the academy as have always entered, having already been socialised into its ways of doing things, its 'habitus', to use Bourdieu's term (Bourdieu, 1977, 1988, 1992).

The fact that many people who have achieved academic success, including many of those who are now teaching new students, are not aware of the various linguistic micro-skills and rhetorical macro-strategies that they deployed in doing so, does not mean that those skills and strategies are irrelevant or that they can only be achieved by osmosis. These linguistic features can often be isolated and identified. This does not however mean that they exist apart from the academic discourses and performances in which they are embedded, they are rather an important intrinsic part of those discourses and performances and need to be acknowledged as such.

Changing Rhetoricities

Rational discourses do not arise, fully fledged as it were, without the benefit of language. Indeed, use of language is often the marker of new thinking, of new discourses. Tensions can arise between traditional expectations of rhetorical enactment in academic discourse and new or emerging rhetoricities. Such issues include the extent to which contemporary theorisations, such as those around the theme of globalisation, including the role of English as a lingua franca, those around post-colonial studies and post-structuralism more broadly, are changing our epistemological assumptions and thereby also the rhetorical instantiation of academic discourse. For example, in so far as traditional academic rhetoricity is based on the European Enlightenment legacy of seeking out the truth, or discovering new knowledge, so a rejection of those epistemological assumptions and new forms of rhetoricising academic understanding, such as the epideictic rhetoric of 'new historicist' discourse, which Susan Peck MacDonald (1994) takes to task, may be transforming traditional notions of what constitutes 'good' academic prose, or at least, diversifying them. I have suggested that at the micro-rhetorical level, the use of the forward stroke (/) to combine two concepts, sometimes traditionally opposite in meaning, is an effect of post-structuralist or deconstructionist theorising, whereby the notion of undecidability takes on epistemological significance, and the determinacy of logical opposites is questioned (Turner, 2003). The notion of alternative discourses has been explored, for example, in the edited collection by Bizzell *et al.* (2002), as well as in Thaiss and Zawacki (2002). Mao has also written an informative piece on the dominant tendency in Chinese American writing to structure the argument via analogy (Mao, 2005).

The Languaging of Academic Writing

Learning to use language in the ways demanded of academic culture cannot be divorced from successful learning in that culture. Language use and academic performance are inextricably interlinked. For example,

Ivanic's (1998) analysis of four kinds of identity that students have to negotiate in their writing points up the complexities of what might be called
the languaging of academic writing. Her examples include the writing of
many L1 students who feel a sense of alienation from the kind of language
they are expected to use, as it is not what they are familiar with in their
daily lives. Others feel that their own experience of life and the knowledge
they have is excluded, when, either they are denied its relevance, or it
proves difficult to feed it in textually into the established disciplinary discourses they are working with. Such psychological and textual difficulties
affect not only their writing but also the quality of their learning.

Lillis (2001) focuses on 'non-traditional' (both first language and ESL)
students and highlights their difficulty in getting to grips with the 'conventions' of academic discourse. These conventions relate to rhetorical
processes such as being explicit, giving definitions, and picking out the
main points, that tutors in all disciplines encourage their students to do,
without further elaboration of what these rhetorical processes actually
require. Language, then, is at the core of students' engagement, whatever
their backgrounds, in and with academic discourses and with processes of
academic assessment.

Languaging and Interculturality

The contemporary context of diversity in higher education in itself creates conditions for the foregrounding of language and the cultural presuppositions implicit in language use. It is intrinsic to the rationale for this
book that all of the above-mentioned categories of student, as well as their
'traditional' counterparts (presumably by traditional, policy documents
mean white, indigenous, middle class students) contribute to the contemporary diversity of higher education. The diversity of languages which
the students speak, along with the diversity of languaging practices which
they bring with them, means that the institutions are naturally sites of
intercultural communication. On the one hand, this operates on an everyday, temporal dimension, relating to interaction between student and student, and between tutor and student. On this dimension, intercultural
communication is already in the academy. It happens in every discipline;
it happens in the coffee bars; it happens in the libraries. Such a naturally
occurring process must of itself institute an awareness of language and
languaging. Arguably, not enough is done educationally to draw on this
rich resource, but its availability is manifest.

On the other hand, languaging and interculturality may be seen to
be operating along a dimension of historical time, whereby a culture of

languaging, of using language in ways that have come to be recognised as academic, is deeply embedded in cultural history. This genealogical dimension, whereby intercultural communication means recognising the sedimentation of intellectual cultural values as well as more general social and cultural attitudes towards language and languaging in the academy, which may not always align with those in students' lives outside the academy, is also important, and constitutes a core theoretical strand of this book. As illustrated in the following chapter, issues of language use in academic performance circulate predominantly in a deficit discourse. This is because the centrality of language use in academic success tends to be ignored. When language becomes visible, that is, when attention is drawn to it, this can only be because it has not been used 'properly'. However, accommodation to the 'proper' or 'conventional' norms of academic language use can also be seen as a matter of intercultural communication. The students concerned may speak the same language, but they are unfamiliar with the social and cultural context of its use, in particular the norms associated with academic writing. While what are often seen as problems of intercultural communication are recognised for international students accommodating to a British, or more generally, Anglo-centric culture, similar difficulties can arise for English speaking students unfamiliar with the effects of deeply rooted, taken-for-granted ways of speaking or writing in an academic context.

Reflexive Practitioners

It is not only the students but also the tutors of course who are participating in intercultural communication. I would submit that all practitioners in language – related pedagogies in the contemporary context of higher education are participating in intercultural communication, even if they do not always fully recognise it. This is the case in both what might be seen as the horizontal sense of contemporary face-to-face interaction, and in the genealogical sense of what might correspondingly be seen as vertical time, going back into the depths of intellectual history.

This leads to the suggestion that teachers of languaging processes in the academy are also 'reflexive' practitioners, reflecting back on the textual practices that they are both participating in inducting their students into. Such teachers are likely to be already 'reflexive' practitioners as advocated by for example, Schon (1991, 1987) and Wallace (1991), which is reflecting on their practice in order to refine it and improve it. As reflexive practitioners, however, they are invited to recognise their position as placeholders or 'subjects' of culturally constructed value systems, in their turn positioning their students within the same value system, or possibly choosing not to, in recognition rather of where their students are coming from, or of changes in epistemological/rhetorical discourses. Such teachers then are not only skilled professionals, but also contributors to the flows (Appadurai, 1996, 2001) of contemporary cultural processes. They are acting politically in the way that Gee suggests is the contemporary role of the English teacher. He states:

> The English teacher can cooperate in her own marginalisation by seeing herself as 'a language teacher' with no connection to social and political issues. Or she can accept the paradox of literacy as a form of interethnic communication which often involves conflicts of values and identities, and accept her role as one who socialises students into a world view that, given its power here and abroad, must be viewed critically, comparatively, and with a constant sense of the possibilities for change. Like it or not, the English teacher stands at the very heart of the most crucial educational cultural and political issues of our time. (Gee, 1990: 68)

Language Pedagogies as Objects of Cultural Theory

The discursive worlds of pedagogic practice, such as language teaching and the teaching of academic writing, and contemporary critical and cultural theorising seldom come together. There have been discussions around the extent to which culture or cultural studies is/should be included within language teaching, for example, in Byram (1997b) and Corbett (2003); how culture is inevitably inscribed in language and therefore impinges on choices of what to teach and how best to illustrate it, see among others Valdes (1986); Hinkel (1999a) and Kramsch (1993, 1998); as well as how to value the multilingualism of language learning students Risager (2006, 2007). Pedagogies for intercultural communication have also been specifically constructed and debates wage around how best to implement them, for example, Buttjes and Byram (1990), Byram (1997a), Byram and Morgan (1994), Guilherme (2002, 2007) and O'Regan and Macdonald (2007). However, in focusing on both the integral role of language to academic performance, as well as representations of language in the academy, I see language itself, along with the pedagogical practices relating to language in the academy, as objects of cultural study and subject them to a cultural – theoretical approach.

Chapter 3
Language in the Academy:
The Discourse of Remediation

Introduction

In this chapter, I explore the prevailing discourse of remediation in which language issues in higher education circulate, and critique the predominant technicist model for language work, which goes alongside it, as well as the institutional marginalisation of this work.

Shock, Horror! Language Problem!

Accounts of gruesome grammar and spurious spelling have become a mainstay in newspaper articles and educational reports of various kinds, bemoaning the decline in standards of language. One such, an article by Alison Utley in *The Times Higher* (13 February 1998), reported on research which revealed evidence of decline in writing skills at both old and new universities. A more recent one, by Donald MacLeod in *The Guardian*, (9 February 2006), states that:

> universities are dismayed by the poor levels of literacy and numeracy among school leavers who arrive in higher education expecting to be "spoon-fed". (MacLeod, *The Guardian*, 9 February 2006)

The article is based on a Nuffield Review report (2006), which includes comments such as the following from admissions tutors and other lecturers:

> I was able to skim the cream of candidates, but even they do not necessarily know how to use an apostrophe. (13)

> They cut and paste essays from the web. Reading books is a skill which has been lost. (16)

> They can't even write in sentences. Their spelling is appalling. They can't be understood. (14)

> They graduate with a 2:1 but they still can't spell or write English. (14)

Another report by the Royal Literary Fund (Davies *et al.*, 2006), which has sponsored creative writers to help improve student writing in universities, makes 'terrifying reading' according to an article by Philip Henscher in *The Independent* (23 March 2006). Those writers have been 'shocked' by work which is 'so incoherent that it's difficult to discern what argument is being furthered'; and by students 'unable to spell simple words' and 'with no grasp whatsoever of punctuation'. Reasons for the current and fairly recent decline are usually attributed to changes in curricula and assessment practices. The reports cite a stronger focus on assessment and league tables by the schools and getting good grades by the students, as the major culprits. As the Nuffield report put it:

> 'This leads to spoonfeeding rather than fostering of independence and critical engagement with subject material.' It went on: 'Learners who may have achieved academic success by such means at A-level, are increasingly coming into higher education expecting to be told the answers'. (Nuffield Review report, 2006: 2)

The issue of recrimination over language use is not new. Going back more than 20 years, Hobsbaum (1984) also writes of the 'decline of literacy' in students across the curriculum, in his specific case, at the University of Glasgow. He saw the problem as being the fact that students were encouraged to present notes rather than 'ordered prose' in essays and reports. He also maintained that the fact that students no longer had a working knowledge of Latin had contributed to their difficulties with grammar and writing. Interestingly, the contemporary correlate to the lack of knowledge of Latin is the decline in learning modern foreign languages. Now it is this and not Latin that is seen as having a knock-on effect in students' lack of knowledge of grammar. It is somewhat grotesque that one of the reasons for the decrease in numbers of students learning foreign languages in Britain is that they do not need to because of the global dominance of English. This in turn is a problem however, as native speakers of English are increasingly unable to write it properly, because they need to have studied foreign languages in order to have knowledge of grammar!

While the melodramatic style of reporting academics' views on their students' use of English may simply be a popular journalistic convention, it nonetheless serves to intensify the evaluative polarising of the issues around the written and students' writing, and firmly embeds them within a pathologising framework. Students are stigmatised as weak or remedial, and language or writing specialists are positioned as technicians with a mechanistically conceived role of making either the text or the student writer 'better'.

Language and the Metaphysics of Transparency

What is perpetuated also in the melodramatic style of reporting language in deficit is a prelapsarian discourse, whereby the benefits of a lost tradition are appealed to while the contemporary condition only needs their restoration. What is 'lost' may be concretely alluded to, as in the pedagogic practices, underlying principles of learning in higher education, or subjects studied, which were mentioned in the quotes above. However, the roots of the relentlessly remedial condition of language may ultimately lie in what the social historian of language, Crowley (1989), has characterised as 'the metaphysics of transparency'. As he put it:

> The desire for the perfectly transparent language can properly be described as one of the metaphysical problems that emerges consistently in the history of western thought. (Crowley, 1989: 64–65)

Foucault detects a similar desire in the work of the 'nominalist' philosophers such as Hobbes, Berkeley, Hume and Condillac, in what he terms the classical age, and indeed uses the same phrase. He sees 'a perfectly transparent language' as their ideal objective, which he characterises as follows:

> the great utopia of a perfectly transparent language in which things themselves could be named without any penumbra of confusion, either by a totally arbitrary but precisely thought-out system (artificial), or by a language so natural that it would translate thought like a face expressing a passion language. (Foucault, 1970: 119)

This deeply rooted cultural conception of language, that it can represent a pre-existing reality, whether the external reality of the physical world or the internal reality of thought, leads to the assumption of language unproblematically mediating between ideas and their expression. In this assumption, language and knowledge inhabit separate, clearly defined spaces, but the former should ideally be able to perfectly (and hence invisibly) represent the latter. While functional approaches to language, a social constructionist understanding of knowledge, and post-structuralist notions of the subject have undermined the transparency conception for language, the effects of its long dominance remain, and continue to pervade many social practices, not least the deficit discourse in higher education.

While a post-structuralist understanding of language drives the arguments in this book, it is the constitutive role of an outmoded conception of language, namely, the transparency conception, in determining attitudes towards languaging in the academy and the status of language work that is the focus here. The issue is its genealogical embedding and its continuing ability to exercise power, rather than its conceptual efficacy. A constitutive role for language is in effect ignored in the discourse and structuring of higher education institutions, where language issues circulate predominantly in a deficit discourse and where language work is securely located on the periphery. The ideal of transparency, and hence invisibility for language has helped to create these conditions. Language is only visible, as it were, because of its failure to live up to transparency. As exemplified further in this chapter, as much as it surfaces at all in the higher education context, language surfaces as a problem. When all is going well and the message is successfully delivered, 'language' is not noticed. However, when the message is not successfully delivered, or the 'appropriate' message is not even attempted, it is 'language' which needs 'remedial' attention. The construction of deficit around language and language work is linked to the assumption that there is a direct line between rationality and epistemic clarity. This assumption implies that language gives unmediated access to knowledge and must therefore be transparent. It is the strength of this transparency conception for language that paradoxically masks its workings.

Language and Social Stigma

A further strand of powerful influence sustaining the deficit discourse comes from the authoritarian prescriptivism of 'correct' English usage embodied in the reference works of Fowler (1926), Partridge (1947) and Gowers (1954). As Bex (1999), a sociolinguist, has documented, their prescriptions are not socially neutral. In fact, in their origins, they were elitist, classist, sexist and nationalist. In his review of the book in which Bex's chapter appears, Coupland refers to these prescriptions as 'sexist', 'smug' and 'bigoted' (Coupland, 2000: 625). Despite the negative associations of this tradition among progressive educators, including language teachers and writing practitioners, the sociopolitical influence of the existence of such prescriptions is such that an ethos of fear and negative evaluation continues to taint discussions around text and language. Also, the fear of getting things wrong often inhibits students in their writing. This is the legacy of power and social status being linked to how language is used. Linguistic prescriptions are an integral part of the politics of establishing and maintaining a standard language. Crowley (1991), for example, has documented those debates in the 19th century from the perspective of Ireland, where the notion of a standard language was strongly related to the locus of political power, namely in southern England, and not Ireland.

Establishing Standard English

Such debates over what constitutes standard English are ongoing, as exemplified in the edited collection by Bex and Watts (1999), and surfaced prominently in the context of the grammar debate surrounding the instantiation of a new national curriculum for the teaching of English in England in the 1980s, recounted in Cox (1991) and Carter (1997).

The symbolic value of grammar is wide ranging. It stands for social regulation, political order and moral propriety in general. Lapses in grammar, punctuation and spelling are therefore deemed to indicate a much wider societal, moral and educational decline. This ethos can be seen in the following quote from a newspaper article written by the public school headmaster, John Rae, at the height of the debate over grammar in the national curriculum. As with many things, the permissive ethos of the 1960s was apparently to blame.

> The overthrow of grammar coincided with the acceptance of the equivalent of creative writing in social behaviour. As nice points of grammar were mockingly dismissed as pedantic and irrelevant, so was punctiliousness in such matters as honesty, responsibility, property, gratitude, apology and so on (*The Observer*, 7 February 1982, cited in Cameron, 1995).

Summing up the link between language use and social and academic snobbery, the following quote from Cameron (1995) is particularly apposite:

> Linguistic bigotry is among the last publicly expressible prejudices left to members of the western intelligentsia. Intellectuals who would find it unthinkable to sneer at a beggar or someone in a wheelchair will sneer without compunction at linguistic 'solecisms'. (Cameron, 1995: 12)

The availability of this widespread social prejudice enables it to feed into (whether consciously or unconsciously) the marginalisation of language work in the academy, and furthermore to sustain a technicist model of easily putting things right, that predominates for this work.

The Technicist Model of Language Work

Other than in what Bernstein calls a 'difference as deficit' framework (Bernstein, 1990), institutions of higher education seem unable to deal with language issues, which they would prefer did not exist at all.

Language problems are analogous to cuts and bruises, remediable by dint of the first aid kit wielded, in the case of second language speakers of English, by the EAP staff, or by study skills or academic writing developers, if they are dealing with native speakers of English. This technicist model for language work is the institutionally dominant one. It is aided and abetted in the context of second language speakers by the combined effects of demand for easily measurable and easily processed university entrance criteria and the successful marketing of global language tests such as International English Language Testing System (IELTS) or Test of English as a Foreign Language (TOEFL). These global screening tests have become part of the regulatory framework of universities where a language test score is a prerequisite to registration on the programme of study, at both undergraduate and postgraduate levels. Their scores slot comfortably into a checklist of easily ticked off registration requirements and preparation for those tests, often also referred to, not inappropriately, as 'language training', is distorting students' perception of the role of language use in academic performance, and encourages a mechanistic approach to learning and teaching. Students seem to want to 'train' to reach the appropriate entrance level score or band rather than to engage with the language as an essential, and integral, part of their engaging with, and being assessed in, their subject of study. As has been argued elsewhere (Turner, 2004), there is a need for a much more robust conceptualisation of language work, particularly in the university context, one which recognises its intellectual rigour and arduous labour, for both students and teachers. The technicist model positions the students of academic literacy in deficit, and institutionally marginalises their teachers. It also underacknowledges the complexity of language work, the multiplicity of factors involved that have to be attended to at any one time, from the micro-level of the letter, through choice of register, and the various features that give coherence and cohesion, to the rhetorical macro-structure of any particular genre.

In critiquing the technicist model for language work in the academy, the aim is not to deny the importance of grammar or individual word choice. It is simply too glib, an easy point-scoring exercise, to debunk any focus on form, such as sometimes occurs in the academic literacy literature. Approaches to writing are now so varied and contested that it becomes easy to link any focus on form with the reified, decontextualised, approach to language teaching, often debunked in examples such as *la plume de ma tante est verte*. Here the unlikelihood of ever uttering such a sentence in 'real life' is ignored in the interests of practising the genitive construction and the agreement of gendered nouns with the correct adjectival form.

With the spread of communicative pedagogies, such an approach is now seldom found in both language teaching and writing pedagogies. Nonetheless, it can be convenient to continue to position teachers and teaching in this way in order to argue for the supremacy of a different approach. For example, Canagarajah (1999: 150) talks of teachers 'who begin by aiming to stamp out errors may conceive of writing as no more than the acquisition of form – a set of correct grammatical and rhetorical structures'.

While this quote resonates with the concerns of the often socially elitist prescriptivist tradition, as discussed in Bex (1999), and its assumptions of uncontestable correctness whose forms can be easily prescribed and taught, which of course Canagarajah is positioning himself against, I would like to take issue with the implication that many writing teachers today think in terms of 'stamping out errors'. There may well be some writing teachers who think that writing is primarily about the acquisition of correct or relevant forms, but this does not necessarily go along with an attitude of 'stamping out errors'. This rather negative conceptualisation fits well with the melodramatic outbursts described above in journalistic articles, but blurs the nuancing that is actually required for academic writing. Students do need to be aware of how their choices at the level of the sentence relate to coherence for the reader of the text overall, as the example given in the following section shows.

The Euphemism of Proofreading

Helping to sustain the technicist model of language work is the fairly recent proliferation of proofreading as a practice in higher education. Sometimes this is organised by graduate students for their international peers, sometimes the students' union provides a service, and generally, notices on campus, offering the services of proofreading and editing for a fee, abound.

While publishers are increasingly dispensing with the roles of proof-readers and copy editors, as electronic technologies make the process easier (Graddol, 2001), it seems ironic that proofreading is increasing in higher education. Proofreading has always played a role in writing peda-gogy, but generally a very minor one. As in the professional context of publication, it is similar to checking the 'proofs' before they go to print. In the pedagogic context, it is also the final stage, giving one more look through an essay or report, before handing it in. The assumption is that changes will apply to spelling, punctuation and possibly sentence-level grammar, only. No re-structuring of text should be involved.

I do not wish to belittle the role of proofreader here, it has a place, whoever does it, and all academic writers benefit from it. However, the issue is that in collapsing more widespread language-related work into the heading 'proofreading', the intellectual and meaning-related importance of working with language is in effect being diminished. It seems that the proofreading analogy for language work enables this work to be minimised, sidelined and sanitised. It masks the academic discomfort embodied in what I call 'the pharmakon of academic literacy' (discussed further below), enabling the fact that language has to be attended to at all, to be tidied away comfortably into a readily available slot.

The housekeeping metaphors of 'polishing' or 'tidying up' the language give the term 'proofreading' its default meaning, and imply surface work and limited effort. Scott gives an example from her collection of subject tutors' advice to students:

> This is basically fine but the English needs tidying up. Get a friend to proofread it for you. (Scott, 2003: 7)

However, to talk of proofreading, in the context of 'improving' or 'tidying up' the work of international students for example, is to create a euphemism. This arises in the contrast between the kind of work that 'proofreading' traditionally relates to, and the potentially extremely complex rewriting, checking back with the original writer to clarify meaning, and rewriting that is, usually involved in any one-to-one academic writing tutorial. To give an example, this is a sentence from a student's work:

> Walter Benjamin discerned the danger of such a contention to which German leftist politicians are seen to have been deeply embedded, anticipating its easy association with fascism.

From the perspective of the reader, should the preposition 'to' be related to 'contention', in which case the past participle 'embedded', which comes later, does not fit? Does the reader then understand that the German leftist politicians were perhaps 'opposed' (instead of embedded) to the contention? It may also be that the student has got the tense wrong in his use of the passive, and that he meant something like the 'German leftist politicians were deeply embedded in a way of thinking which could easily be associated with fascism'. Alternatively again, and the meaning would be similar to this latter sentence if so, it is possible that the student has confused the sound similarity of 'wedded' with 'embedded' and written the latter instead. Such mistakes are easily made when working in another language, and happen, albeit probably more often in speech, in the mother tongue too. What is clear is that the student is communicating a quite complex idea, one that he fully understands, but in writing it in English, he has condensed it or conflated different aspects of it, or perhaps just made a mistake in his choice of English preposition, such that it is not clear to the reader exactly what is meant.

Often the L2 student is perfectly capable of explaining what is meant, when difficulty in comprehending their texts is pointed out, but this means discussion rather than simply 'proofreading' or as is the case in the above text, guessing. Such a process then takes time. The disentangling of one sentence such as the above, especially surrounded by similarly dense text, can take as much as half an hour to sort out. The minimising of time is of course another role that the association of language work with proofreading serves. This minimisation is wryly summed up in the title of a paper by Orr and Blythman (1999) 'Have you got ten minutes? Can you sort out this dissertation?'

On the Institutional Periphery

As illustrated in the somewhat melodramatic discourse discussed above, when the norms and expectations of academic writing are apparently not adhered to, this is a remedial problem. Concomitantly, the role of 'language units' or 'writing centres' is seen as a remedial 'service', peripheral rather than central, to the mainstream operation of the university. In the context of international students in particular, the 'language support' class is what might be termed a 'cinderella' class, put on ideally at times which interfere least with 'mainstream' education. Its brief is effectively to 'mop up' the problems of academic literacy in a foreign language and culture, as invisibly as possible. Even in the United States, where there is a much longer tradition of teaching academic writing, see, for example, Bizzell and Herzberg (1990); Russell (1991); Brereton (1995) and Davidson and Tomic (1999) for overviews, the situation is not much different. Despite the embedding of teaching rhetoric and composition in the higher education curriculum, there remains a culture of marginalisation. As MacDonald states:

> Rhetoric and composition studies, […] remains a somewhat despised stepchild at many universities, particularly at the research university. (MacDonald, 1994: 4)

She also notes other work dealing with the low status of composition studies, especially at what are known as research universities. They include an explicit focus on overwork and underpay by Connors (1990); the politics of composition by Miller (1991); advocacy for writing across the curriculum programmes (Strenski, 1988), as well as showing the pressures operating against such programmes at research universities. From a somewhat different perspective, Holbrook (1991) looks at the feminisation of composition studies, which, in social status terms, is another indication of the marginalisation of this work.

The teaching of modern foreign languages is also plagued by its positioning vis-a-vis literature. As with most dichotomies, elaborated most prominently by Derrida, for example (Derrida, 1978, 1981), there is a non-stated hierarchy involved. In this case, literature is the privileged term. The language teaching parts of modern foreign languages degrees are usually not deemed as important as those involved with literature. In terms of physical location also, modern foreign language courses often 'state' their marginalisation by being taught outside the departmental boundaries of the degree being studied for. They are located in this case in language centres, which usually do not have the same academic status as discipline-specific departments.

There is a hierarchy involved also in linguistic versus literary analysis. For example, in the punning title of their book, *Seeing through Language*, Carter and Nash (1990) illustrate both the value of language analysis for deeper interpretive insight and the invisibility/transparency of language. While they stress that it is important not to regard language merely as a window onto something else and that it 'is a medium that is, active in the transmission of the message' (Carter & Nash, 1990: 24), they also recognise the reluctance of related endeavours in the academic community to accept the value of language analysis. They talk about the tendency of courses in literature and communications, for example, 'to look *past* language at the more 'important' ideas or content that a text contains' (Carter & Nash, 1990: 24).

The Pharmakon of Writing

In this section, I look at the prevailing remedial discourse for language through the lens of the ancient Greek word for 'remedy', namely *pharmakon*. As well as remedy, however, *pharmakon* also means poison. This paradoxical concept, with its dual meanings of poison and cure, constitutes an appropriate metaphor for the context of language in the academy. It encapsulates the ambivalences and complexities that derive from a focus on language in the academy, particularly at the interface between language issues and institutionally embedded preconceptions of the academic. This is the intellectual tradition within which writing itself is situated, and where the pharmakon metaphor has already been used, as discussed below.

In his dialogue *Phaedrus*, Plato invoked the notion of a pharmakon, with its dual meanings of poison and cure, to characterise the 'gift' of writing. This gift, so the myth goes, was declined by the Egyptian King Thamus, when he was offered it by the god, Thoth. Writing is a dangerous gift 'because it substitutes mere inscriptions – alien, arbitrary lifeless signs – for the authentic living presence of spoken language' (Norris, 1987). This suspicion of writing, which seems to be shared by Plato, hails from its lack of immediacy, its inauthenticity in relation to the authority of self-present speech. The association with the spoken word and truth, which is handed on in dialogue between the teacher and receptive student, means that writing is seen as a threat to truth, and by implication, morality. It may create a useful archive, but it threatens real memory, as people no longer need to remember. Much worse, it threatens to break the ties between teacher and student, and with them the eternal truths that are passed on from generation to generation. This predicament repeats itself wherever philosophy refuses to acknowledge its own textual status and aspires to pure contemplation of truth independent of mere written signs. Writing derives from the realm of repetition, it 'mimics the true form of knowledge by exploiting the resources of a dead, mechanical notation' (Norris, 1987: 34). Derrida traces this pattern of thinking about language, truth and reality down through the history of western thought, in the texts of Plato, Kant, Hegel and Husserl (Derrida, 1981). It is at the heart of what Derrida calls the 'metaphysics of presence', which predominates in western philosophical history.

The Pharmakon of Academic Literacy

What I am suggesting here is that the pharmakon phenomenon is reiterated in the contemporary context of higher education. This is the case where issues of performance in language come to the fore. In other words, academic literacy, as a cultural value system, is a metaphorical pharmakon, both poison and cure. It is poison to an institutionally embedded perception of the academic, a kind of 'symbolic cultural capital' (Bourdieu, 1977, 1984), whereby the understanding and communication of knowledge is effected in a unified manner, without the intrusion of language difficulties. In other words, it is the transparency assumption for language that prevails. However, the teaching of academic literacy has come to be seen as a cure for the ailing language of student performance in academic tasks. Effecting such a cure helps maintain the standards associated with an academic 'habitus' but the need for the cure in the first place offends the intrinsic academicism of the cultural capital embodied in this habitus.

The self-sufficiency of academic study must not be tarnished by acknow-ledgement that it needs the support of language or rhetorical structuring in the same way as 'logos' or the self-sufficiency of speech as reason, must not be diminished by accepting the gift of writing.

The dilemma for Plato was that while disparaging writing, he was at the same time writing down for posterity, the wisdom 'voiced' by Socrates. The dilemma for contemporary academic institutions is that with the emergence of the relatively new pedagogies of academic literacy and English for Academic Purposes, the self-sufficiency of the academic mis-sion, mediated through its various and ever multiplying disciplines is endangered by the necessity of acknowledging the substantive role of lan-guage and languaging in academic performance. This role has been repressed but is now asserting itself in the academy through the pedago-gies of remediation. The dilemma for the academic literacy pedagogies is that they are only tolerated while they remain remedial. To put this another way, the remedial positioning of language work is necessary in order to maintain the culturally embedded and socially embodied 'habitus' of being academic.

From the Ivory Tower to the Ivory Ghetto

It could also be said, paradoxically, that the practice of academic liter-acy has been created out of a denial of its existence. What it encompasses, study skills, an understanding of the rhetoric of argumentation, the abil-ity to suspend familiarity in ways of speaking and writing in order to adapt to culturally embedded ways, in some, the ability to do this also in a second language, have all been hidden in the traditional academic pedagogy of osmosis. The notion of how to study has traditionally not been addressed in higher education. Just as academic dress, the 'gown' in the town, is no longer so visible, so are its mores, its taken-for-granted assumptions no longer so readily recognised and practised. More explicit practical measures have therefore had to be taken. Diversity in student population has necessitated some diversity in pedagogy.

As already mentioned, these induction pedagogies or 'support' peda-gogies are not treated as equals, but are marginalised in the institutional discourse, and the institutional structure, of the academy. Speaking spe-cifically of the EAP context, but it extends to all the so-called 'support' work, Swales has felicitously named this institutional marginalisation the 'ivory ghetto of remediation' (Swales, 1990: 11). This phrase is felicitous in that its allusion to the 'ivory tower' of a bygone elite context for higher education points up an underlying continuation of elitist assumptions in academic culture. The tower may have tumbled but its value system persists in its attempts to prop up its 'fallen' standards. Such a prelapsarian discourse, adverting to a past when not only was the ivory tower impregnable to unwanted forces of society and commerce, but language issues did not intrude, forms the backdrop to academic literacy, as both textual practice and pedagogy.

Rewriting Remediation

Given the backdrop of a discourse of remediation within which language issues circulate, foregrounding languaging issues and language pedagogies becomes in itself a matter of institutional politics. While there is a case for not bemoaning the marginalisation issue, one which Johns (1997: 154) makes, when she says that we should not 'wring our hands and bemoan our marginality', there is also a case for addressing this issue directly, asking how and why it has come to be that way, and 're-writing' it or 'writing back' to it. Acknowledging the theoretical resonance of those terms from post-colonial studies, where 'writing back' refers to literature written in countries previously colonised by the United Kingdom, as, for example, in the title of the Australian book on post-colonial literature by Ashcroft, Griffiths and Tiffin (Ashcroft *et al.*, 2002), the concern here is with the conceptual and social positioning of language and language work. In this case, it is a question of writing back to the conditions of becoming of both the marginalised status of language and language work, and the preferred rhetorical renderings of languaging practices in the academy. Here, the use of the term 'languaging', elaborated further in the next chapter, is seen in a modest way as helping to change the discourse.

Chapter 4
Languaging in the Academy: Language as Dynamic Practice

Introduction

In this chapter, in contradistinction to the deficit discourse for language in higher education and the technicist model of remediation that goes along with it, I foreground the notion of languaging. This term points to a much more dynamic and constitutive model for language, issues around language and how language is expected to be used in academic contexts in contemporary higher education.

The concept of languaging accentuates the active, the liveliness and the performative aspects of working with, and using language. As such, it has much to contribute towards a theoretical re-framing of issues around language and intercultural communication.

The Dynamics of Languaging

Languaging is not the most usual term for language work, nor for discussing language issues. However, it is chosen here because it conveys the dynamic cultural process that using language is. Making a verb from a noun as in 'to language' accentuates the processual, the shifting, the fluid. This corresponds with trends in current theorising on social and cultural life and processes. As Street (1993: 23–43) has put it: 'culture is a verb'. The participial form 'languaging' is even more dynamic, conveyed also when used as an adjective. Such motion-based thinking is widespread in the contemporary humanities and social sciences and is revealed also in the choice of metaphors for the theoretical analysis of social process. The choice of 'liquid' for example, in the sociologist Zygmunt Bauman's series of books on late modernity illustrates this point (Bauman, 2000, 2003, 2005), as does the choice of 'flow' in the work of the anthropologist Arjun Appadurai (1996, 2001).

While the term 'languaging' may be used in a psycholinguistic way to refer to the mental processes of meaning-making (Ivanic, 2004: 223), as it were in abstraction from actual texts, the emphasis here is on its social and cultural contexts of production and reception. In my use of the term, I draw on Phipps and Gonzalez (2004), who use it in the context of modern language teaching, further elaborated on in an interview with Phipps by Crosbie (Crosbie, 2005). Phipps (2006) then transported the concept from the teaching and learning of modern languages to the context of tourism studies and the enrichment which learning the language of the country visited brings to the tourist. In their book on teaching modern languages, Phipps and Gonzalez confess that languaging 'may be a slightly uncomfortable term at first' but justify it in terms of the 'unease that precedes new ventures and discoveries' (Phipps & Gonzalez, 2004: 71). At its core, they suggest, languaging is a question of agency, 'of individuals accumulating powers and understandings to enable them to become actively critical social beings' (Phipps & Gonzalez, 2004: 73). In the empirical context of this book, higher education, 'becoming actively critical social beings' is germane, I believe, to what most academics would want for their students. It is certainly what theorists of learning in higher education espouse, for example, Marton *et al.* (1984) and especially, Barnett (1990, 1997, 2000, 2003).

In this book, language is seen as crucial to the process of being critical, as understood in the western educational tradition (see the final chapter for further discussion) and 'languaging' is seen as integral to academic performance. In the context of higher education, this includes interaction in seminars and various kinds of performance through academic writing. The term also applies here to the rhetorical moves that have become conventions of language use in the academy, as well as those that are changing the conventions. The dynamics of languaging in higher education is part of the transformative potential of higher education. As in the case of learning foreign languages which offer opportunities for 'mutual understanding, agency and transformation' as Phipps (2003: 7) has put it, experiencing and developing the different uses of language in the different genres that higher education offers, as well as interacting with students and tutors from different backgrounds provides a rich seedbed for personal growth and individual agency. In this process, languaging is not open-ended, however, there are constraints. These are embodied not least in the inherited ways of doing things in the academy, which are imbued with cultural values that have arisen at different points in intellectual cultural history. This can make the experience of languaging strange and unfamiliar also for individuals whose mother tongue is also that of the medium of instruction. The dynamics of languaging can include painful learning, as well as the joys of experiencing a different languaging self.

Languaging in the academy is for many like learning to operate in a foreign language, whether or not the language is foreign. The academy itself is cultural. It works with assumptions and expectations that have become stabilised in genres such as the essay and tutorial. At the same time, what might be seen as traditional assumptions and expectations are being challenged, not least by those from different academic cultures, with different languaging backgrounds.

Language and Languaging as Constitutive in Higher Education

By contrast to the underprivileged position of language in relation to content as mentioned in the previous chapter, the conceptualisation of language that is promoted here is one that has come with the so-called 'turn to language' in the social sciences in particular, namely the view that language is constitutive. For example, in their discussion of this 'turn' Filmer *et al.* state:

> If there is one key development that stands out above all others in more recent trends in social theory, it is the change that has occurred in the view of language. Broadly speaking, there has been a shift from seeing language as referential (i.e. that it refers to a reality existing beyond language) to seeing it as representational and constructive of reality. That is, to say, the perception has increased that language is the means by which humans socially construct their worlds. (Filmer *et al.*, 1998: 24)

Arguments for the constitutive role of language in knowledge and social construction generally are dominant in post-structuralist theory. Weedon (1987), for example, looks at the social construction of women, and sees both the socio-historical and cultural conditions for the expression of female identity, and the linguistic form of the expression belonging to the same order of discourse. Cameron (1995) provides another example of how a constitutive conceptualisation of language, as 'part of the explanation' changes an approach to a discipline. In this case, she is looking at a language-based discipline, namely sociolinguistics, and in particular, the relationship between language and identity. In traditional approaches, categories such as class and gender are relatively stable, whereas in critical approaches, they are unstable. She states:

> whereas sociolinguistics would say that the way I use language reflects or marks my identity as a particular kind of social subject, ... the

critical account suggests language is one of the things that *constitutes* my identity as a particular kind of subject. (Cameron, 1995: 15–16)

Such a critical theoretical perspective acknowledges that social reality both constructs and is constructed in and through discourse, as Cameron puts it elsewhere: 'through acts and practices of speaking and writing' (Cameron, 2001: 51).

It is those acts and practices of speaking and writing, in the specific context of higher education, that form the empirical and conceptual backdrop to the focus here on the constitutive role of language, and using language in academic performance, in higher education. Language and languaging play a role in every discipline, not only in their textualisations but also in how they are taught and assessed. They are imbricated in epistemological shifts and theoretical frameworks. They play a role as carrier of the past and mediator of future discourses.

The pedagogic practices of higher education itself, such as the seminar, the tutorial and the lecture, alongside assessment tasks such as the essay and other genres of academic writing are seen here as quintessentially languaging practices, although not often positively acknowledged as such. Language and how it is used is then integral to student success in getting a degree.

Languaging in English

While the locus of analysis for this book is contemporary higher education in the United Kingdom, there will be resonances with other predominantly English-speaking institutions in the 'western' intellectual tradition, such as the United States, Canada, Australia and New Zealand, to name Kachru's 'inner circle' (Kachru, 1985, 1992a), if not also with his postcolonial 'outer circle'. In addition, in what he terms the 'expanding circle', European and Asian institutions are increasingly adopting English as the medium of instruction, and it certainly has a prominent place in the school and higher education curriculum.

For many higher education institutions in traditionally English-speaking countries, the desire of increasing numbers of international students to study in a traditionally English-speaking environment is seen predominantly in an economic light. This is because the fee-paying status of 'international' students is increasingly necessary to the financial well-being of those institutions. Whether economically driven or not, however, the increase in international students studying in English means that the ability to perform academically in English has become increasingly important. This has brought issues of language to the fore. Arguably, it is also this context, which could help to bring traditional institutional perceptions of language out of the doldrums of remediation.

It is often pointed out that English is not a culture-free or neutral language; see, for example, discussions in Pennycook (1994b) and Fitzgerald (2003), even if there is a tendency in some sociopolitical contexts to treat it as such. Furthermore, the current political and economic dominance of English on the world stage has also brought with it debates around ownership of the language (Norton, 2000; Quirk & Widdowson, 1985; Widdowson, 1997), and its geopolitical effects (Canagarajah, 1999, 2002a, 2006; Phillipson, 1992), as well as the emergence of Englishes (Kachru, 1992b; Kirkpatrick, 2007; Smith, 1987), and the viewpoint of English as a lingua franca (House, 2006; Jenkins, 2000, 2006; Mauranen, 1993; Seidlhofer, 2002), among others. An ontological understanding of English is therefore very much in flux, and its multiple contexts of use, on a global scale, extremely varied, with different and complex social, educational and political priorities at issue.

This contemporary flux around English contributes to the constraints and challenges confronting international students studying in English, in inner circle academic institutions. Conversely the inherently intercultural experience and expression of those students also contribute to the ongoing flux and transculturation (Zamel, 1997) of English. While this intercultural context is acknowledged and exemplified in later chapters, it is seen as important also to focus on the relative stability of rhetorical conventions in the use of English in the academy. The issue here is not merely to describe those conventions however, as if they were something self-contained, separable, and simply applied, it is to look rather at how the currently preferred ways of using English in academic contexts have been generated as an integral part of intellectual and cultural history. The perspective then is a reflexive one, looking back at how rhetorical conventions and the norms of their evaluation have arisen in the context of a western cultural genealogy.

A Genealogical Approach to Languaging in the Academy

Since Foucault, the word 'genealogical' foregrounds the power dimension in cultural legacies. In other words, what is inherited in terms of values, assumptions and expectations of behaviour is inherently an effect of what has gained cultural and political power or, in Bourdieu's terms 'cultural capital' (Bourdieu, 1977; Bourdieu & Passeron, 1977). Over time, this symbolic capital is invested in different social contexts in such a way that its workings gradually become invisible, and its values taken for granted. Individuals routinely act in accordance with those values, and they are thus perpetuated.

In terms of intellectual history, the methodological framework of genealogical critique might be said to have begun with the 19th century philosopher, Friedrich Nietzsche. In his book *The Genealogy of Morals* (Nietzsche, 1956), he questioned the source of the meaning and value of core moral concepts in western cultural history. So such concepts as good and evil were no longer seen as absolutes but as historically contingent, and subject to changes in meaning in accordance with shifts in social and cultural power. This notion of contingency is central to the contemporary methodological framework of genealogical critique. Foucault's approach to genealogical critique was similar. In his work on medicine (Foucault, 1973c), punishment (Foucault, 1977), madness and sexuality (Foucault, 1973a, 1978), for example, Foucault brings out the fact that the process by which certain aspects of cultural and social life gain political and social dominance is ultimately contingent. He recounted, for example, the different conceptualisations of madness from the middle ages onwards and showed how they both reflected and enacted the dominant social power structures of the times. He did the same in relation to sexuality. Linked to the notion of contingency of what did become dominant in the regulation of social practices is the aspect of what was therefore 'hidden' knowledge. Thus Foucault concerned himself with what had been left out of account in the constitution of European Enlightenment Reason, as it were, themes such as madness, and badness.

What Foucault has become most famous for are his attempts to reveal the underlying rationales as to how large populations, such as those of nation states are governed. This process of what he calls 'governmentality' is enacted through social and political technologies of regulation, whereby the governed subjects in effect collude in, or at least co-operate with, what is deemed best for them, for example, in matters of public health or in maintaining safer societies. This process is perhaps most acutely described in relation to Jeremy Bentham's idea of a panopticon, for the purposes of keeping sight of prisoners at all times. Within the structure of the panopticon, prisoners who would be at all times subject to possible surveillance, would begin to police themselves, and behave as it is expected they ought to behave (Foucault, 1977).

The Regulation of Rhetorical Practices in Academic Pedagogy

Contemporary issues of governmentality, such as how the regulation of psychic well-being has become a major preoccupation of government strategies in advanced liberal democracies, have been taken up in a Foucauldian manner by Rose, in what he terms 'governing the soul' (Rose, 1989). The concern in this book is with the regulation of rhetorical practices in academic pedagogy. The genealogical critique here addresses contemporary attitudes towards language and the practices of languaging in higher education. This includes both the rhetorical norms of tutor–student interaction and academic writing.

An Insider Perspective

According to Dreyfus and Rabinow:

> Foucault introduces genealogy as a method of diagnosing and grasping the significance of social practices from within them. (Dreyfus & Rabinow, 1982: 103)

This implies also that the investigator is involved in, 'and to a large extent produced by, the social practices he is studying' (Dreyfus & Rabinow, 1982: 103). Such is the case also for this book. I am an insider/practitioner of academic literacy and EAP in the academy. I have, to some extent, been moulded by the work that I do and my perspective of it comes from within the academy. In particular, I have the privileged position of observing students unfamiliar with the workings of academic writing and academic discussion, as I try to induct them into the workings of pedagogical demands and expectations, against which, for the most part, they will be assessed. As already mentioned, this unfamiliarity can be experienced by both indigenous and ethnic minority, so-called 'home' students from families unfamiliar with UK higher education, as well as international students, whose languages and cultural styles of interaction are very different.

Within this situated context of contemporary higher education, my focus is also on the contingency of what has become powerful as well as on the processes or forms of regulation which maintain that power. While Foucault's and Rose's analyses were acted out on a much wider stage, concerning the social polity in general, my concern is a much more modest one, the discourse in which language circulates in the academy, and the presuppositions behind how language is, or should be, used. At the same time, however, it is the modesty or 'low-profile' of the object of focus that in itself foregrounds a kind of intellectual suppression. The social position of language in the academy, whether with regard to student performance or with the professional teaching of academic language use, is subordinate. It is therefore worthwhile to bring questions such as why it is that the contemporary reception of language use and representations of language in higher education are as they are. The concern here, then, is not so much with uncovering hidden knowledge, as illuminating a feature of contemporary intellectual and academic life that is underrepresented or often misrepresented in the institutional life of academe. Language is not so much 'hidden' as subsumed into invisibility by a dominant discourse of transparency, and its technologies of rhetorical regulation.

Academic Literacy as a Power/Knowledge Effect

In working with a unified notion of academic literacy, there is no intention to deny the contemporary multiplicity of differences in ways of arguing, the preferred genres, and differing power struggles of different disciplines and pedagogic practices. I am rather pointing beyond any specific discipline to the interactional context of tutors and students in higher education, and the normative backdrop prevailing over students' academic performances. As discussed further in later chapters, in addition to being a 'discoursing subject' in specific disciplinary domains, the academic writer is also a discoursing subject within what I call 'the visibilising economy of rationality, language, and knowledge', which was inspired by scientific rationality and the urge to know.

Such a unified notion of academic literacy acknowledges the universalist assumptions inscribed in its intellectual heritage, and the hegemony of values surrounding what counts as 'good' in language-using academic performance. These values ultimately derive from the power of European Enlightenment understandings of knowledge and knowledge production. I am using the unified term, then, in recognition of there being a culture of academic literacy, which is a genealogical effect of European Enlightenment power/knowledge. Foucault's concept of power, or power/knowledge (Foucault, 1980), emphasises the capillary effects of power, whereby dominant social and cultural values, aspirations, procedures, influence or 'discipline' behaviour in non-immediate, but indirect, and widespread, ways. With regard to linguistic behaviour, both spoken and written, this is seen as inscribed with the values of both epistemological and socially dominant power. This includes the dominant understanding of the relationship between language and the communication of knowledge, an understanding of knowledge that interrelates both a Cartesian rationalist understanding of clear thinking and a Lockean empiricist understanding of discovery through sensory perception, as well as how both these approaches take on values from the culture of the mind or academia and learning that the 'Western' tradition has inherited. Academic literacy can then be seen as itself a discipline, that is, 'disciplined' in the Foucauldian sense (Foucault, 1977), by formations of value concerning the use of language, processes of learning, and the communication of knowledge.

From this power/knowledge perspective, the institutional discourse of higher education around language is also a major locus for the perpetuation of values pertaining to language and to language use, which were generated at a much earlier stage of intellectual history. The shock-horror discourse, which erupts when language use is not what is expected, as elaborated in the previous chapter, in effect works to maintain a normative understanding of the role of language and how it should be used.

The Power of Cultural Inscription

Attitudes towards language in the academy on the one hand, and active languaging practices on the other, are indelibly culturally inscribed. However, these issues have tended not to attract cultural theoretical scrutiny. This contrasts with philosophical and literary discourses, for example, where language is recognised as the carrier of metaphysical mystique, and therefore needs to be 'deconstructed', a theoretical approach derived from the work of Jacques Derrida. Ultimately, arguing for the impossibility of any definitive interpretation, as each interpretation is inextricably tied in with an opposing one, any assumption of a firm foundation on which to stand is dislodged, and the grasp of meaning is infinitely deferred. The assumption of western metaphysics, that language can convey meaning, as if transparent, is denied. Language in effect colludes in the structuring of texts which makes any definitive meaning impossible, and at the same time provides the resources for a deconstructive analysis. This is constitutive of the metaphysics of presence, which Derrida discerns in the philosophical history of western culture.

It is important to recognise that western metaphysics is culturally inscribed both in attitudes towards language and in how language, in this case, specifically English, is used in higher education contexts. As well as the transparency conceptualisation for language discussed in the previous chapter, there are a number of other currents running from and throughout different points of cultural history, which have influenced the norms and practices regarding language and language use. In the 18th century, for example, Jonathan Swift's *Proposal for Correcting, Improving and Ascertaining the English Tongue* (Swift, 1957), which was a plea for the stabilising of language, to make it a site of certainty, to 'make Words more durable than Brass' (Swift, 1957: 17) signals the political importance allotted to codifying and controlling language. The continuation of this means of social control may be seen in the role of the 20th century prescriptive grammarians mentioned also in the previous chapter. Such processes may be seen as technologies deployed in the 'governmentality' of language and how people use it. As Leith points out in his history of the standardisation of English, the 'preoccupation with fixity has often functioned as a kind of brake on the natural tendency towards variation and change' (Leith, 1983: 33). The social and political desire for fixity of the language may be said to have triggered moves for its codification, most eminently exemplified in Samuel Johnson's long laboured over dictionary, published in 1755 (Johnson, 1755). The powerful effects of such codification remain in the contemporary normativity of aspects of language use, especially in relatively stable contexts, such as that of the academy.

In locating genealogical roots, or even mapping genealogical routes, it is important to remember that the process is not one of a simple, mechanical cause and effect logic. It is rather a case of recognising and acknowledging the 'always already', a much used trope in continental philosophy, appearing regularly in the work of Althusser, for example Althusser (1971), and Derrida. It suggests the impossibility of locating an absolute origin on the one hand, while on the other, recognising the continuing workings of a certain kind of understanding or set of cultural values. Its conceptual significance in cultural studies, for example, is discussed in Tudor (1999: 96). Here, the concern is not with the specific pinpointing of cause and effect in the language we use in specific contexts, but rather the understanding that deeply entrenched cultural value systems invisibly mobilise our psycholinguistic schemata, our uptakes to specific speech acts, the preferred rhetorical ordering of academic writing, and our pedagogical practices in general. These value systems in effect inform how we have come to speak and write academically. The normative practices of the academy, then, such as the tutorial or the essay, are not simply to be understood as linguistic genres to be analysed and converted into pedagogical techniques enabling students to perform better in them. While there is undeniably pedagogical merit in this, the focus here is rather on illuminating such languaging practices as themselves cultural artefacts, inscribed by power relations working over centuries.

Languaging and Performativity

While in a very concrete way, it is often the case that intercultural encounters enact the deferral of meaning that Derrida theorises, it is not particularly helpful to dwell on this in the practical pedagogical contexts of teaching language, or indeed in the everyday occurrences of using language in academic genres. Mismatches in pragmatic uptakes and misunderstandings of words in context may be routine in intercultural encounters, thereby delaying a sense of understanding, but such empirical languaging contexts are not the stuff of philosophical enquiry. Nonetheless, they are theoretically relevant as they reveal the social and academic accomplishments that language and languaging perform. For this reason, throughout this book, I often talk of languaging in specific contexts in the academy as performance. However, what I also want to advert to is the more recently developed notion of performativity, whose theoretical resonances play out both in an understanding of the dynamics of languaging in conformity with deepset expectations, and in how intercultural languaging in particular exerts a transformative potential on the context of its operation. The notion of performativity signals productivity and reiteration. In this respect, it can refer to both the perpetuation of traditional kinds of more or less ritualised performance, but also the production of something new, which comes into being with the performance. It is in this latter sense in particular that it has been used in identity politics, for example, Butler in the performance of gender and other political roles (Butler, 1997, 2006); Pennycook on the social and cultural identification with popular cultural forms such as rap and hip-hop (Pennycook, 2007); Canagarajah on language learning, identity and identification (Canagarajah, 2004), and in a number of different social contexts in Bell (1999). Performativity therefore also signals the potential for change by doing, a process which is never ending.

The theoretical notion of performativity is indebted to Derrida's deconstructive practices, and his notions of différance, citation, iterability, spectres and so on. It derives particularly from his deconstruction of Austin's theory of speech acts (Derrida, 1977), in which he disrupts Austin's dichotomy of constatives and performatives and shows the reliance of both on the principle of iterability, which in effect subsumes the notion of the constative within that of the performative.

The Intercultural Performative

The notion of the intercultural performative acknowledges the empirical production of a specific space – time enactment of intercultural communication and theorises this performativity as both a historicised act and a transformative agent, in this case, in the ongoing construction of contemporary international higher education. Austin's notion of the speech act is regularly invoked in the practical context of intercultural encounters, usually to point out where an intended illocutionary force in a particular social context is not taken up by the other participant, or where the same speech act in the same context has a different illocutionary force, or where a different speech act performs the same illocutionary force in a different language. Such contrastive cultural and linguistic issues are in effect the basis for pragmatics (Blum-Kulka *et al.*, 1989; Leech & Thomas, 1990; Thomas, 1983, 1995).

What has achieved less attention, however, is the bi-directionality of the intercultural encounter. The illocutionary force of the mismatched uptake is also being mismatched, and so on in what is more like a Deleuzian rhizomic pattern than a diametrically cross-cutting one (Deleuze & Guattari, 1983). So, for example, in what I have called the discursive dance of the intercultural performative (see Chapter 13), a British tutor interprets a Japanese student's difficulties with writing her MA thesis as difficulties in structuring the writing. As seems often to be the case when international students seek help with their essays or similar, it is the assumption of difficulties with the language which comes to the fore. However, the student wonders why he is telling her this (which she already knows about); leaves communication of what she really wants to know to the senior student she has brought with her and ultimately decides that because this is the course convenor and not her personal tutor, she does not have to tell him everything he wants to know, including at what point in time she might submit her first draft. The communication in the tutorial is twisting and turning as different assumptions from different cultural background norms for the basis and context of the communication come into play, sometimes at different points and at other times simultaneously. What I have foregrounded in this tutorial encounter, however, is how the interpretive space of the institutional genre is being destabilised, as different kinds of performative acts occur within it.

The Temporal Bi-Directionality of Performativity

There is also a temporal dimension to the bi-directionality which the theoretical notion of performativity foregrounds. Here, performativity points backwards as well as project forwards. It points backwards in history to show how what is now has come to be, and simultaneously forwards from what is now to what might become/is becoming. Taking up Butler's (1997) notion of the 'citational' nature of identity, Bell (1999) sees it operating in what she calls *'The Performativity of Belonging'*. In her introduction to the edited collection, she discusses the work of Fortier, one of the contributors, as follows:

> the highly ritualized movements that one performs in Catholic Mass are the incorporation of norms, a 'stylized repetition of acts' that cultivate the sign and the sense of belonging. (Bell, 1999: 3)

It is repetition which constitutes the sense of belonging. As Bell puts it:

> Through embodied movements, the citation operates to recall and reconnect with places elsewhere that, through those very movements, are re-membered; at the same time, a site of diasporic belonging is created. (Bell, 1999: 3)

In the case of the intercultural tutorial encounters discussed in Chapter 10, how the tutor performs his role enacts traces of the Socratic dialogue, thereby pointing back to, and perpetuating an already well-established cultural template. At the same time, however, the languaging of international students as they communicate with their peers and their tutors in the western contexts of institutionalised educational practices, by its nature, transforms those practices. Their performativity has transformative effects.

The overall situation is one of mobility, concrete movement across geographical borders, as well as mental and intellectual mobility across established culturally engendered student or tutor subject positions. Elucidating such subject positions in relation to their own genealogical cultural formations and value systems, and showing how each may be transforming the other, is merely one, albeit janus-faced, perspective on the ongoing production of international and intercultural subjects, within the context of higher education.

Further data and discussion on intercultural communication will be in focus from Chapter 8 onwards. In the meantime, in the following few chapters, I would like to look backwards at how we have got to where we are in terms of what is expected, and valued, in written academic discourse.

Chapter 5

Occidentalist Inscription: The Historical Construction of Contemporary Representations of Language in the Academy

Introduction

A major focus of previous chapters was a critique of the institutional discourse around language issues in higher education. The representation of language in this discourse tends to be either negative or invisible. Issues of language use in academic performance then circulate predominantly in a deficit discourse. By contrast, the centrality of language use in academic success tends to be ignored. This is because a cultural ideal has developed whereby language should be invisible. Such an invisible language allows the more important message to be more readily available. As a result, when language does become visible, that is, when attention is drawn to it, this is assumed to be because it has not been used 'properly' (Turner, 1999c). It must therefore be in need of remediation.

The aim of this chapter is to explore how the discourse around language has come to be as it is. The locus of exploration is predominantly the culture and power that grew up around scientific rationality, from its emergence in Europe in the 17th century through to its consolidation in the 18th century, when it was an integral part of the wider power structure associated with the European Enlightenment. The cultural and social power that created the dominance of scientific rationality, and the cultural and social power which scientific rationality itself accrued and wielded, is implicated in both the subordinate positioning of language within a language-content dichotomy, and in how language was conceptually constructed, as well as in the rhetorically preferred ways of using language, especially in academic discourse. Dominant conceptualisations of language, as well as the preferred ways in which it embodies rhetorically, the dominant cultural values, are therefore seen as part of the wider intellectual heritage of western culture.

An Occidentalist Perspective

In looking at the wider intellectual heritage of western culture and its effects on language, the approach taken here is 'occidentalist'. The term 'occidentalism' derives its intellectual resonance from Said's notion of 'orientalism' (2003), a complex concept which is not a purely descriptive term, but one which reflects back on those who purport to describe the mores and cultures of the 'orient', namely those from Europe, from 'the west'. In other words, the notion of orientalism contains within it a critique of the west's involvement in the construction of the orient, which was at the same time, colonised by the imperial west. The term 'occidentalism' then is a more explicitly reflexive concept. It adverts to the practice of western knowledge gathering and turns it back on itself. It reflects back on how the western intellectual and cultural tradition has constructed its own view of what constitutes knowledge and how best to find or achieve it.

This means that, for example, an occidentalist perspective recognises how a powerful conceptual notion such as modernity has been framed and constructed by dominant western philosophers, scientists and political thinkers. It also acknowledges that their dominance would not have been possible without the imperialist and violent politics of colonialism and slavery. In acknowledging this intellectual and political history, then, the notion of occidentalism puts the European Enlightenment project in the frame for critique. It also recognises the continuing power of the values inscribed in that project and looks for contemporary instances of their disruption and change.

While Nietzsche, in his questioning of the source of the meaning and value of core moral concepts in western cultural history, such as guilt, may be said to have begun the process of occidentalist critique (Nietzsche, 1956), it is from the perspective of post-colonial experience and theorising that it has been more widely explored. This is the case in the book by Venn (2000), entitled *Occidentalism: Modernity and Subjectivity*, whereby he makes the case that the west's formation of modernity grew alongside its colonisation of the 'new world'. Without colonisation, and without slavery, the economic and conceptual dominance of Europe, for example, the European Enlightenment ideals of fully understanding the world through 'man's' power to reason, could not have been possible. As Venn puts it:

> Occidentalism ... is the conceptual and historical space in which a particular narrative of the subject and a particular narrative of history have been constituted; these have become hegemonic with modernisation, having effects throughout the world because of the scope of the project of modernity and the global reach of European colonisation. (Venn, 2000: 2)

While Venn's project is to 'break' with that conceptual space, aiming to:

> dislodge from post-Enlightenment philosophical discourse a number
> of critical elements that enable one to indicate a discourse of being
> which opens towards a different postmodernity, a transmodernity,
> one which is the correlate of a postcoloniality to come (Venn, 2000: 2).

Here, the aim is not so much to break with this conceptual space, but to
recognise its continued existence in attitudes towards language and its
embodiment in language use, specifically, the rhetoricity of academic
discourse. Such recognition also acknowledges its historical contingency
and the possibilities for a different becoming, and in that sense it is also
critical.

The European Enlightenment project to describe, categorise, and therefore know the world, was not only a project with literal colonial ambitions, but also one which developed a colonising mindset, namely, one
which sought to capture and appropriate 'other' knowledge, in the same
way as it appropriated raw resources and commodities. This colonising
mindset also wanted to determine what constituted knowledge. It is felicitously summed in Hall's curt phrase: 'the west and the rest' (Hall, 1992).
Traces of the colonising mindset remain in how we talk about contemporary knowledge production. We continue to talk of 'pushing back the frontiers' of knowledge, and for the practitioners within, it is important to be
'at the cutting edge' of discovering new knowledge.

The internalised conceptual link between the process of colonisation
and dominant epistemologies is also made explicitly by Young in his *White
Mythologies*, as follows:

> the construction of knowledges which all operate through forms of
> expropriation and incorporation of the other mimics at a conceptual
> level the geographical and economic absorption of the non-European
> world by the West. (Young, 1990: 4)

What I want to do here is bring this conceptual mimicry to the textual
context of rhetorical embodiment. It seems that the dominant epistemological and cultural values of the European Enlightenment have constructed a rhetoricity, which inscribes those very values.

The Epistemological Importance of Clarity

During the 17th and 18th centuries, when not only the discovery of new
knowledge, but also the importance of its communication became

paramount, the fear that language might get in the way of a pure transfer of knowledge was either explicit or implicit in many of the debates of the time. From Descartes' notion of 'clear and distinct' ideas through to Locke's metaphor of the conduit, see further below, language is caught up in a 'discourse of transparency' (Turner, 1999a: 49), which is further related to the epistemological importance of making knowledge visible. The culturally embedded nature of the transparency conception for language, its rootedness in western metaphysics, as Crowley (1989) has put it, gives it a strength, which readily enables the construction of language as an invisible medium.

Scientific rationality is perhaps most cogently expressed in Descartes' famous dictum, 'cogito ergo sum'. His faith in the ability of 'man' to ascertain the truth by reliance on his own reason or ability to think, marked a cultural shift towards valuing the power of reason, and no longer only relying on experience. The method of reasoning which Descartes propounded was based on doubt or scepticism. As Venn puts it:

> It is a scepticism which has one main aim: to proceed to the systematic exclusion of all those ideas, sentiments, feelings, desires and values which could be thought to belong to an old decaying order, or to be competing to replace it, and to the exclusion of everything which threatens the purity of a Reason that alone becomes the source of knowledge and of truth. (Venn, 1984: 135)

This emphasis on reason had implications also for language. In the old order of knowledge, or *episteme* as Foucault calls it in his book *The Order of Things* (Foucault, 1970), language *was* transparent, in the sense that it was also the repository of truth. In other words, the truth could be read off from the correct interpretation of language. The power of 'correct' interpretation was of course only vested in those, such as priests, with the authority to do so. With the new explanatory structure of the classical age, or modernity, however, rationality and logic came to be regarded as primary. As Venn states:

> This explanatory structure replaces the previous schema based on 'signature' and on representation, that is, to say on the idea of a *signus dei* imprinted in the world, knowledge of which was also knowledge of God [Aquinas]. The world became no longer transparent; those authorized to read its language could no longer speak its truth. Language itself and its authoritative texts – scriptures or theological and philosophical works – could no longer be trusted to reveal the secret of the order of things. (Venn, 1984: 35)

What is interesting in the context of this substantive epistemic shift to the predominance of human reason, and the point I want to emphasise here is the continuing conceptual importance of visibility. The locus of interpretive power may have changed, but the mode of cognising has not. Seeing clearly, whether as an effect of what God has revealed, or as a result of the exercise of human reason, is at issue in both cases. This conceptual framing is paramount in Descartes' method of isolating 'clear and distinct' ideas. In his book on the rationalist philosophers, Cottingham outlines its importance as follows:

> Descartes insisted that no concept should be allowed in a philosophi-
> cal or scientific explanation unless it is either transparently clear or
> capable of being reduced by analysis to elements that are clear.
> (Cottingham, 1988: 32)

The association of rationality with clarity is therefore made at the outset, when the autonomous thinking subject, Descartes' cogito, comes into being.

Language and the Communication of Clarity

The importance placed on clarity of thought transferred easily to clarity of linguistic expression, although there was a definite hierarchy involved. As well as creating a link between 'clear and distinct' ideas and clear and distinct linguistic expression, scientific rationality, in privileging knowl-edge, conceptualised the communication of knowledge as a conduit. The conduit conceptualisation is made explicitly in Locke's (1975 [1689]) *Essay Concerning Human Understanding* as follows:

> For Language being the great Conduit, whereby Men convey their
> discoveries Reasonings and Knowledge, from one to another, he that
> makes an ill use of it, though he does not corrupt the Fountains of
> Knowledge, which are in Things themselves; yet he does, as much as
> in him lies, break or stop the Pipes, whereby it is distributed to the
> public use and advantage of Mankind. (Locke, 1689, Book III. Chapter
> 11, Section 5: quoted in Harris and Taylor, 1997, 2nd edn: 127)

This quotation foregrounds the way in which meaning/knowledge is separated from language. Language is seen as a necessary adjunct, the means whereby knowledge, which is discovered and stored in the mind, is represented and communicated to other minds. It is the scientific dis-coveries that are important: language becomes important only in as much as these discoveries have to be communicated as clearly and correctly as possible.

The need for language to be a transparent conduit then was given impetus from the need for an emergent scientific rationality to assert its dominance. The conduit model for language seems appropriate in that it suggests directness and security, keeping the way 'clear' and free from error in the transmission of what were themselves tightly boundaried and contamination-free clear and distinct ideas. Both Descartes, the archetypal rationalist, and Locke, the archetypal empiricist, seem locked into the same value system for language, a discourse of transparency, in which knowledge becomes clear by the utilisation of the correct method and is clearly conveyed by the medium of language.

The conduit model remains embedded in the lexical resources of English, as can be seen through a cognitive metaphorical analysis. Such analyses, epitomised in the title of Lakoff and Johnson's (1979) book *Metaphors We Live by* (Lakoff & Johnson, 1980) display the conceptualisations underlying conventional ways of speaking about or 'looking at' everyday topics. In his examination of the 'conduit metaphor' for communication, Reddy (1979) found that it was responsible for 70% of expressions in English for communication. For example, we 'put things into words', 'get ideas across', 'transmit messages' and so on. These expressions imply that language is a pre-existing, transparent, container for communicating with each other. While linguists such as Halliday (1978) explicitly reject the conduit conceptualisation for language, in favour of a 'social semiotic' model, which emphasises both the reflecting and shaping force of language in society, the conduit model remains in the numerous linguistic expressions, which perpetuate the cognitive metaphor. They may be seen as the linguistic inscription of a powerful epistemological assumption.

The Mathematisation of Language

What Locke's quotation above also highlights is the fear that natural language users might not be up to the task of conveying knowledge correctly that they might 'break or stop the pipes'. As a result of this widespread social fear on the part of scientists/philosophers of the time, a great deal of effort in both the French and British scientific/philosophical establishments of the 17th and early 18th centuries went into improving language, so that it might live up to the ideal of clarity. These efforts often took the form of changing language into a system of mathematical symbols.

Leibniz, for example, worked on what he thought of as a 'universal language', an 'algebra of thought' which would 'synthesize into one system the merits of a deductive logic and those of a Cartesian logic of discovery' (Baker & Hacker, 1984: 22). As Baker and Hacker further state:

> Such a language would provide an exact and structurally perspicuous system of symbolization for the precise expression of all actual and possible scientific knowledge. (Baker & Hacker, 1984: 23)

This idea was enthusiastically acclaimed by Descartes for its benefits to the exercise of correct judgement. As he wrote to fellow mathematician, Mersenne:

> The greatest advantage of such a language would be the assistance it would give to men's judgment, representing matters so clearly that it would be almost impossible to go wrong. (Letter to Mersenne, 20.11.1629 quoted in Baker & Hacker, 1984: 23)

The concern to mathematise language in order to communicate more clearly was taken up also in England by Bishop Wilkins. His *Essay towards a Real Character and a Philosophical Language* (Wilkins, 1968 [1668]) was designed to make signification 'unambiguous and pure' (see Crowley, 1989). Similar ideas continued into the 20th century with the logical positivists. For example, Bertrand Russell's philosophical quest in *The Philosophy of Logical Atomism* (Russell, 1918) was to work out the basis for the 'logically perfect language'. He argues that:

> in a logically perfect language, there will be one word and no more for every simple object ... A language of that sort ... will show at a glance the logical structure of the facts asserted or denied. (Russell, 1918: 58, quoted in Crowley, 1989: 65)

In the 17th century as well as in the 20th century, and taking in also the attempts of the etymologists, such as Bishop Trench, in the 19th century to find the 'true' meanings of words, the aim, as Crowley puts it, was 'to guarantee the status of language as the vehicle of truth and clarity' (Crowley, 1989: 65).

Ironically, it was only in the efforts of cryptography rather than clarity that any mathematically encoded language was used successfully. Robert Hooke recorded his *Descriptions of Helioscopes* in Wilkins' *Real Character* because he wanted only initiates to know the secrets of his balance spring watch; see the discussion in Jardine (1999). The use of cryptography reveals the other side of the desire to communicate knowledge, namely the desire to capitalise on its technological successes. As Jardine points out:

> coded announcements were a way of 'place-keeping' for ideas that would be divulged later when they had been fully worked out. (Jardine, 1999: 322)

They were particularly suited to procuring patents or royal licence. After filing for a patent, including with the application a sealed envelope containing a coded explanation of the process, the inventor ploughed as much funding as he could into resolving the technical details of the invention, then returning to claim the patent. While this is a supreme example of clarity in the exercise of instrumental rationality, it also points up the difficulties of attaining the communication of knowledge to the degree of clarity that the scientists and philosophers of the 17th century envisaged.

The Politics of Style

The drive to change and improve language in the interests of both communicating knowledge and retaining its 'purity' was not restricted to ignoring natural language completely and inventing new symbolic systems. In 17th century England, the Royal Society's declared purpose was not only to advance science but to improve the English language as a medium of prose. This latter purpose is achieved, according to Bishop Thomas Sprat in his history of the Royal Society, by endorsing 'mathematical plainness' for language and, to the same effect, rejecting all 'amplifications, digressions, and swellings of style'. (Sprat, 1958 [1667: 113]). This latter formulation was also an oblique reference to the French scientific academy, who were seen as rivals to the Royal Society. The French academicians were perceived by the English as interested in style and eloquence for its own sake.

Interestingly, in this social and political drive to improve the use of English in writing, there were other linguistic casualties. In his study of proverbs, Obelkevich (1987) draws attention to their ousting from polite and learned society, with the demand for the 'correct, classical, and polished style' (Obelkevich, 1987: 59) of prose. He writes:

> Proverbs were put in a bad light by changes in learned culture itself – for example, by the emergence in the late seventeenth century of new models of literary prose style. Rhetoric as the guide to writing was replaced by grammar; metaphors were attacked, notably by the Royal Society, as emotional and untruthful; the ornate, 'cornucopian' style of the past, with its oral residue, gave way to a plain, clear 'correct' and more 'written' style. (Obelkevich, 1987: 58)

By the middle of the next century, in the 1740s, it was clear that the process of proverbs losing the social prestige they had enjoyed in the 16th
century was complete. Obelkevich cites Lord Chesterfield advising his
son at this time, that:

> a man of fashion never has recourse to proverbs or vulgar aphorisms.
> (Obelkevich, 1987: 57)

Consonant with the changes in prose style was the desire to 'lay bare'
knowledge, and not distract by language. As embodied in the expression,
the 'naked truth' knowledge was conceptualised as being found or 'uncovered' in its simplest, purest, completely untrammelled state. This preference for truth/knowledge to be completely naked is yet another instance
of cultural investment in the concept and value of clear visibility.

Knowledge as Seeing Clearly

It is perhaps helpful to go back to 17th century knowledge production
practices in order to gain an appreciation of how seeing clearly became
such an important epistemological criterion. Observation, that is, literally
seeing with one's own eyes was the procedure by which new knowledge
claims were made and ratified. Much effort at the time was therefore
invested in improving the technological apparatus, which allowed what
was invisible to be better seen. This applied to improving telescopic lenses
as well as equipment for use in experiments. The use of an air pump in
experiments designed to get a better understanding of respiratory and
circulatory systems in the body was one such.

The Royal Society of London was the site of arbitration over whether
what the scientist/experimenter saw was the truth or not. Here, the acceptability of claims made on the basis of particular experiments was usually
to have the experiment done publicly, observed by fellow members of the
Society. Robert Boyle, a son of the Earl of Cork, was a key proponent of
this process, providing both an air pump, one of the most important pieces
of apparatus for the experiments of the time and devising the strategy of
getting witnesses to an experiment to sign a register. Replications of the
experiment were encouraged and the more witness signatures there were,
the more the results of the experiment became established knowledge
(Shapin, 1984; Swales, 1990: 111).

With the instantiation of *The Philosophical Transactions of the Royal
Society* in 1665, empirical observation with the eyes was extended to written observations of their own experiments made by scientists in letters to
the President of the Society. Here, the ambivalence in meaning of the

word 'observation' between what is seen and what is said or written can be seen as apposite, as the written representation of knowledge was influenced by the observatory manner in which its claims arose. Such letters outlined experiments and their findings, and often included translations from other European languages (Jardine, 1999), thereby widening the scope for establishing and adjudicating claims. Other people would write in, picking up points for criticism or asking for clarification. Jardine (1999) illustrates the ethos of fierce competition between the empirical scientists, the makers of practical apparatus such as Hooke, and the rationalists, of whom Newton is a prime example. This rivalry, and disagreement, is clear also in the letters to the Royal Society, taking issue with Newton's claims for his experiments on optics, which Bazerman discusses in his rigorous analysis of Newton's writing of the *Opticks* (Bazerman, 1988). Bazerman's extensive study, which along with the set of interrogatory letters from members of the Royal Society, includes Newton's lectures and revisions to his accounts of his experiments, reveals the extent to which Newton honed his rhetorical style in order to meet the sociopolitical, and methodological demands of his time. As such, this book provides a powerful example of the production of rhetorical norms in relation to 17th century knowledge production practices.

The Rhetorical Visibilisation of Observation

In keeping with the wider ethos of discovery of the time, as well as in extrapolation from the conferment of authenticity to knowledge claims through direct observation, one of Newton's tasks is to make his experiments and their findings visible to his readers. As Bazerman puts it:

> His overall rhetorical problem is to give an account of his findings so that they appear as concrete fact, as real as an earthquake or ore found in Germany even though the events that made these facts visible to Newton occurred in a private laboratory as the result of speculative ponderings and active experimental manipulations. Newton constructed an orderly narrative, rejecting possible causes … for the elongation of a prism for example, until the final, inevitable cause is revealed by the experimentum crucis. (Bazerman, 1988: 90)

By apparently stumbling upon findings, Newton is hiding the fact that they are based on speculations over which he has long laboured in the laboratory. At the same time, he is making visible for his readers the processes that he is going through, so that they can enact them, as it were, in their own minds. Newton's decision to rhetoricise his experimental results as a journey of discovery both inscribes the ethos of discovery of the times, a time of European colonial expansion as well as of knowledge, and panders to the empirical scientists in his audience, whom he needs to persuade, and whose preferred methods are inductive.

However, where Newton's rationalist predilections come through is in the fact that he not only wants to persuade his fellow scientists of the viability of his experimental procedures, he also wants to convince his wider readership of the reasoning process associated with the experiment. This requires a different rhetorical strategy. Bazerman refers to him hitting on the strategy of 'interpretive command', which:

> has the advantages of increasing the appearance of generality to the claims and lending the universal force of geometry. (Bazerman, 1988: 117)

An example of Newton deploying this strategy is shown in a later account of his findings to the Royal Society, where he begins:

> Let alpha represent an oblong piece of white paper. (Bazerman, 1988: 115)

Such a formulation corresponds to the beginning of a geometric proof, following the pattern of deductive logic. This contrasts with his previous, predominantly narrative style, where he recounts his experiments in the past tense and foregrounds his own agency and the practical constraints under which he was working. The following is an example:

> the refractions were as near as I could make them. (Bazerman, 1988: 91)

With the authority of deductive logic, and the incontrovertibility of geometric proof, Newton lends authority to his own argument. Bazerman talks of Newton, 'marching' the reader through 40 pages of narration and discussion, 'creating a tactile and ideal proof of the theorem' (Bazerman, 1988: 122). Both of these major rhetorical strategies, which Newton has recourse to for different purposes, are visibilising ones. On the one hand, there is the concretude of the journey of discovery narrative and on the other, the mapping out of geometrical-style proof.

Language and the Representation of Visibility

Moving forward to the 18th century, and the field of natural history, we find another example of the intertwined relationship between knowledge and visibility. Natural history is the field which Foucault chose for his discussion of what he refers to as the 'classical episteme' (Foucault, 1970). Not only did this field exemplify par excellence the process of creating identity and difference through its close attention to classificatory procedures in the establishment of plant genus and species, it also illustrated the preferred alignment between language and the 'observing gaze' (Foucault, 1970: 132).

Natural historians in the second half of the 18th century, as with the experimental scientists of the Royal Society in the 17th century, thought of themselves as engaged in discovering something that was already there. While there were competing systems of classification, the natural historians were all engaged in a common project, namely as Eriksson puts it: 'the faithful representation of nature's own plan' (Eriksson, 1980: 66, quoted in Pratt, 1992: 29). By contrast, Foucault sees the Linnaean project as rather one of:

> a new field of visibility being constituted in all its density. (Foucault, 1970: 132)

This new field of visibility also has implications for the conceptualisation and use of language. As Foucault puts it, natural history:

> has as a condition of its possibility the common affinity of things and language with representation; but it exists as a task only in so far as things and language happen to be separate. It must therefore reduce this distance between them so as to bring language as close as possible to the observing gaze, and the things observed as close as possible to words. (Foucault, 1970: 132)

While Foucault is mainly concerned here with the coming into being of classifying processes and the social and epistemological power this function took on, what is of interest for my argumentation is the role imputed to language. It is the mediator of both the 'observing gaze' and the close analytical description of flora and fauna:

> natural history reduces the whole area of the visible to a system of variables all of whose values can be designated, if not by a quantity, at least by a perfectly clear and always finite description. (Foucault, 1970: 136)

The visibilising and classifying of botanical knowledge is thus dependent on the descriptive and representational power of language. Language is invested with the role of 'mapping' knowledge, without drawing attention to itself as part of the map. In other words, it has to be transparent.

Mapping Discovery

Given the visibilising or knowledge-mapping role of language, social and epistemological power is then vested in those whose role it is to make the linguistic maps. Such men are the European, male, observer scientists, not least the natural historians. In her book titled *Imperial Eyes*, Pratt (1992) effectively makes the conjunction between a visibilising epistemology and the European colonial project, whereby not only the eyes 'capture' or 'posess', but their role is nonetheless also important in the imperial project. In this vein, she compares the natural historian plant gatherers, as they scour the globe, to imperial ambassadors. She quotes Linnaeus's words to a colleague:

> My pupil Sparrman has just sailed for the Cape of Good Hope, and another of my pupils, Thunberg, is to accompany a Dutch embassy to Japan; … The younger Gmelin is still in Persia, and my friend Falck is in Tartary. Mutis is making splendid botanical discoveries in Mexico. Koenig has found a lot of new things in Tranquebar. (Pratt, 1992: 27)

The global scope of the natural history project mirrors both the European Enlightenment's desire for total knowledge and global dominance. The *pursuit of truth*, as it were, runs alongside the European colonial enterprise of 'discovery' of new territory. The inverted commas around the word discovery here signal the understanding of the current postcolonial era, which jibes at its imperial ancestors for their outrageous pomposity in claiming discovery. As Pratt wryly puts it when discussing the texts of the 'verbal painters' of the Victorian age:

> As a rule the "discovery" of sites like Lake Tanganyika involved making one's way to the region and asking the local inhabitants if they knew of any big lakes, etc. in the area, then hiring them to take you there, whereupon with their guidance and support, you proceeded to discover what they already knew. (Pratt, 1992: 202)

Here, it seems that the exploratory zeal of European imperialists/colonisers has been invested in the Victorian psyche to the extent that discovery must also be invented. Making a discovery becomes important in itself as does the descriptive 'laying bare' of knowledge, that is, what is discovered, in language. The notion of expository prose takes on a new significance here. It is literally exposing knowledge, while also embodying the psycho-symbolic importance of (European) discovery and the need for it to be communicated.

The Visibilising Economy of Language, Truth and Knowledge

To the extent that knowledge had to be 'uncovered' or 'laid bare', language had both to reveal what was found and at the same time mask its own role in doing so. Therefore, in terms of the communication of knowledge, language played the important role of making it visible, of being its visibilising force, but at the same time making itself, the medium of communication, invisible. This interplay between visibility and invisibility is key to the relationship between language, knowledge and reason. It is also symptomatic of the European Enlightenment mentality and the wider value system of Occidentalism.

Occidentalist Rhetoricity

In the above outline of conjoined aspects of scientific, social and rhetorical history, the aim was to place the conceptualisation of language within the wider symbolic and cultural landscape of confidence in man's reason, the desire for knowledge, and imperial ambitions. In other words, the importance to the discoverer of knowledge of communicating it, and the psychological impact of an imperial mindset that was both colonising, and literally, 'mapping' the world, see, for example, Pratt (1992), had its effects also on rhetorical organisation. In symbolic terms, the mapping of rhetorical organisation, for example, in the relaying of discoveries or the description of plant categories, paralleled also the physical mapping of the world that was part of European colonisation. In this sense, then, I speak of occidentalist rhetoricity, reflexively acknowledging the historical and cultural influences that have come to constitute what continue to be the preferred ways of writing academically in English. Another way of putting this is to state that the rhetorical norms of academic writing are a legacy of the European Enlightenment's self understanding of seeking out the truth and discovering new knowledge, while making the role of language in this process, invisible.

The paradox arises then that an ideally invisible medium has the task of making clear or visible. The tensions arising from this paradox are at the heart of languaging in the academy, its rhetorical practices, and its subordinate positioning. On the one hand, the cultural construal of transparency for language enables the rhetorical labour of language to be ignored. On the other hand, language is not invisible, despite its construal as such, but is helped to appear so by a rhetorical ordering which parallels the logic of deductive reasoning and the consummate clarity of exposition, reinforced not least by Descartes' exaltation of 'clear and distinct' ideas as the methodology par excellence for ascertaining truth.

In other words, a rhetoricity of transparency is effected by rhetoricising invisibility, that is, by creating in the rhetorical ordering and use of language, the effect of invisibility through conformity with principles of logic and a visibilising conceptualisation of the representation of knowledge. In the next chapter, I want to look further into the issue of rhetorical values as cultural legacy, and how their embodiment in what is by now a traditional rhetoricity for academic writing, is sustained and perpetuated.

Chapter 6

Disciplining Language: Rhetorical Values and the Regulation of Academic Writing

Introduction

In the previous chapter I highlighted how language was conceptualised in relation to scientific rationality, as well as how the rhetoricity of written language, that is, its textual embodiment, was affected, and indeed effected, by epistemological assumptions which were supported by related social and political concerns. In other words, language and how language was used was intimately involved with the power politics of the age. What this meant for language was that it was caught up in a paradox. On the one hand, it was charged with representing new knowledge so that it was visible, and on the other hand, it should ideally maintain its own invisibility.

In this chapter, I look more specifically at how the rhetorical values, which have formed to support this paradox around visibility and invisibility, have their own related and specific cultural history. These rhetorical values of clarity, concision and brevity, reached their apogee in the 18th century with the widespread demand for and enactment of polished prose. Furthermore, they have become so established that they continue to shape assumptions and evaluations of what constitutes 'good' academic writing.

The continuing importance of these rhetorical values means that they wield power. They act like a form of regulation, ensuring discipline and order in how language is used in writing. This rhetorical regulation is maintained in the metalanguage of evaluation for academic writing as well as in textbooks and pedagogic practices. I see it working in a similar way to what Foucault construed as 'power/knowledge' (1980). In this case, it is a question of rhetorical power/knowledge embodying, circulating and enacting particular epistemological and culturally related values.

Inscribing a European Rationalist Rhetoricity

A major emphasis throughout this book is placed on the fact that preferred ways of using language are interrelated with wider cultural processes. Of particular relevance to academic writing is the power that
accrued to scientific rationality from the mid-17th century onwards. With
scientific acclaim, the natural philosophers/scientists of the 17th and 18th
centuries also accrued social power and their work wider cultural value.
This was not least the case for their views on how language should be
conceived as well as how it should be used. While the attempts at creating
artificial languages failed, the principles underlying such projects were
nonetheless successful in that they transferred to prescriptions for how
natural language should be used. Such prescriptions may be seen especially in the case of English where, Bishop Sprat (1958 [1667]), enjoined a
'mathematical plainness' for language, and, to similar effect, rejected all
'amplifications, digressions and swellings of style'. Such *prescriptions* had
an effect on actual language use, so that they became rhetoricised, that is,
they were *inscribed* in language.

The rhetorical inscription of clarity and simplicity in language use,
such that no attention was drawn to the language itself, was not only
deployed in the communication of knowledge, but also in literature. For
example, in his discussion of the late 17th century/early 18th century
novel, Watt (2000) describes the prose style of Daniel Defoe and states
that he:

> .. fully exemplifies the celebrated programme of Bishop Sprat. (Watt,
> 2000: 101)

He further elaborates Sprat's programme and Defoe's compliance with
it as:

> A close, naked, natural way of speaking; positive expressions; clear
> senses; a native easiness; bringing all things as near the mathematical
> plainness as they can: and preferring the language of artisans, coun-
> trymen and merchants before that of wits or scholars. (quoted in Watt,
> 2000: 101, from Sprat, 1667: 113)

Watt also makes clear the link between Defoe's prose and the values of
scientific rationality:

> The simple and positive quality of Defoe's prose, then, embodies the
> new values of the scientific and rational outlook of the late seven-
> teenth century. (Watt, 2000: 102)

Defoe's work as a novelist is also related to Descartes' philosophical realism, and the epistemological problem of dualism that it raised. According to Watt:

> Defoe would seem to occupy a very central position between the subjective and the external orientations of the novelist: the individual ego and the material world, as the result of Defoe's use of formal realism, are both given a greater reality in his novels than in previous fiction. Indeed, the fact that his narrative point of view, that of the autobiographical memoir, shows itself to be so well suited to reflect the tension between the inner and the outer world, suggests that the Cartesian shift to the point of view of the perceiving individual ego was itself calculated to make possible a more sharply defined picture of the outer as well as of the inner world. (Watt, 2000: 295)

The importance of sharp definition, of clarity, of boundaries and of the reality of both an external and internal world represents values and concerns that came with scientific rationality in 17th and 18th century Europe. It is a mark of the power of scientific rationality that its values permeated wider social and cultural practices.

What is of particular interest here is that its values were also rhetorically inscribed. This may be seen as an effect of what Foucault calls 'power/knowledge' (Foucault, 1980). This is a process of governing or regulating, whereby the actual sources of power and knowledge are not themselves visible but the value system or 'regime of truth' that is constructed operates well anyway, through a number of 'disciplining' or regulatory technologies.

The Disciplining of Language: Making Visible while Remaining Invisible

As was emphasised in the previous chapter, the social and political economy within which scientific writing had to operate, was a paradoxical one, whereby knowledge was made visible, but the means of doing so, that is, in language, ideally remained invisible. This interaction between visibility and invisibility works in a way similar to Foucault's analysis of power, in *The Birth of the Clinic* (Foucault, 1973c). Here the visibility of the sovereign as all powerful gives way to the invisibility of disciplinary technologies of power. Instead of the sovereign, it is the subjects themselves on whom these technologies operate, who are made most visible. The process is similar also with regard to the techniques of surveillance that Foucault discusses in the historical contexts of how prisoners were treated and how medical practices were developed (Foucault, 1973b, 1977). Foucault emphasises the capillary effects of power/knowledge, its 'net-like' organisation. He states:

> Power must be analysed as something which circulates, or rather as something which only functions in the form of a chain. It is never localised here or there, never in anybody's hands, never appropriated as a commodity or piece of wealth. Power is employed and exercised through a net-like organisation. And not only do individuals circulate between its threads; they are always in the position of simultaneously undergoing or exercising this power. They are not only its inert or consenting target; they are always also the elements of its articulation. In other words, individuals are the vehicles of power, not its points of application. (Foucault, 1980: 98)

While individuals, in this case writers, as the vehicles of rhetorical power will be the focus of the next chapter, it is rather the textual embodiment of rhetorical values in academic writing that is the focus here.

To make a conceptual analogy then, I characterise the rhetorical practice of academic writing as policed by a visibilising economy of rationality, language and knowledge, in which language is 'disciplined' by the demands of the other two, particularly as they were promoted throughout the period of the European Enlightenment. Whilst academic writing must make as visible as possible the knowledge it is conveying, it ought itself to remain invisible. This invisibility is maintained if language operates in the visibilising way that is desired. Just as the human body is disciplined by technologies of surveillance, such as the panopticon and the medical examination, the 'body' of written language is disciplined by culturally embedded rhetorical values, including the rigours of an explicit step-by-step deductive logic, conceptual precision, and clear and concise representation, in other words, a visibilising rhetorical technology of clarity, concision and brevity. The emergence of these values in intellectual cultural history will be discussed further in the following section.

The Observing Gaze and the Production of Knowledge/Clarity

The social, cultural and cognitive importance of science and the extent to which it infiltrated the European imagination can be seen also through its links with the major social, political and economic driving force in Europe from the 16th century onwards, namely colonisation. In the title of her book on travel writing, *Imperial Eyes*, Mary Louise Pratt bears witness to this conjuncture. The phrase 'imperial eyes' captures both the epistemological importance of the observing gaze of the scientist and the possessive gaze of the coloniser. The textual sources for Pratt's book are travel writings, and they include work written in the 16th century, ranging through to examples from the 19th century. The writings from the second half of the 18th century onwards are very much tied up with the natural history project of plant classification, associated predominantly with Linnaeus. The importance of making things visible, which arose from this project, and the implications this had also for how language was used, was discussed in the previous chapter. What brought this project and the interests of travel writers together was the global scale on which it was carried out. It was necessary to describe the internal flora and fauna that were to be found in the different types of landscape around the world. Of particular interest here is the fact that on their travels, the writers began to mimic the scientists. As Pratt puts it, they:

> began to develop leisurely pauses filled with gentlemanly 'naturalising'. (Pratt, 1992: 27)

In some cases, these pauses grew in scale so that:

> the observing and cataloguing of nature itself became narratable. It could constitute a sequence of events, or even produce a plot. (Pratt, 1992: 27)

However, in this process, it was not only the case that the plant classification project was infiltrating travel writing, travel writing, by its incorporation of the finding and describing of plants, was also playing an important role in cementing the authority of European science:

> Narrative travel accounts were 'central agents in legitimating scientific authority and its global project alongside Europe's other ways of knowing the world, and being in it.' (Pratt, 1992: 29)

Pratt further characterises natural history as an epistemological shift. She states:

> Natural history as a way of thinking interrupted existing networks of historical and material relations among people, plants, and animals wherever it applied itself. The European observer himself has no place in the description. (Pratt, 1992: 32)

Rhetoricising Objectivity

The final sentence in the above quote is a revealing example of how objectivity was rhetorically instantiated. Not only was the prototypical

European observer/scientist/knowledge maker determining the boundaries of what should count as knowledge and defining its contents as clearly as possible, he was also deleting his own role in the process. Rhetorical clarity and epistemological objectivity were inextricably linked, while human agency was masked. Such masking continues to be the norm in the maintenance of an impersonal stance in academic writing. It also often forms the basis for late twentieth century feminist arguments against the masculinist bias of academic textual rhetoric. For example both Code (1995) and Threadgold (1997) talk of the 'disembodied subject' of academic writing.

In the 17th century, it was the need to privilege Reason itself that may be seen as accounting not only for textual disembodiment, but also a linked need to banish emotion. An example of this privileging can be seen in two different versions of how an experiment on a live dog is relayed. The example comes from (Jardine, 1999: 116). In the more personal and emotion-revealing version, which was written by Robert Hooke in a letter to Robert Boyle, the text is as follows:

> The other Experiment (which I shall hardly, I confess, make again, because it was cruel) was with a dog, which, by means of a pair of bellows, wherewith I filled his lungs, and suffered them to empty again, I was able to preserve alive as long as I could desire, after I had wholly opened the thorax, and cut off all the ribs, and opened the belly. My design was to make some enquiries into the nature of respiration. But I shall hardly be induced to make any further trials of this kind, because of the torture of the creature; but certainly the inquiry would be very noble, if we could find a way so to stupefy the creature, as that it might not be sensible.

Here Hooke's own agency in performing the experiment is foregrounded, and while he brackets the information of how he felt about it, he nonetheless shows his emotions.

The other account is that written up in the Royal Society's records:

> A Dog was dissected, and by means of a pair of bellows, and a certain Pipe thrust into the Wind-pipe of the Creature, the heart continued beating for a very long while after all the Thorax and Belly had been opened.

In this latter version, there is no agency. The use of the passive serves as a distancing and depersonalising procedure, and the matter-of-fact tone is devoid of emotion. There is also no mention of the cruelty inflicted on the dog. A similar rhetoricity of a distant observer and a generalised process, sanitised from human emotion, continues to be valued in the academic essay.

Objectivism and Distancing

Newton's *Opticks*, closely analysed by Bazerman (1988) for evidence of how Newton had developed his rhetorical strategies in the interests of greater persuasive power, also served as a source for the systemic functional linguist, Halliday, who similarly discerned the emergence of a new mode of scientific writing in it, but focused more on the evidence it yielded of syntactical change. In his charting of differences in the way of using language in scientific writing between the time of Chaucer's *Treatise on the Astrolabe* (c.1390) and Newton's *Opticks* (1730 [1704]), Halliday finds that a major difference in Newton's text is the occurrence of logical relationships, characterised by nominalisations of processes or properties, and causal verbs. He gives the following example, which comes at the end of a paragraph in Newton's text:

The unusual Refraction is therefore perform'd by an original property of the Rays. (*Opticks*, 358), cited in Halliday

He also lists examples from an increased number of verbs relating to cause or proof such as:

depends on, accelerates, produces, arises from, is performed by, requires an understanding of, cannot be handled by. (Halliday, 1994: 140)

Half a century later in Joseph Priestley's *History and Present State of Electricity*, the number of such verbs has increased, and after another hundred years, by the time of James Clerk Maxwell's (1881) *An Elementary Treatise on Electricity*, Halliday estimates 'there are some hundreds of them in current use' (Halliday, 1994: 142).

The focus on explanation, which this textuality exemplifies, revealing, or literally, *laying out* the truth of things, as the Latin etymology of the word has it, obscures human agency, even though it is usually the scientist's setting up of particular experiments that has enabled the explanation. This is a further significance of Newton's textual rhetoric of geometric proof, namely the removal from the text of the thinking subject, who is also the individual doing the experiments. In relation to Bazerman's work on Newton, for example, Threadgold speaks of 'the gradual disappearance of the embodied masculine subject of science from the scene of his scientific activities' (Threadgold, 1997: 21). She makes the point also, in reference to more recent work on science writing (Knorr-Cetina, 1981), that contemporary accounts of the production of scientific reports are similarly disembodied. Here, the textuality is linked to constraints of governmental, institutional, organisational, managerial and political pressures. The surrounding social and political conditions may be different, but the rhetorical subject position nonetheless remains.

Mirroring Values: Rhetorical Inscription and Metarhetorical Criteria

What was foregrounded in the above sections was that in the course of intellectual history, ideas and practices that wield cultural or episte-mological power do not only have social effects, but also have rhetorical effects. In other words, both the epistemological and cultural importance of clarity and objectivity in the conduct and construal of European scien-tific rationality created the conditions for their rhetorical importance in writing. Together with logical concision and linguistic brevity, they have become rhetorically inscribed in language use, such that they are now the taken-for-granted rhetorical norms deemed appropriate for academic writing.

In speaking of rhetorical effects, I am not simply referring to their polit-ical effectiveness, but rather to the fact that the values that were persua-sive were also incorporated, literally embodied, in the way texts were constructed. This is what I mean by rhetorical inscription. The rhetorical inscription of clarity and objectivity was particularly an effect of the suc-cess and power of European scientific rationality.

What is interesting about this rhetoricity is that its values mirror the epistemological preferences for the well-defined clarity of ideas or objects of study, thereby constituting a verisimilitude between the conception of the ideas and their representation in language. What I would like to high-light also is that the values of this rhetoricity serve as criteria for what is deemed to be 'good' rhetorical ordering, 'good' text, or 'good' language. The following excerpt from a contemporary book review will serve as an example of this evaluative metarhetorical framework. It comes from the Times Higher Education Supplement, of 8 April, 2005: 28, and is a review of Anthony Kenny's *A New History of Western Philosophy: Vol. One: Ancient Philosophy*. The review was written by James Ladyman.

> Kenny's prose is exceptionally clear and his sentences rarely span more than two lines. He conveys his subject matter with a light touch of which only the greatest of writers are capable. Often the text is almost deceptively simple to read as Kenny exercises his great skill at summarising ideas in a pithy phrase. (Ladyman, 2005: 28)

In the first place, the eulogistic praise for the prose indicates the importance of language to the ideas that are conveyed. So language matters. However, it is also a good example of the metalanguage for evaluating how language is used. This metalanguage pivots around the perception of clarity, concision and brevity. What is more, both the language of commendation and the style at the source of the commendation are constituted in this evaluative metalanguage. This is just as the 18th century knowledge producers and polished prose enthusiasts wanted things to be!

The rhetorical inscription of those historical epistemological values continues to dictate what counts as good writing. Clarity, concision and brevity continue to be the dominant expectations of academic prose, as well as the criteria used to make the metarhetorical judgements of whether it is good or bad.

The Cultural Construction of Rhetorical Values

The cultural valorisation of clarity has a long history in the western tradition, going beyond even that of the growth of European science and knowledge production. Before the epistemological association with objectivity, clarity was linked with morality and the conveying of truth and sincerity. This cultural connectivity goes back to the time of the ancient Greeks, and the pedagogic training in rhetoric. Speaking specifically of academic writing, Nash (1990) represents it as follows:

> There is a Western tradition of academic writing, a tradition observed in schools and institutions of higher education in Europe and the United States. This tradition, preserved from Classical times and mediated to us through the clerical institutions of the Middle Ages, involves precepts of rhetorical structure and recommendations for the management of language in the composition of texts. It also involves corollary assumptions about the morality of the compositional act; that the writer will scrupulously pursue truth in argument and narration, strict accuracy in ascertainable fact, lucidity in exposition (Nash, 1990: 28).

It is the situatedness of academic writing within this longstanding tradition that marks it out as a specific literacy practice, with a social and intellectual history as well as continuing contemporary expectations of delivering the goods of what might be seen as 'goodness, truth, and beauty'. These are the values of a Platonist metaphysics, which Nash's characterisation of academic writing echoes.

Moving on to the mediaeval period, additional, specific rhetorical values come to the fore. Mediaeval learning emphasised in particular the rhetorical values of concision and brevity. This was in association with showing logical proofs, an activity of particular value in the scholastic tradition. In his book on medieval learning, Piltz (1981) makes explicit reference to this value system as follows:

> It is a mistake to use verbose proof when it can be expressed concisely. (Piltz, 1981: 96)

He also refers to the well-known definition of the difference between logic and rhetoric (in its traditional sense of persuasive argumentation) in relation to the fist and the palm of the hand; see also Billig (1987). Piltz gives its source as Alcuin, the teacher of the Emperor Charlemagne, who had asked the question, thus:

C: What distinguishes logic from rhetoric?
A: As the fist can be distinguished from the palm of the hand. Logic combines reasoning in as few words as possible. Rhetoric, rich in words, is allowed free reign in the sphere of oratory. One compresses words, the other extends them.

From Alcuin, De dialectica (Patrologica Latina 101: 952–953) quoted in Piltz (1981: 23).

In Billig's case, where he is concerned with the field of social psychology, rhetoric is seen as metonymic for a more open, indeed open-ended, mode of 'arguing and thinking' in contradistinction to the dominant mode of logic, which is criticised as encouraging closed thinking. However, it is the more tightly formed style of logic that continues to be valued in academic writing, in English at least. This is especially the case if the writing concerns the development of an argument.

In historical terms, however, beyond the context of demonstrating philosophical proofs, a logical style of ordering thinking has not always been so prominent. This can be seen in the following cultural historical example from Obelkevich's (1987) study of proverbs. In this excerpt, he is contrasting 18th century 'tightly knit' prose with the earlier 16th century style of Tudor prose in which proverbs thrived:

> Not only was there a resemblance between the fluency of sixteenth century writers, with their proverbs and commonplaces, and that of oral poets and story-tellers, with their stock epithets and formulae. There was also an oral quality to the very texture of Tudor writings: loose and

informal, it had room for digressions and illustrations, proverbial and otherwise; it was closer in structure and spirit to the aggregative oral mode of the story-teller than to the tightly knit prose which would eventually triumph in the eighteenth century. (Obelkevich, 1987: 56)

This excerpt shows how a logical style, here embodied in the phrase 'tightly knit prose', was part of the stylistic cultural ethos in which proverbs were no longer welcome. The shift from 'digressions' and 'the aggregative' to 'tightly knit prose' has been an enduring one. The value of logic, where its steps are clearly marked in tightly focused prose, continues to hold sway.

Proverbs in Intercultural Perspective

It is also interesting to note as an intercultural aside, that proverbs, have not gone through the process of social disparagement in East Asian cultures, as was the case with their use in 'polite' or educated discourse in English. They are in fact culturally highly valued (Turner & Hiraga, 2003). As Hinkel (1999b) also notes in her study of the contrasting use of rhetorical devices in writing, they are often used in Chinese, Japanese, Korean and Indonesian writing, 'when authors feel that they need to strengthen their position by referring to the assumed common knowledge embodied in proverbs' (Hinkel, 1999b: 98).

Twentieth Century Cooperation

From a 20th century philosophical position of identifying the logic of communication, namely Grice's cooperative principle (Grice, 1975: 46), the values of clarity, concision and brevity in language use continue to thrive. They are embodied in his maxims of manner:

Avoid obscurity of expression
Avoid ambiguity
Be brief (avoid unnecessary prolixity)
Be orderly

His maxims of quantity also focus on brevity:

Make your contribution as informative as is required (for the current purposes of the exchange).
Do not make your contribution more informative than is required. (Grice, 1975: 45)

Grice's maxims are often used, or at least implied, in the teaching of academic writing. They therefore serve to justify and consolidate those rhetorical values. Whilst Grice's maxims have been critiqued as idealisations by Birch (1989), who saw them as exemplifying 'an ideology of closure and completeness', they nonetheless have wielded influence, not least in ELT. Birch's critique may also be applied to the maintenance of ideal rhetorical values:

> Grice's maxims exist in a *virtual* world and are used to try to explain in an ordered, neat way how the *actual* world works (Birch, 1989: 36)

It nonetheless remains the case that tightly ordered logical exposition, concision in choice of lexis, clarity and economy of style continue to be the rhetorical norms within which academic writing pedagogy and expectations of a smooth read, operate. Together, they constitute a visibilising textual economy, whereby the reader is led along a route of clearly identified argumentation, without detour and distraction.

Power/Knowledge and the Maintenance of the Rhetorical Technology of Clarity, Concision and Brevity

What is of particular interest here is not only the fact that rhetorical inscription was the result of socially prestigious practices at particular moments in intellectual cultural history becoming widely valued and acted upon, but also the fact that the same rhetorical values continue to frame what constitutes 'good' academic writing in contemporary higher education. Significantly, this means that academic writing should not be seen as autonomous or given. It is not an autonomous set of skills or a discrete set of rhetorical values that have arrived independently, or been designated as such by some kind of decree. It is rather a cultural practice that has been invested with rhetorical values that are themselves the effects of wider cultural processes. Those values continue to be espoused, and are maintained by specific technologies of practice, which both control and perpetuate them.

In other words, the values of clarity, concision and brevity can themselves be seen as a regulatory technology for academic writing. They are sustained by a power/knowledge network of regulatory practices, which maintain their rationale and perpetuate their value system. This means that the institutional practice and pedagogy of academic writing itself, for example, in as much as it continues to promote the values of clarity and the explicit mapping out of argumentation, can be seen as a locus of power/knowledge, maintaining rhetorical values which at the same time perpetuate European Enlightenment values and its visibilising economy.

The continuing validity, and indeed perpetuation, of this value system can also be seen in the titles of some textbooks on professional communication. For example, (Lanham, 1983) talks of the C-B-S style, which stands for 'clarity', 'brevity' and 'sincerity'. Another key text on rhetorical organisation, widely deployed in the United States, is by Williams (1989). It has the title: *Style: Ten Lessons in Clarity and Grace*. This book has gone into several editions, and together, these books among others show the enduring nature of rhetorical values for writing, which are deeply rooted in the western intellectual tradition. In their continued advocacy of those values, they also constitute a locus of power/knowledge for the continued dissemination and circulation of the rhetorical values.

The Regulatory Technology of Feedback on Writing

The evaluative metalanguage of feedback on writing constitutes a further regulatory technology, policing the body politic of rhetorical correctness. It is aligned with and supports the paradoxical construction of language, whereby in a kind of rhetorical magic, it makes visible while itself remaining invisible. In other words, the metalanguage of feedback mirrors the preferred academic rhetoricity. In earlier studies of typical feedback comments, I identified two major conceptual frameworks Turner (1992, 1999a). They were *clarity of focus* and *tightness of structure*. Adverse comments such as 'you do not focus your ideas clearly enough', 'this is all over the place', 'pay more attention to structure' and 'your argument is too loosely drawn' are indicative of these conceptual frameworks, as are their positive counterparts, 'good concise analysis', 'tightly structured' or 'tightly knit'. Here the values of 18th century polished prose continue to prevail.

The positive evaluation of clarity is pointed up also in frequent references to its polar opposite, 'vagueness'. For example, Myers (1996), in a corpus of his own feedback on students' written work, notes the numerous times he uses the word 'vague' and how it is always used negatively. Similarly looking at comments on students' texts, Lillis (2001); Lillis and Turner (2001) identified the ubiquity of the injunction 'be explicit', also from the semantic field of clarity. What was interesting about this exhortation, and indeed from the students' perspective, confusing, was that it had a number of different meanings, relating to differing tutor expectations in the context. They are listed as follows (Lillis & Turner, 2001: 59):

- Make clear link between claim and supporting evidence.
- Avoid vague wordings (etc.)
- Check that it is clear what this, these refer to.

- Make clear why a particular punctuation was used.
- Say why particular section was included.
- Make links between sections.
- Show that you understand key terms.

In her study, Lillis (2001) focuses on 'non-traditional' (both first language and ESL) students and highlights their difficulty in getting to grips with the 'conventions' of academic discourse. As well as cognitive-rhetorical processes such as being explicit, these conventions also included giving definitions, and picking out the main points. Tutors in all disciplines are likely to encourage their students to do those things, but without further elaboration of what these rhetorical processes actually require in terms of actual linguistic realisation. While evaluative and exhortatory comments on student texts index preferences of rhetorical organisation, the fact that they are rhetorical preferences, and indeed culturally rooted, is often not overt, nor even well understood as such by those making the comments. This was also shown in Lea and Street's (1998) research, where lecturers talked about the need for structure and argument, without elaborating on what that entailed in actual writing.

It is somewhat ironic, then, if not insidious, that while the virtues of clarity are routinely extolled, it is an ethos of vagueness that prevails in the reality of assessing student academic writing. As Lillis's work has shown, attributions such as 'vague' set up nothing more helpful for the student than a sense of vagueness about what they are expected to do. Being told their work is vague, or that they need to be more explicit, feeds into student perceptions of what Lillis has termed the 'institutional practice of mystery' (Lillis, 1999).

The Student Perspective

The emphasis on logical ordering is striking to many international students who find themselves having to rethink their approach to writing and find a way into this writing style. When they talk about academic writing in English, and say, as they often do: 'it is very logical', this is not a simple benign statement of the obvious, or one relaying a sense of what would be expected. It is rather a sign of difference. It designates a site of struggle for them. Injunctions to tighten the structure or express the argument more clearly, therefore, are often a source of confusion for international students who believe they have expressed themselves as clearly as they could. This points up the fact that the rhetorical style of prioritising logical ordering is culturally specific.

It is of course not only international students who have problems with rhetorical ordering and metarhetorical injunctions from their tutors. It is also an issue for native speakers who are not yet familiar with working on and with academic texts. As shown in the examples from Lillis above, the struggles of such students are beginning to be documented. A number of other studies take up students' perceptions of academic writing, including Ivanic (1998), and Canagarajah (2002b); so the issue that it is a site of struggle is no longer completely hidden, as the assumption of rational thinking equals clear and transparent language would have it be.

Expression in language and cognitive analysis go together, but it tends to be only the cognitive ability that is valued. However, as many writing teachers can testify, attempts to write out ideas may also help to clarify them. Writing is an important part of the process of both thinking and learning, as is testified, for example, in Mitchell and Evison (2006) and Langer (2007). Also it is seldom the case that writers can express their thoughts as if fully fledged before they transfer them to the page or screen. The relationship between thinking and writing is at best symbiotic rather than mechanistic, but the power/knowledge network around the rhetoricity of clarity, concision and brevity, militates against acknowledging this.

The Dual Face of Clarity

What seems to be at issue in the fact that tutors tend to take for granted that students will understand their rhetorically focused comments is an assumed veridicality between the process of thinking or reasoning and its rhetorical organisation. This veridicality assumption can be seen also as accounting for the eulogistic praise delivered in the book review above. The praise for the rhetorical values of clarity and concision is in harmony with the conceptual framework they embody. This is also the unity of form and content that lives up to the cultural ideal of transparency.

However, the assumptions of a 'rightness' of 'good' or 'polished' academic prose and the ubiquitous expectation of this cultural ideal, bring with them their own problems in the context of contemporary academic writing practices. For example, they account for the ready availability of the deficit discourse. As soon as the epistemological, the culturally valued, and the rhetorical, do not appear in unison, the clarion call of deficit rings out. This is the point at which language becomes visible, when there is a problem. 'Good' language use is 'unmarked' because it is effectively a rhetoricisation, a matching in linguistic form of culturally entrenched, and deeply valued, patterns of thinking. This set of longstanding unexamined assumptions and expectations has created a disjunction between what counts as good writing, and actual practice and experience.

It is almost impossible to argue against clarity, its value is so linked not only to good writing, but to the moral landscape of honesty and integrity, the assumption that nothing will be hidden, as well as to an aesthetics of grace and elegance, as illustrated in the textbook title mentioned above. However, there is at least one exception to the normatively positive evaluation of clarity, and that comes from the critical pedagogue, Henri Giroux (Giroux, 1992). He critiques the 'stylised aesthetic of clarity' (1992: 25), and the fact that it is seen as a 'common sense requirement'. For him, clarity constitutes 'a troublesome politics of erasure by claiming to represent a universal standard of literacy' (1992: 24). Furthermore, the strength of assumptions of clarity set up a resistance to complexity, which Giroux sees as thwarting the take-up of contemporary theorising in educational discourse.

The question I have asked here is: how has clarity come to have the status that it has? By locating the construct of clarity in the historical context in which it became predominantly associated with rationality and objectivity, the evaluative metalanguage of clarity can itself be seen as a social construct. Historicising 'clarity' in this way, as well as highlighting the power/knowledge network that sustains it, goes some way to dislodging the complacency that goes with treating it as 'common sense'.

The Rhetoricity of Occidentalist Reason

While the scope of rhetorical regulation is not as broad as the regulatory practices of major social projects such as public health or sexual behaviour, as in Foucault's work, it is nonetheless powerful and deeply affects the culture of higher education. In their commentary on Foucault's genealogical method, Best and Kellner (1991: 51) state the following:

> Genealogies attempt to demonstrate how objectifying forms of reason (and their regimes of truth and knowledge) have been made, as historically contingent rather than eternally necessary forces.

The 'objectifying forms of reason' at issue here are those related to scientific rationality itself. It has engendered a rhetoricity with an ability to permeate all academic disciplines. Through its technologies of rhetorical regulation, it continues to inform what constitutes 'good' academic writing.

The issue here is not about the rhetoric of reason, nor is it about the cultural importance of seeking to persuade, whose traditional strategies are meticulously outlined in, for example, Perelman (1981). It is also not about how rationality is best conceived and promoted, as in, for example, Myerson (1994) but about the rhetoricity of academic writing and academic practice, as it takes place prototypically between tutors and students. Such rhetoricity is an effect of power/knowledge, disseminated largely through the project of the European Enlightenment, whereby ways of thinking and reasoning have been enfolded into written rhetorical practice.

While still powerful, however, this 'objective', 'rational' rhetoricity is also seen as culturally and historically contingent. The converging forces in intellectual cultural history that have privileged the concept of clarity, for example, and the creation of rhetorical norms in writing that are perceived to conform to that conceptualisation are ultimately contingent. For this reason, I talk of 'occidentalist' rhetoricity, both rooting, and 'routing' continuing preferred rhetorical practices in higher education, in and through western cultural and intellectual history. Things might have been different, they could yet change.

Chapter 7
Power/Knowledge and the
Construction of Rhetorical Subjects

Introduction

The previous chapters have identified the effects both on the conceptualisation of language and on the rhetorical values for how language should
be used, especially in writing, of what I have called the visibilising economy of scientific rationality and knowledge. This economy is operated by
three interlinked discourses. They are the discourse of transparency within
which language is conceived, the discourse of clarity within which language use, especially in the context of academic writing, is evaluated and
the discovery discourse within which knowledge is laid bare.

In this chapter, I look more specifically at the subject position of academic writers as it has been constructed within this visibilising economy,
and whose position as academic writing subjects continues to enact its
power/knowledge. The notion of the Cartesian cogito, for example, has
become so deeply cognitively and culturally embedded that it wields
invisible power, enacted by rhetorical subjects who play out (or write
out) its role as clear, rational and autonomous thinkers. Similarly, the universalist discourse of the European Enlightenment, and its totalising view
of knowledge has created rhetorical writing subjects who take up a position of its observing gaze, and command textual, as well as epistemic
control over what is observed and explained. These rhetorical subjects
and their textual subject positions continue to enact what constitutes
good academic writing.

Subjects and Subjectification

The notion of the subject has gained prominence in contemporary theorising in a range of disciplines. It is particularly associated with French
theorists such as Althusser (1971), Barthes (1993), Foucault (1973c, 1977,
1980, 1982), Lacan (1977), Lyotard (1984) and Deleuze and Guattari (1983),
among others, who use it in relation to the constitution of 'subjects' and

'subjectivity' as a social and cultural process, creating a sense of self or consciousness. It effectively inverts the dominant understanding of the self as an *a priori* autonomous individual. It also diminishes the importance of explanation based on cause and effect logic, viewing subjects and subjectivities as effects of complex social and historical processes.

Given its derivation from use by French theorists, the meaning of the term subject in a theoretical sense in English is not always readily available. For language teachers, or those responsible for teaching academic writing, for example, it is more likely to be thought of as a grammatical term or as a specific academic discipline, such as geography or history, as taught in a school curriculum. In fact, it is the politico-legal use of the term in English, as in 'the Queen's subjects', which is more appropriate as a jumping off point for an understanding relating to processes of power. Students of semiotics or cultural studies, on the other hand, may be more familiar with the term, as once again, in its derivation from French structuralist and semiotic theory, it is frequently used to refer to how the viewer of films or the reader of texts is positioned, hailed, or 'interpellated' (Althusser, 1971), as a reading or viewing subject (see Silverman, 1983, for an overview).

From their perspective on how the individual or 'subject' is viewed in psychology, Henriques *et al.* (1984) refer to terminological problems in English deriving from the translation of the French verb 'asujettir', which means both 'to produce subjectivity' and 'to make subject'. They state that they use the term 'subjectivity' to stand for both a sense of self-awareness and of subjectification. This complies with Foucault's use of the word subject. In his essay on The Subject and Power, Foucault also refers to two meanings of the word 'subject':

> subject to someone else by control and dependence, and tied to his own identity by a conscience or self-knowledge. Both meanings suggest a form of power which subjugates and makes subject to. (Foucault, 1982: 212)

Subjectivity and Power/Knowledge

In the work of Foucault, subject formation is linked with power/knowledge. Foucault's concept of power/knowledge recognises the subtle and insinuative workings of power, how it is closely allied with what is deemed to constitute knowledge, and how it affects and constrains how people behave. Foucault was concerned not to analyse the workings of power/knowledge in a top-down manner, as the exercise of power is traditionally understood (Foucault, 1980). He saw his project as the exact opposite of that of Hobbes in *Leviathan* (Hobbes 1985 [1651]) where the concern was with the consolidation of power and the stabilisation of society in strong central government. He did not want to ask 'why certain people want to dominate' but rather:

> how things work at the level of on-going subjugation, at the level of those continuous and uninterrupted processes which subject our bodies, govern our gestures, dictate our behaviours, etc. ... We should try to grasp subjection in its material instance as a constitution of subjects. (Foucault, 1980: 97)

This is not to see such subjects as the powerless, as it were. Everyone is the subject of power in Foucault's sense, which he further refines as 'something which circulates' (Foucault, 1980: 98). For him, 'individuals are the vehicles of power, not its point of application' (Foucault, 1980: 98). In *Discipline and Punish*, Foucault emphasises the experience of subjectification to invisible power. He writes:

> The man described for us, whom we are invited to free, is already the effect of a subjection much more profound than himself. (Foucault, 1977: 30)

This power/knowledge approach to subjectivity/subjectification undoes the predominant assumptions of what the philosopher Richard Rorty terms 'foundationalist epistemology' (Rorty, 1979), whereby the subject as 'knower' objectively discovers and analyses the 'known'. Foucault critiques the knowledge practices that have created this duality, and at the same time sees those knowledge practices as having created that dominant form of subjectivity. In other words, the knowing, discovering, autonomously reasoning human subject is an effect of power/knowledge rather than an autonomous originator. As Colebrook puts it:

> the formation of the subject through practices of the self is not to do away with the subject so much as to reverse its logic and causality; the subject is an effect of practice. (Colebrook, 1999: 126)

In his discussion of plagiarism, Pennycook (1996) has used the term subjectivity in a similar way. He puts it thus:

> If, instead of a Self or an Identity, we consider the notion of subjectivity, or indeed subjectivities (we are, in a sense the fragmented products of different discourses), then we arrive at more or less a reversal of the speaking subject creating meaning. We are not speaking subjects

but spoken subjects, we do not create language but are created by it. ... the question then becomes not so much one of who authored a text but how we are authored by texts. (Pennycook, 1996: 209)

It is the notion of subjection or unconscious subjectedness to a system of assumptions and expectations that informs my use of the terms 'subject' and 'subjectivity'. This in turn locates the function of both tutors and students in their modes of spoken and written interaction within a broader, valorised, genealogy of intellectual culture. In this chapter, I am particularly concerned with the subjectivity of academic writers and the rhetorical regulation to which they are subjected.

Academic Writing Subjects

By speaking of academic writing subjects, I am theorising the process, whereby student academic writers, for example, are constrained by the rhetorical practices they are writing within. Here, the concepts of agency and rhetorical convention are interrelated. This makes it possible to speak of both writing and reading subjects, writers and readers who are subject to deeply embedded and culturally valorised norms of language use.

As was discussed in the previous chapter, the rhetorical power/knowledge to which they are subjected is an effect of the power of scientific rationality, which emerged out of 17th century Europe. The methods of inquiry associated with it, the values attached to its mode of communication, and the social status invested in its already mostly socially elite practitioners, all achieved social and cultural dominance. Reinforced through the optimism and exploratory zeal of the European Enlightenment, epistemological and methodological precepts have inflected both the use of language in particular ways and created an evaluative matrix for language use. This process of embodying scientific rationality within rhetorical contours, is part of a wider historical and cultural process of naturalisation, whereby over time, ways of using language which are associated with value, in this case, the enactment of scientific rationality, are no longer noticed as forms in themselves. This is how the invisibility of language and the clarity of writing have been constructed. This is also how a normative rightness has been construed which is noticed only in the breach.

The naturalisation of discursive practices and how this reinforces hegemony is a point made forcefully by Fairclough (1995). As he states:

A particular set of discourse conventions (e.g. for conducting medical-consultations, or media interviews, or for writing crime reports in newspapers) implicitly embodies certain ideologies – particular

knowledge and beliefs, particular 'positions' for the type of social subjects that participate in that practice, (e.g. doctors, patients, intervie-
wees, newspaper readers), and particular relationships between
categories of participants. (Fairclough, 1995: 94)

As a result of the process of gaining power and being maintained, rhetorical norms have become taken for granted, seen as common sense, and
therefore susceptible to the remedial discourses which surround them
when they do not conform to widespread expectations. These remedial
discourses are in effect regulatory discourses, sustaining a rhetorical
power/knowledge. Their rhetorical subjects are disciplined as it were, by
wearing rhetorical straitjackets whose contours have been defined by the
epistemological assumptions underlying the European Enlightenment
mentality of knowledge production and reception.

The Subjectification of the Cartesian Cogito

Assumptions about the academic writer and the consequent evaluation
of her/his writing work implicitly in institutions such as universities
where the notion of academic writing is tied up also with assumptions of
rationality and its unitary, clear-thinking subject. This subject is inscribed
in Descartes' notion of the cogito, 'I think therefore I am', and projects an
individual rational, male, subject, in control of 'his' thinking and by extension 'his' writing. In his study of the essay, albeit as a literary genre rather
than an academic one, Good (1988) also discerns Cartesian influence, as
well as the importance of an observer. As he states:

> the essay presupposes an independent observer, a specific object, and
> a sympathetic reader. It also presupposes a language capable of ren-
> dering and communicating observations, whether physical or mental.
> Its starting point is like that of Cartesian philosophy: an isolated self
> confronting a world of which nothing is known for certain. (Good,
> 1988: 4)

As Good is concerned to differentiate the literary essay from Descartes'
scientific project of finding a suitable method for hitting on certain knowledge, he emphasises the more 'spontaneous and unsystematic' qualities of
the essay. However, it is the assumption of finding certain knowledge, and
being able to relay clearly the truth of the matter, sustained by the stance
of an independent observer that continues to invest the implied subjectivity of the academic writer and the rhetoricity of the text. This continuing
value system in effect subjectifies the writer. The language of academic

writing then, is not, as traditionally assumed, a neutral medium conveying ideas independently formed in the mind of an autonomous subject, but rather an effect of conformity to the socio-rhetorical norms engendered by the belief in Cartesian rationality. Similarly, student writers are as much *subject to*, as subject or agent *of*, rhetorical conventions. So to 'write well' and to 'think clearly', and above all their interrelatedness are not so much straightforward possibilities, available to every individual, but rather a mediated effect of epistemological and ontological assumptions and conceptions of rationality.

While there is a certain irony, in the present context, in using a theory which rejects the autonomy and freedom enjoined in the Cartesian subject, to maintain the continuation of this subjectivity within the position of the academic writer, it is nonetheless consistent with a poststructuralist position. In his inaugural lecture at the Collège de France in 1970 (Foucault, 1970), as well as in an essay titled 'Politics and the Study of Discourse' (Foucault, 1991), Foucault critiques the mind-body dualism of Cartesian rationality, which separates the mind of the writer from the linguistic codes that s/he writes in. As he states:

> to challenge the idea of a sovereign subject which arrives from elsewhere to enliven the inertia of linguistic codes, and sets down in discourse the indelible trace of its freedom; to challenge the idea of a subjectivity which constitutes meanings and then transcribes them into discourse. Against these ideas I would advocate a procedure which maps the roles and operations exhausted by different 'discoursing' subjects. (Foucault, 1991: 61–62)

He thus subverts the conventional understanding of the autonomous subject. However, the enduring power of the effects of the conventional conceptualisation, even if it itself is no longer contended, continue to work in our assumptions of the writing process, as well as in our assumptions that if the individual is rational s/he can write. This means that, in addition to being a 'discoursing subject' in specific disciplinary domains, the academic writer is also a discoursing subject within the visibilising economy of rationality, language and knowledge.

The Rhetorical Subject of Essayist Literacy

The use of the term 'essayist literacy' derives from the Scollons (Scollon & Scollon, 1981), and is used also by Gee (1996). The Scollons use the term to embody the values of what they call the 'modern consciousness' in contradistinction to the values of Athabaskan culture, which they are studying. Whereas essayist literacy values decontextualisation and distancing, Athabaskan culture values known relationships between writer/speaker and audience. Riddles, for example, are an important genre, teaching the importance of guessing meanings and reading between the lines, rather than assuming an explicit relay of information.

The Scollons acknowledge their debt to the work of Berger, Berger and Kellner on 'the homeless mind' (Berger *et al.*, 1973) as the basis for their understanding of essayist literacy. I suggest that what I'm calling the sub-jectified Cartesian cogito and what Berger and Kellner called the 'home-less mind', are part of the same cultural phenomenon, or 'modern consciousness'. This consciousness has its roots in the ethos of the European Enlightenment. However, the notion of subjectification prioritises the effects of power and the genealogical embedding of what has gained intel-lectual dominance within European history, rather than a comparison with a different cultural tradition. Nonetheless, 'essayist literacy' and the rhetoricity of rationality have the same cultural roots.

Cultural Values and the Essay

Gee talks of both the reader and the author of 'essayist prose' as 'fiction-alisations' (Gee, 1996: 60). For him, the reader is 'an idealization of a ratio-nal mind formed by a rational body of knowledge of which the essay is a part'. The author is a fiction because 'the process of writing and editing essayist texts leads to an effacement of individual and idiosyncratic iden-tity' (Gee, 1996: 60). He further talks of the essay's 'illusory quality of seeming to be explicit, clear, complete, closed, and self-sufficient' (Gee, 1996: 27). In this way, he effectively confirms the existence of what I have termed the evaluative metalanguage of clarity, but he focuses on its illu-sory nature, rather than the continuing assumptions of its viability.

In his study of the rise of the essay form from the time of Montaigne, van Peer links it to the rise of the bourgeoisie and bourgeois values within society at large. He talks of:

> its [the essay's] emphasis on free enterprise and equality, on liberty and the possibility of social critique and detachment from time and tradition, on the freedom of ideas and expression, on refined manners and exquisite yet honest style, on the quest for disinterested under-standing and truth. (van Peer, 1990: 201)

He further suggests that the essay itself became an instrument of main-taining the ideals of bourgeois society, as 'through the various social insti-tutions, such as the family, the press and the salon or the literary coffee-house', its discursive purposes were internalised by the individuals reading and writing them. The essay therefore played a strong role in both creating a bourgeois sensibility and maintaining an ethos of 'civilised' society. As such, it is a heavily laden cultural artefact, whose values remain embedded in what counts as good academic writing.

The continuing values of essayist literacy and importance of the essay form itself can be seen in the following quote concerning what constitutes a 'good' essay in the humanities:

> The transparency of the essay – the quality that makes it a form of expression and a tool of assessment at the same time – is a transparency of artifice. Students have to learn that combining their subjectivity with an apparent objectivity is one of the hallmarks of a 'good' essay. The line is a very fine one between being too personal and being too dry and rigid; but treading that line becomes the mark of a good student in the humanities. At times, being competent in the rhetorical and diplomatic skills of essay- writing is as important – if not more so- than knowing your subject. (Andrews, 1999: 12)

Here, the merits of 'transparency' continue to be extolled, but 'transparency' has shifted from being a conceptualisation of language, to the enactment of rhetorical skills in achieving this effect. Transparency then has become rhetoricised, that is, enacted in rhetorical production, valorised and naturalised.

The Reading Subject and the Reception of Academic Writing

This production and reception of transparency chimes well with the characterisation by Barthes (1990) of the 'readerly' text, whose main attributes are 'unity, realism and transparency' (Silverman, 1983: 242) and which 'depends upon a linear reading or viewing' (Silverman, 1983: 245). While Barthes' analysis relates to literary and cinematic texts, the reading position it sets up, the expectation of a 'smooth read', something that does not require too much effort, applies well to the reception of academic writing.

Bazerman is also aware of the analogy between Newton's new-found rhetorical strategies and the notion from literary theory of the 'closed text'. As he states:

> In what modern literary theory would call a closed text, Newton does the thinking and experimenting for the reader, with the reader needing only to comprehend each step as he is presented with it. (Bazerman, 1988: 117)

As mentioned in the previous chapter, in relation to the rhetorical technology of 'clarity', an expectation is set up whereby the reader is led along a route of clearly identified argumentation, without detour and distraction. Nonetheless, students new to academic culture, whether native or non-native speakers, can have difficulty in delivering an adequate performance of the naturalised rhetorical and aesthetic values of essayist literacy.

The Rational Writing Subject as Textual Map-Maker

The project of European colonialism, the epistemological importance of discovery, and the deductive delineation of logical proof, which are all culturally interrelated, all have a literal concern with mapping, or mapping out. Mapping the world in a spirit of colonisation and capturing of knowledge makes its mark also on textual mapping. The process of mapping knowledge began literally with maps. As Jardine's overview of the age shows, scientists and mathematicians were crucial to the project of 'discovering', and knowing the world, solving problems of navigation by explaining the movements of the heavens and of the sea and thereby also lending value to the mapping techniques of cartography (Jardine, 1999). While such cartographers were producing knowledge of the world by mapping its contours, Newton is a prime example of how the rhetorical mapping of knowledge was also being carried out. Rhetorical action as clearly signposted logical exposition, as well as making visible the empirical process of experiment may be seen as another product of the age. It is affected by the same confidence in 'man's Reason', which in turn is imbued with the certainty of deductive logic.

Descartes was a mathematician, and Newton's success in persuading his colleagues in the Royal Society, by laying things out as in a geometrical proof, is symptomatic of Cartesian influence. Charged with the authority of the Cartesian 'cogito', as it were, the rational subject, usually either a scientist or a philosopher, or both, could lay out the world of knowledge from his standpoint. The shape of argumentation is usually described as linear, as in association with the traditional western assumption of logic. The writing of argument then should afford the reader consistency of gaze, as it were, and enable a steady walk through the argumentation. The 'consistency of gaze' of course is also an effect of the position the writer takes up in order to promote the argumentation. If the writer is clear on her/his position, then the gathering of ground (i.e. facts and justifications) around that position enables its identification within the wider landscape. Such geographic metaphors are conventional in the domain of inquiry or knowledge acquisition. The pursuit of truth, as it were, is linked with a territorial imperative to clear the ground, stake a claim, and construct a vantage point. As with colonisation, so it is with knowledge production. Even in already established 'fields' of knowledge, there is an impulsion to 'push back the frontiers' and for the practitioners within, to be 'at the cutting edge'. The symbolic effects of such a general colonising mindset continue in the expectations of how a student writes an academic essay, as much as in those of a researcher leading the field.

The Topic Sentence and Surveying the Scene

Just as with the European Enlightenment mentality, where scientific rationality is poised to conquer all, the individual writer must take up a position, from which she/he can survey the relevant field, and chart an appropriate argumentational route through it. In the pedagogic practice of academic writing, the role of topic sentences may be seen to be performing a similar function. They serve an overview function, and begin a move-ment from the general to the particular, or from making a claim to support-ing it. As such, the continuing importance of topic sentences in academic writing practice, is perpetuating a rhetorical norm, which is in itself per-petuating a particular kind of 'monarch of all he surveys' (Pratt, 1992: 197) subjectivity.

This writer subjectivity is inscribed symbolically in the functional impor-tance of a good introduction, also. Berkenkotter and Huckin draw explicit attention to such importance in a scientific article. Notably, they state the significance of a visual overview, as follows:

> In a good Introduction you can almost get the entire paper and back-ground. A good Introduction, in a way, is like Kentucky Fried Chicken. The Colonel used to say if the gravy is good enough you can throw away the chicken. And you can almost throw away the paper, if the Introduction is set up well, because *you can see the field, you can see where it all fits, you can see what they did.* (my italics) (Berkenkotter & Huckin, 1995: 59).

The Inscription of a Specific Cultural Subjectivity

A link between map-making and textualising is also made by Pratt (1992), but in a different way. She discerns in the earlier discourses of travel writing that she looks at, the construction of a certain type of European consciousness or cultural subjectivity, related to circumnavigat-ing the world. Here, she emphasises the fact that circumnavigation applied not only to the actual voyage, but also to the book of the event. The opportunity to sail round the world in print, as it were, was an important factor in the construction of a 'world historical subject' who is 'European, male, secular, and lettered' (Pratt, 1992: 27). Pratt uses the following quote from Defoe to illustrate this early 18th century subjectivity:

> [he may] make a tour of the world in books, he may make himself master of the geography of the universe in the maps, atlasses and measurements of our mathematicians. He may travell by land with the historians, by sea with navigators. He may go round the globe with Dampier and Rogers and kno' a thousand times more doing it than all those illiterate sailors. (Daniel Defoe, *The Compleat English Gentleman* (1730); quoted in Pratt (1992: 27))

In other words, accounts of circumnavigation were culturally as important, if not more so, than the actual voyage. The process of mapping the world was not simply the technical project that it seemed; it was helping to shape a particular European imperialist consciousness. Knowledge of the world in a geographical sense has the psycho-symbolic effect of facilitating the acceptability, indeed expectation, of mastery in the imperialist sense. The scientific accounts of gentleman scholars such as Newton may similarly be said to have been feeding a sense of mastery and control. As Bazerman put it when Newton hit on his rhetorical strategy of positing abstract geometry rather than his own actions as the basis for description of his experiments, this gave him 'interpretive command' (Bazerman, 1988: 117).

In the academic essay, it can be said that writers act in control of their texts in as much as they have been subjectified by assumptions of autonomy and control and enact the rhetoricity that conforms to those assumptions. The continuing vocabulary of 'mastery' and 'control' over text, grammar and argument is a legacy of this traditional understanding. The individual assessed on the extent to which he/she is in control of the argument in an academic essay may be seen as a genealogical trace of this value system, whereby the individual writing subject is enacting 'mastery and control'.

Objective Subjectivities

In the quote cited previously from Andrews, he talks of students 'combining their subjectivity with an apparent objectivity' and relates this to the dangers, on the one hand, of 'being too personal', and, on the other, of 'being too dry and rigid'. This illustrates well the traditional dualism that has been formed, whereby 'subjectivity' and 'objectivity' constitute two different and separable entities. The power invested in reason exemplified by the Cartesian cogito privileges abstract processes of thought, as in a geometric proof, for example, rather than feelings. The mind–body dualism advocated by Cartesian philosophy creates a disembodied, distant 'voice' or what has more recently been critiqued in philosophy as 'The View from Nowhere' (Nagel, 1986) which privileges objectivity, and creates a negative 'other', namely subjectivity, which connotes a narrow, individual or unresearched opinion. Each of these conceptualisations will have different effects on the shape of academic writing. Andrews hopes that elements of each will be brought together, and shows an awareness of how difficult these rhetorical effects are to achieve. The assumption is that students will work to achieve them. Essay writing is seen as a set of skills, where traditional objectivity remains the norm, but should be ideally leavened by intrusions of the individual personality.

The position here is more reflexive, acknowledging the historical production and naturalisation of a rhetoricity, which has been shaped by the power invested in the notion of a scientific rational observer. The rhetoricity associated with this rational subjectivity, complexly, is one where the rhetorical subject position is one of conveying objectivity. In other words, rather than being an *a priori* 'neutral' means of writing, objectivity is a rhetorical product. It is the result of the inscription of scientific rationality in rhetorical norms.

The notion of subjectification cuts across the distinction between subjectivity and objectivity. The academic writing subject does not so much convey objectivity as s/he is subject to it.

Rhetorical Regularisation

As well as conveying his own authority as a scientist, Newton as a leading scientist was also helping to shape a new epistemic reality, and along with that, rhetorical norms, whose genealogical traces may still be seen in the values attached to academic writing. In other words, he was also shaping a new rhetorical reality. Newton's success in convincing his peers brought him a degree of social power, at one time becoming president of the Royal Society, and he remains an iconic figure in the history of science. As such, his extensive work on getting the rhetoric 'right' for his book on Optics, at an important period in European history when empiricists and rationalists were competing with each other in their methodological approaches make his rhetorical success an important instance in the process of creating normativity for academic writing. As Bazerman says (1988: 324) Newton's devising of rhetorical strategies in order to persuade his audience were also creating an ideal for scientific generalisation.

The ideal of Newtonian science structured as a comprehensive deductive system of great generality can be seen as fostered by Newton's discoveries of the most advisable procedures for winning his arguments. (Bazerman, 1988: 324)

Newton's *Optics* was reprinted several times and accrued status and admiration, thereby affording the opportunity for his rhetorical structuring to be replicated in different contexts and with different subject matter. Such a process need not have been consciously undertaken, but a popular text is likely to have effects on what counts as accessible style and generate norms of accessibility. In the preface to an early 20th century edition of the *Optics*, Albert Einstein shows its enduring effects, as rhetorical artefact as much as source of knowledge, in his praise of Newton's 'joy in creation and his minute precision ... evident in every word and every figure' (quoted in Bazerman, 1988: 124).

'Minute precision' is obviously a positive evaluation and symptomatic of a range of rhetorical virtues embodying economy and elegance as well as exactitude and certainty. It is not unsurprising that these are also virtues of the 'exact sciences'. They can be seen also in logicians' desires for language, such as Russell's 20th century notion that 'there will be one word and no more for every simple object ... '(Russell, 1918: 58), quoted in Crowley (1989). These aesthetic values along with the norms of academic writing, such as logical exposition, concision in choice of lexis, and economy of style continue to meet the expectations, which academic writing pedagogy requires, and academic readers demand. The point to be emphasised here is that they are not simply *a priori* givens; they have been culturally produced and maintained.

Chapter 8
Subject to Confucian Rhetorical Culture

Introduction

As the numbers of students from China, Japan, Korea and Taiwan, for example, have markedly increased in UK institutions in recent years, they serve as the main exemplars of intercultural communication in this book. While such students by no means represent the extent of international diversity in contemporary higher education, their often widely differing assumptions and expectations offer an enriching perspective on it. This is not only the case with regard to the differences they bring with them, they also point up what is entrenched and taken for granted in a western institutional context. Given this entrenchment, the behaviour of such students is not always appropriately interpreted, giving rise to such negative stereotypes as 'passive' or 'silent' students (see also the discussions in Chapters 11 and 12) or from a western perspective, what is worse 'uncritical' students (see in particular, the discussion in Chapter 14).

Over the next few chapters, I explore intercultural interactions in terms of genealogical cultural differences, where Socrates and Confucius serve as metonyms for the respective, powerful value systems. On the one hand, genealogical traces of the Socratic dialogue can be seen in western educational practices, particularly as they relate to the roles of tutor and student. What is foregrounded here in particular is the importance attached to verbalisation, and the ways in which higher education tutors elicit verbalisation from their students. On the other hand, Confucian and Taoist principles in the understanding of teaching and learning may be seen as a genealogical counterpoint to the valorisation of the dialogic in western intellectual cultural history.

Confucianism in East Asian Culture

While Confucianism has its roots in Chinese culture, going back more than a hundred years before Plato, when Confucius himself was alive,

551 BC–479 BC, its principles and teachings have also influenced life in Korea, Japan and Vietnam as well. As Yum (1994: 76) notes, as well as being the official doctrine of many Chinese dynasties, until the Cultural Revolution in the mid-20th century, and readopted in the nineties thereafter, Confucianism was also adopted as the official doctrine of the Yi dynasty in Korea for 500 years, and the Tokugawa Shogunate in Japan for over 250 years (1603–1868). It is therefore not unreasonable to assume some similarities in how Confucian principles have permeated social practices in those countries, whether or not they have been, or continue to be, officially sanctioned or explicitly proclaimed. Such principles in fact need not be consciously adhered to in the minds of the participants; they are rather culturally inscribed and witnessed in repeated behaviour patterns, often from early schooling onwards, and so form part of routine behaviour.

One example of how similar practices permeate the different national contexts comes from the widespread use of a single classic textbook for teaching the writing of Chinese characters. As the Scollons (Scollon & Scollon, 1995: 125) point out, this textbook known as *The Three Character Classic (San Zi Jing)* is used in the learning of both classical Chinese writing and Chinese ethical philosophy, and 'has been used in Confucian education in China, Japan, Korea, and Vietnam for as long as eight hundred years' (Scollon & Scollon, 1995: 125). The text goes back to the Southern Song Dynasty (AD 1127–1279) and is based on Confucian classics such as *The Analects* and the writings of one of his foremost disciples, Mencius. It therefore embodies the ethical position taken by that school of thought that all humans are born good. It begins with the following words:

Ren zhi chu, xing ben shan
Xing xiang jin, Xi xiang yuan (Scollon & Scollon, 1995: 125)

The lines are translated as:

Man by nature is good; people's inborn characters are similar, but learning makes them different.

Lee cites a longer version (and alternative translation) of this poem from the *Three Character Classic*, which provides a fuller version of Confucian educational principles:

Men, one and all, in infancy are virtuous at heart.
Their natures are much the same, the practice wide apart.
Without Instruction's aid, our instinct grew less pure.
By aiming at thoroughness only can teaching ensure.
…

To feed the body, not the mind – fathers, on you the blame!
Instruction without severity, the idle teacher's shame.
If a child does not learn, this is not as it should be.
How, with a youth of idleness, can age escape the blight?
...
Diligence has its reward; play has no gain.
Be on your guard, and put forth your strength. (Lee, 2005: 26)

I have quoted Lee's version of this poem in full, because it seems to encapsulate many of the values which infuse the attitudes and behaviour, including the linguistic behaviour of East Asian students in intercultural educational settings. They include an emphasis on instruction, the importance of working hard, the responsibility of the family, as well as the teacher for a child's learning, and the conception of the teacher as an extension of the family.

In her discussion of Confucianism, Yum (1994) elaborates four principles for good conduct which influence styles of communication. They are:

(1) *jen* This is translated as 'humanism' or 'warm feelings among people'. Yum also represents it as 'like a seed from which springs all the qualities that make up the ideal man'. The actual practice or embodiment of jen is related to reciprocity. Confucius said that practising jen is not to do to another man what you yourself do not want. Quoting McNaughton (1974), Yum suggests this principle operates as follows: If there's something that you don't like in the person to your right, don't pass it on to the person on your left. If there's something that you don't like in the person to your left, don't pass it on to the person on your right (McNaughton, 1974: 29).

(2) *i* (yi) This is translated as faithfulness or loyalty. Yum suggests that it is easier to understand through its opposite, personal interest or profit. It is 'that part of human nature that allows us to look beyond personal, immediate profit and to elevate ourselves to the original goodness of human nature that bridges ourselves to other people' (Yum, 1987: 77).

(3) *li* This is translated as propriety, rites, or respect for social forms. Yum explains that this is the outward form of the Confucian ethical system, as opposed to *jen* and *i*, which represent its conceptual content. As an objective criterion of social decorum, *li* was perceived as the fundamental regulatory etiquette of human behaviour. Mencius claimed that li originated from deference to others and maintaining an attitude of reserve as regards one's own feelings. According to Confucius, li followed from *jen*, that is, from being considerate to

others. On the other hand, propriety without humanness was perceived to be empty and useless.

(4)   *chih* (zhi) This general principle is associated with wisdom or a liberal education.

The third principle *li* is incorporated in 'the book of rites' (*Li Ji*), one of the five Confucian classics. This book is concerned with proper conduct in maintaining the five relationships, including ways of speaking within those relationships. The five relationships are those between: prince and minister; father and son; husband and wife; elder and younger; and between friends. These predominantly hierarchical relationships are an important backdrop to understanding Confucian styles of communication. Conducting those relationships in the proper way, that is, saying the right things in the right way at the right time, as it were, was seen as important in the maintenance of order in society more generally. One of the implications of this, as Kirkpatrick, for example, has stated, is that 'individual expression had to be harnessed' and 'motivation to communicate was severely inhibited' (Kirkpatrick, 1995: 284). Many of the implications of speaking with propriety or maintaining silence as appropriate are illustrated in real examples and discussed in the following chapters.

Confucian Subjects

In contrast to the values associated with the performance of a kind of Socratic dialogue, discussed in Chapters 9 and 10, Chapters 11 to 13 explore a different cultural genealogy. This is illuminated by the rhetorical action performed by East Asian students as they participate in international education in western institutional contexts. It shows, for example, the promotion of a proactive silence, which tends to conflict with a preference for speech and dialogism in the western academic cultural tradition. Their action is in tune also with the cultural importance of following the teacher as an exemplary model, and with the spatial conceptualisation of the 'way' of learning, which is a translation of the word Tao, and therefore the crux of Taoist philosophy. A number of illustrative examples of how the differing perspectives interact in intercultural communication are provided.

As much of what is written in Confucian texts concerns principles of teaching and learning, it is not surprising that an educational context brings them to the fore, and that further, in an international intercultural context, they stand out. The argument being made here is that Confucian values, especially as they are embodied in ways of communicating, continue to be available to East Asian students, whether or not the students themselves are actually conscious of them as such. This means that even in interaction with 'western' tutors in western educational contexts, East Asian students can take up subject positions which have been formed culturally over the long period of influence of Confucianism, and its infusion into social as well as educational norms. This is not to suggest that Chinese, Japanese, Koreans and Vietnamese all order their ways of communicating with each other in exactly the same way in all contexts. Nor conversely, should it be assumed that the communicative styles of Europeans and Americans, including the English-speaking styles of Britain and America, are always the same. Nonetheless, such culturally embedded styles of communication become particularly prominent as 'different' when they occur in the course of intercultural communication, in this case, in western educational institutions. For example, in an initial classroom encounter, a question addressed to the whole class by a western teacher, may not result in any response from a group of East Asian students, if this is not a situation the students are familiar with. With educational globalisation of course, and it appears, the hegemony of western style pedagogy in this process, such situations occur less frequently, but it was certainly my first experience of such a classroom encounter.

The potentially negative consequences of such experiences are warned against by Scollon (1999), who states:

> Western teachers unaccustomed to a classroom full of Asian students all too frequently feel that their words are going to waste because they do not get the feedback they are accustomed to not only in terms of comments and questions but in head movement and facial expression. It is all too common in such a situation to fall into a downward spiral of lowering our expectations and simplifying our language, using more direct questions that tend to elicit simple yes/no answers and decrease the possibility of dialogic exchange. This has the effect of further lowering teacher expectations in a vicious circle that amounts to failure to speak to students in a way that is capable of fully benefiting them by providing the rich language environment they need in order to learn. In this we risk letting not only our students go to waste but ultimately our words. (Scollon, 1999: 27)

My aim here is not to pathologise East Asian students for their ability to give their western teachers culture shock, nor to assume that they cannot adapt to or take on board the underlying precepts and styles of communicating that are prevalent in western educational institutions. Many do this successfully, and without necessarily changing their sense of self or identity. Indeed, this was what happened in the case of a student who came to appreciate the importance of talking through what was going on in his work as an artist, as a means to developing his practice. This example is discussed in Chapter 11.

The potentially deleterious effects of intercultural university classroom contexts are brought out from the perspective of student learning, in Holmes's (2006) New Zealand study. Here, her focus group studies with Chinese students reveal that they feel their ideas are not fully engaged with, and at the same time they are aware that their own practices of face-saving strategies and the maintenance of harmony are contributing to this negative state of affairs. She sums up the situation of their co-learning with New Zealand students as follows:

> Disagreement is silenced by the need to preserve harmony and face, even though internal debate is taking place. New Zealand students, by contrast, voiced disagreement or discontentment with group processes. The way each group interpreted the communication encounter appeared to be a lose-lose learning situation. The Chinese students did not have the opportunity to express their ideas, engage in critical debate and possibly develop their thinking; the New Zealand students did not benefit from the Chinese students' insights or have their own ideas contested by another world view. (Holmes, 2006: 28)

Doing One's Best: An Intercultural Perspective

In discussing this issue of Confucian subjects, it is not a question of positing an ongoing static sameness in how an individual behaves and reacts. Nor is it one of determinism. Rather, the notion of Confucian subjects acknowledges the power/knowledge of thousands of years of cultural influence and social practice and therefore the ready availability of subject positions, in this case in contexts of teaching and learning, which have been motivated by Confucian principles. To give a very simple example in terms of linguistic behaviour, East Asian students often make such statements to their teachers as:

I will work very hard

or

I will do my best

as closing statements after a consultation with a teacher. They function as statements of commitment, whether simply as a matter of course, responding to the context of teacher consultation and their undertaking to do what has been agreed, or as a form of promising redress, if for example, they have been reprimanded for not handing in work or have not attended as often as they should. They are in effect formulaic, part of a 'conversational routine' (Coulmas, 1981) in teacher–student contexts. Their purpose and effect is different from what it would have been if a British student had made the same utterance. This is not only because such utterances by East Asian students occur more frequently, but also because they signal a more general commitment to 'good studentship'. This attitudinal stance is linked to what Singleton, in the context of teaching in Japan, calls 'the spirit of gambaru' (Singleton, 1991), where the verb 'gambaru' translates as 'to do one's best', and the overall spirit is one of effort and perseverance. This 'spirit' or learning ethos is tied up with the Confucian principle of self-perfectibility, de Bary (1983, 2007); Lee (2005) and Li (2009) and the importance of effort in this process, and chimes also with the opening sentence of Confucius's Analects (I.1)

> Is it not pleasant to learn with a constant perseverance and application? (Lee, 2005: 27)

While the sentiment of 'working harder' is rooted in educational principle, its pragmatic use may simply signal polite student behaviour, with no substantive change in the kind of work the student submits. The western teacher/interlocutor however, may be led into expecting work or behaviour of a different quality.

Deconstructing the Parameters for Intercultural Analysis

Scholars in many different fields, including psychology, anthropology and linguistics, have set up a range of theoretical frameworks and analytical criteria for the description of patterns and styles of communication. These include socio-pragmatics; natural semantic metalanguage; interactional socio-linguistics; politeness theory; and discourse analysis. This has meant the proliferation of a number of keywords or concepts, many of which are used outside of their original points of reference. As a result, there have also been theoretical discussions on the adequacy or not of typologies with claims to universality. Such discussions include Wierzbicka's concern with the extent of imprecision in the use of conceptual terminology, especially in cross-cultural research (Wierzbicka, 1991a), and Gumperz and Levinson's discussion of universalism versus cultural relativity (Gumperz & Levinson, 1991). In her discussion of how the variability of their contexts of operation detract from the analytical applicability of the widely used variables of *power* and *distance*, Spencer-Oatey (1996) also points up the difficulty of using the same analytical parameters cross-culturally.

With no underlying assumption here that neutral constructs are possible, or indeed desirable, what I want to draw attention to particularly is the evaluative dimension of variables or concepts whose descriptive acuity seems fine when restricted to the cultural context in which they have been formed, but whose bipolarity has a negative effect when used contrastively with another culture with different norms. In other words, the analytical terms in English, which have been chosen to identify one or the other cultural predisposition, or characterise a communicative value or approach to communication, seem to carry a cultural loading that is diametrically opposed to the value system in a contrasting culture. The choice of analytical concept used in framing any particular cultural perspective, then, can set up in turn a further array of associated differences which may not actually apply, or which at least may be evaluated differently from within another cultural perspective. Especially in the case of East–West comparisons, there seems to be an inevitability of conflicting value systems and cross purposes, as each background perspective relies on precepts which are either completely differently evaluated in the respective systems, or which appear to position the contrasting cultural system in a negative light.

Cultural (In)dependence

A case of diametrically opposed value systems arises for example, with the term 'dependence', which is used to designate what Doi sees as the prevailing cultural ethos in Japan (Doi, 1973). While this is a translation from the Japanese term *amae*, and has been chosen by a Japanese analyst, it seems nonetheless to be an unfortunate choice, given its resonance in English. In an intercultural context in a western-based institution the concept of 'dependence' can redound rather negatively, contrasting starkly as it does with the much valued concept of 'independence', and in particular independent thinking. While Doi, a psychoanalyst, with experience of working in both Japan and the United States, was talking of dependence in largely emotional terms, he also saw it as a structuring metaphor for Japanese society in general. Doi's book has been widely circulated in English and is therefore well known. It could therefore be used to justify any negative perceptions of Japanese students in the intercultural context as lacking independent thinking or being uncritical.

Interestingly, Kubota (1999) critiques Doi's contribution as coming from a widely perceived need for Japanese culture to reassert itself against the overwhelming influence of the United States. This is the movement or tendency known as *nihonjinron,* which proclaims the uniqueness of Japanese culture. Therefore, it seems feasible that the concept of dependence may have been chosen for its striking difference from what is valued in the United States. The problem is that whereas dependence, or better, social interdependence could have positive connotations in the context of promoting social cohesion, and therefore arguably greater success in this respect could be claimed for Japanese society than for British or American society, the evaluative ordering does not similarly transfer to the context of international higher education.

Harmony in Conflict

The intercultural case is similar with the term 'harmony', which is routinely seen as motivating speech patterns in Confucian cultures. While the maintenance of harmony seems to fit well with Confucianism, where 'proper human relationships' are the basis of society (Yum, 1994: 77), and extolled for example, in the *Three Character Classic* (Lee, 2005; Scollon & Scollon, 1995). Despite the fact that it has a generally positive, peace-loving connotation in English, it is not rooted in the same genealogical cultural heritage, and therefore does not have the same value in a different genealogical cultural heritage. In terms of linguistic behaviour, harmony may be contained in the fact that the participants in the discussion maintain the proper speaking relationships, showing due deference to seniors and higher status participants, and not speaking unnecessarily. This does not mean that there is necessarily underlying agreement among all the participants, however. Some might be quietly seething. In contrast, in western contexts of speaking and putting forward opinions, keeping silent might not maintain harmony as what is required is persuasive debate, and the contribution of as many participants as possible is preferred.

The Dilemmas of *enryo* and either/or *Questions*

In her discussion of what she terms 'Japanese key terms and core cultural values' Wierzbicka (1991b) devotes about six pages to the notion of *enryo.* Because of the specific cultural context in which this concept has gained importance, it is difficult to translate into English, but perhaps its most accessible meaning is that of 'restraint'. It is linked to the pressure for conformity often associated with Japanese culture, although under the new pressures of globalisation, this may be changing. Wierzbicka quotes Lebra's comment as follows:

> Pressure for conformity often results in a type of self-restraint called enryo, refraining from expressing disagreement with whatever appears to be the majority's opinion. (Lebra, 1976: 29)

In similar vein, Smith (1983) commented that:

> One way to express enryo is to avoid giving opinions. (Smith, 1983: 83)

Not only is the cultural value of *enryo* linked to the avoidance of expressing opinions, see further the discussion on being critical in Chapter 14, it plays a role also in 'sidestepping choices when they are offered' (Smith, 1983: 87). Wierzbicka quotes an account by Doi, of the discomfiture he felt in the United States, when he was the recipient of hospitality and confronted with numerous choices. His discomfiture lay in the fact that he didn't want to have to make those choices. He was happy with whatever the host offered: tea or coffee; milk and/or sugar; scotch or bourbon. As he said: 'I couldn't care less' (Doi, 1981: 12). In the contrasting context of Japanese hospitality it is rather incumbent on the host to consider what the guest would most like to have and simply present that.

The Inter-Relational Dynamics of Individualism and Collectivity

The notion of harmony is often linked also with the individualism-collectivity dimension, outlined by Hofstede in the field of organisational psychology (Hofstede, 1980). His framework for analysing differences across cultures was the result of observations of difference in corporate cultures across the globe, and of the need for global corporations, notably IBM in his case, to work with and manage personnel in different national contexts, and has been hugely influential. He promoted the use of a measurable index of four dimensions, power-distance, uncertainty avoidance, individual/collectivity and masculinity/feminity, which were used to compare national attitudes and predispositions. A fifth dimension was added, long-term orientation, after a study conducted with Chinese managers and employees. These dimensions and their uses continue to be discussed and critiqued in the business world, and to some extent also in other academic fields, for example, Bond *et al.* (2000).

While the measurability of the dimensions is not of interest here as the aim is not to compare scores on any index, the contrastive dyad individual/

collectivity is of interest because of its conceptual and descriptive relevance, along with the associations of harmony, to East–West communication. This dimension seems at first glance to accommodate quite well to broad differences in approach to communication, namely the relevance of the individual speaking for him or herself, as opposed to orienting what is said according to his/her position within the group, and out of consideration for the ethos of the particular group. Nonetheless, the notion of collectivity is not subtle enough to capture all the forces at play within group-oriented communicative cultures. While it allows for an emphasis on the importance of the group in designating who speaks and how one speaks, for example, according to age or status, it does not differentiate between 'in-group' and 'out-group' communication, which is just as important in East Asian contexts. A further problem with the notion of collectivity is that it can also take on a philanthropic hue when it is seen as an abstract ideal, where the interests of the greater good are served rather than those of the individual.

When set against the characterisation of individualism in the western perspective, the contrastive discourse may take on a moral tone, which is not relevant in the context of origin where the speech style has been identified. I develop my critique of this moralising discourse, which runs along the lines of 'collective' and 'group' = 'good, and individual' = bad for its out of context generalisation. A genealogical approach locates any values in the intellectual and social cultural contexts in which they have evolved, and does not judge them in ethical or moral terms.

This critique is developed below in terms of the ethical discourse that has developed in the social sciences in the United States in particular where a communitarian ethos is argued for over what has come to be seen as the socially bereft results of individualism.

Differing Orders of Discourse: Communicative Styles and Politico-Moral Frameworks

The concept of individualism has itself been at the nub of recent sociopolitical debates within western democracies. On the one hand, individualism stands for the basic democratic rights of each individual, for example, to exercise freedom of speech. On the other hand, however, individualism is also seen as at the root of a range of social ills. This highly negative connotation of individualism arose in some key texts in the social scientific literature of the 1980s and 1990s, especially in the United States (Bellah *et al.*, 1985; Putnam, 1995; Shapiro, 1997), where it was linked to the contemporary plight of the United States, where 'drugs, crime, alienation, family breakdown, loss of good neighbourliness and the like' (Rose, 1999: 181) were only too visible. As Rose points out, this social and political science literature takes its cue from Alexis de Tocqueville, who, writing in the 1830s about democracy in the United States (Tocqueville, 1969), pointed to individualism, and in particular, the facility with which US citizens formed societies or groups around all sorts of things, as the key to democracy. What is bemoaned by the contemporary political scientists is that this predisposition to create civic associations has been lost and the contemporary overly individualistic American goes 'bowling alone' (Putnam, 1995). This image epitomises for those aspiring to a more communitarian ethos, the decay of ethico-cultural networks of civic trust.

Writing around the same period as Bellah *et al.*, Yum (1994) frames her discussion of Confucian social relations in comparison with western individualism, within a similar ethico-cultural discourse (Yum, 1994: 76). Quoting Bellah *et al.* and the pathological state of individualism which they identify, she states:

> Although individualism has its own strength as a value, individualism that is not accompanied by commitments to large entities eventually forces people into a state of isolation, where life itself becomes meaningless. (Yum, 1994: 84)

In tapping into this powerful discourse, however, which is critiquing the contemporary state of western individualism, Yum is in danger of setting up comparisons between western and Confucian communication styles within the same ethico-political discourse. Possibly mindful of adopting such a high moral tone, whereby western values are pitched negatively against the Confucian values of attention to social relations, Yum also points to the negative aspects of the latter, namely the fact that 'individual initiative' and 'innovation' are slow to appear, and that some individuals feel that 'their individuality is being suffocated' (Yum, 1994: 85). These negative effects are however rather mild, compared to the dire social consequences laid at the door of extreme individualism. There is therefore a huge difference in scope between the individualism that may be discerned in western patterns of communication and the individualism that is posited as the source of a range of social and political problems in western democracies. Also, on the collectivity side of the coin, the fallacious inference might be drawn that group-oriented communication patterns might lead to the kind of communitarian social ethos that the American social and political scientists have in mind. These issues are simply not of the same order of contrastive potential. Care therefore needs to be exercised over how the analytical terms available are used, and attention needs to be paid to the differing discourses within which they gain their analytical momentum. They in effect mean different things within different orders of discourse.

Teleological Thinking: Globally Neutral or a Western Hegemony?

One further contrastive cultural dyad that I'd like to discuss here is that of Ballard and Clanchy's (1991) ascription of an 'extending knowledge' approach, applicable to western academic cultures and that of a 'conserving knowledge' approach, to Confucian cultures (Ballard, 1996; Ballard & Clanchy, 1991). The knowledge extending formulation also aligns with the discovery ethos of western colonisation, which was discussed in Chapter 5 in relation to its effects on rhetorical preferences, but also in a spirit of critique for its related colonising dynamic. What the contrastive semantics of 'extending' versus 'conserving' also enables, however, is the critique that on any kind of forward trajectory for knowledge, the 'conserving' cultures are going to be left behind. Kubota in fact makes this critique (Kubota, 1999), labelling the distinction 'orientalist'. However, what she does not acknowledge is that in doing so, she is actually privileging a teleological dynamic, which is deeply embedded in the western intellectual tradition, and might not therefore be expected in intellectual traditions without this cultural history. Buying into western perspectives on progress through the production of knowledge is one thing, but it is not the same as suggesting this perspective has always been universal, or even that it is universally desirable. As Jack (2004) has argued in relation to the incorporation of management practices from the developed nations into developing world contexts, it should not necessarily be assumed that that is the best policy. In the case of a conserving approach to knowledge, nor should such an approach necessarily be assumed to be negative. In fact, a conserving knowledge approach might in many instances be seen as valuable.

I would counter against Kubota's critique that the dichotomisation of 'extending' and 'conserving' knowledge is an effect of 'orientalising' or 'othering', that it is rather a question of unreflexively continuing a deeply embedded, intellectual–cultural mode of cognising. Certainly, the semantic implication is clear that this dichotomy effectively positions non-western cultures as always behind, trying to catch up, but that in itself constitutes the teleological dynamic of an uncritiqued notion of progress.

The point that the cultural historian Robert Young makes in relation to what he terms 'collusive Eurocentrism', is relevant here. Young's example relates to the way in which Marx's thinking is seen to parallel Hegel's even though he is considered to be 'turning Hegel on his head'. Marx may have posited different winners in the teleological trajectory of history, initially projected by Hegel, but he 'did not change the mode of operation of a conceptual system which remains collusively Eurocentric' (Young, 1990). While Marx anticipates ownership of the capitalist means of production by the proletariat and Hegel is concerned with a more abstract philosophical ideal of Spirit or absolute knowledge as the result of human historical progress, the teleological process, or imagined final purpose, determining the trajectory is the same. Privileging this entrenched western dynamic is a mark of its hegemony.

Critiquing the Ready Critique of Othering

It is ultimately too easy to trivialise, or even deter attempts at understanding cultural difference by invoking 'othering' or essentialising. One of the effects of globalisation is that individuals may relate more to global sub-cultures for their sense of self, see for examples, Pennycook (2007) and Holliday (2009) or the notion of cosmopolitan citizens Guilherme (2007), than think of themselves in terms of their national affiliations, but there are nonetheless likely to be instances in which aspects of the cultural genealogies infused into those nationalities come to the fore, regardless of the individual's predominant sense of self. The existence of such deeply running patterns of thinking in intellectual–cultural histories is, however, barely touched upon in intercultural analyses.

Through my use of the term 'occidentalist', I have attempted to mark the embeddedness of certain ways of thinking and certain ways of doing things as an effect of power working over time, and no longer visible as such. This approach acknowledges and tries to reveal the continuing power/knowledge effects of such genealogically embedded modes of thinking, in order to build a reflexive awareness of their working rather than to simply accept them. At the same time, the ready availability of those ways of thinking should not lead to the assumption that they will always be like that or that they cannot be critiqued. For example, the teleological dynamic has already been critiqued by Lyotard as 'grand narratives' (Lyotard, 1984), and this mode of critique has been influential in contemporary cultural and postcolonial theorising. It has opened up spaces of resistance, or the opportunity for those who have been left out of account in the narrative of cultural history as it were, to tell their stories, to give what Lyotard calls in contrast to the grand narratives, 'petits recits'.

By analogy, a similarly reflexive approach to the Confucian tradition could be labelled 'orientalist', but that would be too confusing. What is important is the process of reflexive thinking. In this process, 'de-sedimenting subjectivities', to use O'Regan and MacDonald's phrase (2007), is necessarily involved. I am not however positing a specific kind of re-subjectivised being, or a specific kind of intercultural subjectivity; this would be to reiterate the teleological dynamic.

Conclusion

While there are many different ways of pointing up contrasts in cultural perspectives, values, priorities, which have implications for styles of communication, it is important to remember that the issue of contrastive cultural analysis or intercultural communication is not about imprisoning the communicative or any other behaviour of individuals within neat explanatory categories. The categories serve as a heuristic but they are not impermeable and their lines of demarcation are inevitably squiggly rather than straight. They are also, inevitably, by dint of the intercultural dynamics itself, caught up in an ongoing process of performative transformation.

Chapter 9
The Power/Knowledge Effects of the Socratic Dialogue

Introduction

The focus of this chapter is the cultural power of the Socratic dialogue in the western intellectual tradition. It continues to be valued, both in its own right, and in terms of the ongoing importance vested in the dialogic as a cultural, political, theoretical and practical process. In the context of this book, where the spotlight is on language in higher education, the continuing need to refer to the importance of the dialogic, or explicitly espouse a Socratic approach in the context of teaching or advising students, indicates the continuing valorisation of a longstanding tradition. With valorisation comes power. What I want to emphasise here are the effects of such power, and how they can work implicitly in the academic context. This is where an emphasis on dialogue and talk in the furtherance of learning has in effect been naturalised.

Intellectual Midwifery as Genealogical Pedagogic Practice

At the time of Socrates/Plato, the intellect was deemed the most important faculty. In his history of the western intellectual tradition, Tarnas summarises this point as follows:

> The true structure of the world is revealed not by the senses, but by the intellect, which in its highest state has direct access to the Ideas governing reality. (Tarnas, 1991: 12)

Talking specifically of what the role of the intellect was for Socrates, Tarnas states:

> It was the divine faculty by which the human soul could discover both its own essence and the world's meaning. That faculty required only awakening. However arduous the path of awakening, such divine

intellectual power lay potentially resident in humble and great alike. Tarnas (1991: 38)

The notion of 'awakening' continues to resonate in contemporary educational and social discourse more widely through the trope of 'developing one's potential'. It is also the crux of the 'intellectual midwifery', which Socrates saw himself performing in relation to the delivery of the thoughts and judgements, which he is trying to draw out from his interlocutors, in Plato's dialogues. Those dialogues are characterised by Robinson (1953), one of the many philosophers and commentators on Plato's philosophy, as a methodology deployed in the interests of reaching the truth. He summarises this methodology as:

> the idea that there could be a supreme method for reaching ultimate truth (ultimate truth being truth about "essences" or "forms") which would operate solely by conversation in the form of question-and-answer. (Robinson, 1953: 88)

An explicit example of Socrates' understanding of himself as a midwife in this conversational, truth-reaching process comes in the dialogue *Theaetetus* (Plato, 1961), where Socrates tells *Theaetetus* that his mother was a midwife, and that what he does is similar. He states:

> My art of midwifery is in general like theirs; the only difference is that my patients are men, not women, and my concern is not with the body but with the soul that is in travail with birth. (Plato, 1961: 825)

Tarnas also mentions the fact that:

> Socrates often referred to himself as an intellectual midwife, through his dialectical skill bringing to birth the latent truth in another's mind. (Tarnas, 1991: 40)

This process of inducing an intellectual birth is also described by another commentator on Plato's philosophy, Guthrie, who puts it in terms of Socrates:

> leading men to an understanding of certain unvarying and permanent principles on which to base their conduct ... but his conversations showed him that most men suffered an illusion of knowledge which had to be dispelled before the positive side of their inquiries could begin. (Guthrie, 1961: 108)

Men therefore had first to realise their ignorance before they could develop their knowledge. Socrates' method for reducing men to a state of ignorance or reducing the debate to a fixed starting point was known as the 'elenchus'. Billig (1987) glosses the elenchus in the following way:

> by questioning, Socrates gets debaters to agree to certain propositions and then by further questioning examines the implications of this agreement. (Billig, 1987: 347)

Very similar processes to those discussed in relation to the methodology of the Socratic dialogue and the 'arduous path' towards reaching agreement or basic principles on which to take a discussion forward are observed in the intercultural tutorial data discussed in the following chapter.

Genealogical Critique

The focus of critique here is not simply to take issue with the educational ideology that a tutor's role should be to induce the student into an understanding that he/she has worked out for him/herself, of what counts as knowledge, or good judgement. There is nothing intrinsically bad about this process, and if done well, with its assumptions and expectations acknowledged on both sides of the learning/teaching divide, it may very well be seen as an excellent way of promoting learning. There is, however, a danger in the fact that something is so deeply embedded in an educational culture, and so readily available to practitioners within that culture, that it comes to be seen as 'natural'. Such an everyday or commonsense 'naturalness' also makes it difficult to critique. This is why a genealogical critique is important. A genealogical critique needs to be aware of the investment of past valorisations in contemporary practices and evaluate them anew. This need not necessarily invalidate pedagogical procedures of longstanding, but it means recognising that they operate not only in a local, institutional context, but also in a wider and deeper intellectual tradition. It is at this 'reflexive' level that a genealogical critique functions. The focus is not on the face value of the rhetorical strategies themselves or how effective they are; it is rather on the extent to which these strategies are culturally embedded and what educational, philosophical and cultural values they implicitly espouse.

Genealogical Reflexivity

From a reflexive perspective, the broader cultural value system within which the values associated with the Socratic dialogue operate is occidentalist. This means looking at the values and the dominant modes of knowledge production of the west from within, as was outlined in

Chapter 5. Occidentalist inscription or the power/knowledge investment and continued dissemination of what has been culturally valued and valorised is not simply visible and definable, and so ignorable or dismissable, it is much more porous, working invisibly in seemingly innocuous rhetorical action.

In the contemporary context of higher education, especially in Anglo-centric institutions in the United Kingdom, the United States and Canada, Australia and New Zealand, the presence of many students from East Asian backgrounds, such as China, Japan and Korea, which share a Confucian heritage, two powerful intellectual genealogies interact. Where expectations of a different kind of rhetorical action prevail, the intercultural tutorial in itself can drive the reflexive dynamics of genealogical critique.

Reflexivity in action can in fact also be seen in the following chapter when the students in effect force their British tutors to be more specific about what it is they are trying to get the students to do, and about what their role as tutor is. In further chapters, I look at the intercultural tutorial data from the perspective of the East Asian students, and also explore the genealogical perspective of the Confucian heritage, as well as how hybrid forms of interaction are being performed, but first of all I want to look at how deeply embedded in western intellectual history, the assumptions of value associated with the Socratic dialogue are.

The Cultural Inscription of the Socratic Dialogue

From their origins in ancient Greek, Plato's dialogues have been a source of commentary and inspiration in the western intellectual tradition. This has been facilitated by translations and commentaries, first of all into Latin in the early renaissance period by Marsilio Ficino (1433–1499), then into German in the early 19th century by the philosopher and theologian, Schleiermacher, and subsequently into English in the late 19th century, in what remains a classic translation by Benjamin Jowett, the then Master of Balliol College at Oxford University. Such has been the influence of Plato's philosophy, as expounded in his dialogues, that the early twentieth century philosopher Alfred North Whitehead famously dubbed the history of Western philosophy, 'a series of footnotes to Plato' (Whitehead, 1979: 39).

Not only the content of Plato's dialogues but the form itself of what has come to be known, indeed venerated, as the Socratic dialogue continues to be discussed in multiple European languages. It has become not only a philosophical/literary reference, but a cultural artefact in its own right. The assumption of its effectiveness as both a theoretical construct and practical educational procedure continues to thrive. For example, the conceptual and intellectual significance of the Socratic dialogue permeated cultural theorising in the 20th century. One major thinker, the German hermeneutic philosopher, Gadamer (1975, 1988) looks to the Socratic dialogue as the ideal for human communication. As Bernstein states:

> Gadamer's entire project of philosophical hermeneutics can be read as an attempt to recover what he takes to be the deepest and most pervasive theme in Western philosophy and culture – that the quintessence of our being is to *be dialogical* (italics in original). (Bernstein, 1986: 65)

As a former student of Gadamer's, and taking up many of his philosophical and critical theoretical themes, Habermas develops the notion of dialogue or 'true conversation' into his well-known and influential theory of 'communicative action' (Habermas, 1984, 1989). For Habermas, communicative action constitutes a universalist theory of rationality, serving the interests of mankind as a whole. This communicative rationality is pitted against, and advocated as preferable to, the dominant means-ends rationality, which pervades social practices.

From a somewhat different philosophical perspective, and against Habermas's ultimately teleological position, the American philosopher Rorty (1979, 1989) uses the similarly speech-based metaphor of conversation to frame his theoretical perspective. Rorty criticises the claims to universality of any systematising philosophy, what he terms a 'truth-seeking philosophy' in its search for a 'final vocabulary' and proposes 'an ongoing conversation of mankind' instead.

From yet another theoretical perspective and yet another European language background, but similarly valorising the Socratic dialogue, is the work of the influential Russian scholar Bakhtin (1981). He harks back to the Socratic dialogue as prototype for his notion of 'dialogism' (Holquist, 1990). In addition to the term 'dialogism', Bakhtin further structures his theoretical repertoire in language-based terminology. This includes 'heteroglossia' and 'polyphony' as well as 'intertextuality'. The pervasive influence of Bakhtin's terms in many areas of cultural, literary, and educational studies is a mark of their conceptual dynamism. This in turn reflects the appropriacy of their metaphorical transfer from the real-life vitality of using language and languages, and the multiplicity of its forms of meaning making.

The Intellectual Dynamism of Speech and Language in the Western Tradition

The above three, theoretically distinct, but nonetheless 'western' in terms of intellectual history and culture, traditions attest to the ready availability of the idiom of dialogue or conversation in philosophical and cultural–theoretical thinking. They also acknowledge its cultural roots in ancient Greece, particularly in the work of Plato, as well as how they were interpreted by the renaissance Neo-Platonists. In more practically oriented, and specifically pedagogical pursuits also, the dialogic, especially via Bakhtin rather than Socrates per se, is seen as particularly important. For example, in her discussion of communicative language teaching, Savignon (2007) refers to the work of Bakhtin, and the need for a Bakhtinian 'dialogue of cultures' in the development of sociocultural competence in language learning. Here the dialogic acts as both theoretical construct and the motor of practice in language education.

Dialogically Eliciting Independent Judgement

In other contemporary educational and professional discourses also, in different European languages, the Socratic dialogue is explicitly promoted as a valid pedagogical approach. There are those who consciously draw on Socratic strategies to elicit logical clarity or to provoke understanding in their students. An example of an explicit espousal of a Socratic approach in educational discourse in higher education comes from (Thonus, 1999: 227). She quotes from *The Writing Tutorial Services Guide to Tutoring* used by Indiana University in the United States:

> It is important that you COACH and not fix. … Coaching is more demanding of all concerned. Tutors must keep silent when they are bursting to tell students how to approach an issue or solve a problem. Students learn more when they shoulder more of the responsibility for their educations. To accomplish this, use the Socratic method by asking thoughtful, challenging, and polite questions. … Nudge, don't push – let the student do most of the work. (Thonus, 1999: 227)

Underlying this mode of communication is the educational philosophy of 'finding things out for yourself', a widespread and major assumption of Anglo-centric higher education, as the use of such phrases as students taking 'responsibility for their education' in the quote above shows.

Having students take responsibility for their own learning is also a prominent principle in ELT, but its intellectual resonance with a cultural–genealogical tradition tends not to be acknowledged. It is treated rather as an abstract and separate pedagogical principle, something prized for its own sake. In similar vein, approaches to the teaching of a grammar point, as in the so-called 'inductive' syllabus, whereby the student is led to formulating the grammatical rule for herself/himself through exposure to multiple examples, is not specifically associated with Socrates and drawing out ideas from the students themselves. However, the principle of students coming to understand something for themselves does have Socratic resonance. The notions of 'deductive' and 'inductive' curricula in language teaching, which imply differing degrees of teacher-led and student-led learning, may then be seen as reflecting continuing tensions in educational philosophy that go back to the ancient Greeks. Socrates' arguments against what now would be seen as the 'prescriptive' tendencies of the Sophists may be seen as an early example.

The genealogical inheritance of this tension in educational philosophy is also embodied etymologically in the word 'education' itself. There are two possible sources for the word in Latin: *educere* meaning to 'lead out' and *educare* meaning 'to train' or 'to mould'. While the first derivational source fits well with the Socratic philosophy of questioning and thinking for oneself, the second may be enlisted to support a more top-down approach of 'training' and following models. Debates in education continue to rotate around these principles, in all sorts of fields. The notion as to whether 'teacher training', a conventional usage, should rather be teacher education or teacher development, is a case in point.

The Implicit Workings of the Socratic Dialogue in Contemporary Tutorial Encounters

The heritage of the Socratic dialogue is obviously European, hence its relevance in several intellectual traditions disseminated initially in different European languages. As already mentioned, it is promoted as a valid pedagogical approach in different European languages. However, the institutional practices of higher education vary in the different national language cultures and so tutor–student interactions in small groups, let alone in one-to-one interaction as discussed below and in the following chapter, may be less prevalent in French, German, Spanish or Italian, than in English.

Hitherto, the small seminar or tutorial has been prevalent in the English-speaking world. The one-to-one tutorial in particular is seen as the traditional preserve of the humanities at the universities of Oxford and Cambridge (Palfreyman, 2001; Tapper & Palfreyman, 2000), and is not very prevalent elsewhere, although its precepts of independent thinking and critical dialogue, which furthers that thinking, continue as basic assumptions for the larger-scale seminar. What is of particular interest to the discussion here is the extent to which these encounters implicitly point up the assumptions on which the Socratic dialogue is based. It is the implicit working of such underlying assumptions and expectations, especially from the perspective of the students, that can be the source of problems, militating against the smooth flow of communication between tutor and student and the meeting of desired objectives.

The interanimation of subject positions in particular speech situations or 'speech genres' (Bakhtin, 1986) and the language tradition in which they occur is integral to Bakhtin's notion of dialogism, as well as to the emphasis put on the utterance by his contemporary, Volsoshinov. In taking issue with what he calls 'abstract objectivism', in effect Saussure's system of 'langue' and 'parole', whereby the utterance is seen as something individual, Voloshinov (1973) highlights the significance of the utterance as a social phenomenon. As Hodge and Kress (1988: 19) state:

> Voloshinov's work foregrounds the speech act as an exchange between individuals whose consciousness is already socially constructed.

Similarly, in his discussion of Bakhtin's dialogism, Holquist emphasises the fact that an utterance 'is never in itself originary' (Holquist, 1990: 60). He continues:

> an utterance is always an answer. It is always an answer to another utterance that precedes it, and is therefore always conditioned by, and in turn qualifies, the prior utterance to a greater or lesser degree. Before it means any specific thing, an utterance expresses the general condition of each speaker's addressivity, the situation of not only being preceded by a language system that is, "always already there", but preceded as well by all of existence, making it necessary for me to answer for the particular place I occupy.

The historical continuity that uses of language serve is brought up well in this quote, and the notion of 'answering for the particular place occupied' provides an appropriate analogy for the argument in the next chapter relating to the subject position of the western tutor in the tutorial encounter, as well as to the subject position expected of the student. In other words, the place occupied by the academic tutor, based in a contemporary western institution, in interaction with students, answers to the role initiated in western academic culture by Plato's Socrates. Such an ongoing enactment of deeply embedded cultural and pedagogical assumptions is of interest in itself, marking the power of cultural–genealogical inheritance.

The Dialogic in Intercultural Perspective

The status of the Socratic dialogue as a cultural artefact is particularly pointed up in the context of comparative East–West discourse where its cultural difference, both as a practice and as an object of value prevails. The Scollons (Scollon & Scollon, 1994: 141) capture this cultural comparative difference well in the following formulation:

> The Socratic dialogue remains the iconic image of western language, while the calligraphed poem is that of Chinese.

The above formulation not only highlights the cultural significance of the Socratic dialogue and calligraphy respectively, but the relative cultural weight placed on speech and the written sign respectively. This puts the dialogic very much in perspective as part of a genealogical legacy.

Writing was one of the six traditional arts taught in Chinese antiquity, along with rites, music, archery, charioteering and mathematics (Dawson, 1981: 20). As with the other arts, it was seen as predominantly practical. By contrast, in the context of ancient Greek culture, it is known that Plato treated writing with suspicion, a theme that has continued in the western tradition. On the other hand, the process of saying, of dialogue, has concomitantly been revered in the western tradition. This reverence was attached not only to the practical value of dialogue, in negotiation with others, but also to its conceptual relevance in promoting thinking and understanding.

In contrast to the value associated with writing and the aesthetic importance attached to calligraphy, in the Eastern intellectual tradition, language and talk are often negatively evaluated. For example, there are many proverbs in Chinese and Japanese extolling the virtues of silence and the negative effects of too much talk. Examples from Japanese, which are unusual from a western perspective include the following:

> *The mouth is the origin of trouble*
> *The eyes speak as much as the mouth*
> *What is not said is a flower*

These examples were among others printed in 1997, in number 11 of the journal *The Japanese Learner* as a discussion point for use in language teaching classrooms. One other reported there is the Japanese *ishin denshin*, understood as a form of direct transmission, which according to Scollon and Scollon (1995: 139) is a dominant value in Zen Buddhism. It is thought to have originated in China in the early Tang Period (AD 618–907) and has had a major impact on Chinese, Korean and Japanese cultures. In this tradition, it is believed that the most important things cannot be communicated in language, that language is only useful for somewhat secondary or trivial messages. A discernible note of caution in relation to talk, where it is subordinated to action, can be found in the

Confucian Analects also. As Law *et al.* put it in their discussion of how Confucius saw the learning process:

> He [Confucius] also stressed practice and action in the learning process, (Law *et al.*, 2009: 92), and in this regard, they quote the Analects, 2.13:

> He acts before he speaks, and afterwards speaks according to his actions (Law *et al.*, 2009: 92).

In his appreciation of the value of silence, the western philosopher, Georg Steiner (1961), emphasises how the Buddhist and Taoist traditions can convey the 'shape and vitality' (Steiner, 1961: 30) of silence better than the western tradition. He talks of the importance of contemplation in the Buddhist and Taoist traditions whereby 'the highest, purest reach of the contemplative act is that which has learned to leave language behind it.'

The roles of language, then, in what may be seen broadly as two contrasting cultural traditions of west and east are therefore diametrically opposed. In the western context, language is of inordinate importance, especially in its role of verbalisation in speech, whilst in the eastern Buddhist and Taoist traditions, it is ideally subordinate to quiet contemplation. These traditions may be seen to have residual effects on both the value of talk and verbalisation of ideas and how communication practices are enacted.

Socratic Subjects

In the following chapter, the speech acts of British tutors, in tutorial interaction with Japanese students, are seen to echo strategies of the Socratic dialogue. As these tutors attempt to 'induce' critical, evaluative, comments from the students, it is clear that their elicitations are not at all transparent for the students. On the one hand, their initial utterances reflect the extent to which this mode of interacting with students is taken for granted. It is embedded in 'western' educational culture. On the other hand, as the tutors are forced to restate, and sometimes, explicitly explain, what they want from the students, an opportunity is afforded to analyse and explain the intentions behind the tutors' utterances, as well as point up the rhetorical preferences of the educational culture underlying tutorial practice. However, the focus need not only be on inducting international students, and others unfamiliar with its mores, into the ways of prototypical 'western' academic culture. The reality of intercultural communication in action also affords an opportunity for reflexive critique. In other words, the intercultural dynamics can be a jumping off point for an analysis of how the expectations of tutor-student interaction have come to be as they are.

In further chapters, there are accounts of instances from a range of English-speaking academic encounters across the world, where the norms of the western academic culture invest the students with power to voice their own opinions or make their own judgements, but this in effect disadvantages East Asian students operating in that culture, for a variety of different reasons.

It must be remembered, however, that while it is the intercultural dynamics that brings the deep-seated workings of genealogical inheritance to the fore, this does not mean that familiarity with the underlying expectations of pedagogic interaction in higher education is automatic for UK students either. In an earlier UK-based study, Kress and Fowler (1979) stressed the need for students, who were being interviewed for a place at university, to show independence of opinion in order to affirm their status as members of the discourse community. They were concerned that students from class backgrounds where the interactional norms of academic encounters were less well known were being disadvantaged. Such a locus of disadvantage may be seen as an effect of the workings of power/knowledge whereby the institutional norms wield their power invisibly through commonly occurring speech acts in academic contexts such as a tutorial or advisory session. These power/knowledge effects are insidious in that they help maintain boundaries over who has access to the required knowledge or ways of speaking, and thereby can be, albeit for the most part inadvertently, exclusionary. As discussed also in Chapters 6 and 14, in relation to knowledge about the norms of academic literacy, students entering the university system under the contemporary social programme of 'widening participation' and international students from very different cultural and linguistic backgrounds with different norms of social interaction, may find themselves in very similar, albeit disadvantaged, situations, with regard to knowing how to interact in academic context tutorials, interviews or advice sessions. In other words, they are not yet familiar with the subject positions the academic context in a particular language tradition requires them to take up.

Chapter 10

Socratic Subjects: The Western Tutor as Midwife

Introduction

In this chapter, I look at a range of empirical data from intercultural tutorials, where the intercultural nature of the tutor–student encounters in itself brings to the fore the workings of deeply embedded cultural value systems. These systems operate on both sides of the encounter, in this case, on the part of the British tutors and on that of the Japanese students concerned. This chapter will focus on the pedagogical values and educational philosophy, which lie, implicitly, behind the British tutors' utterances. Here, I see traces of the Socratic mentor in the subject position of the tutor. Such a position is generally available in the wider educational culture, and does not need an explicit acknowledgement of the influence of the Socratic dialogue. However, the fact that it does appear may be seen as an effect of the Socratic dialogue's power/knowledge. Taking up a Socratic position can be enacted as a conscious pedagogic strategy, and learned societies exist which advocate this. However that is not what I am concerned with here. Individual academics might simply explain their behaviour as a tutor as following on in the tradition in which they themselves were taught. It is therefore a mark of the genealogical power structure invested in the value of the Socratic dialogue in both the western pedagogic, and intellectual, tradition that Socratic behaviour on the part of academics does not have to be explained, or consciously acknowledged. It appears as normal, until it is encountered by students from a different pedagogical cultural tradition. Aspects of this different educational cultural background, with different assumptions and expectations of tutor and student communicative interaction, will be looked at in the following chapters, both from the point of view of assumptions about the role and behaviour of a 'Confucian' tutor, and from the perspective of the students.

Re-enacting Socratic Midwifery

In my data of one-to-one intercultural tutorials, it was the difficulties the British lecturers had in eliciting the kinds of responses they wanted from their Japanese students that brought the elicitation strategies themselves into focus. Those elicitations are in fact, at face value, often fairly simple, but it is the underlying significance of how they function in the context that is interesting. While the speech acts vary, their illocutionary force, to use Austin's (1955) terminology, converges in the rhetorical function of 'inducing' comment from the student. The rhetorical purpose of the tutors' elicitations was predominantly indirect, putting the onus on the students to come up with either analysis and critique, or a sense of future direction. It was this deliberate indirectness, coupled with persistence over several attempts to get the kinds of responses they wanted that led me to parallels with a Socratic approach, in particular, the practice of intellectual midwifery. In their attempts to induce such critical commentary, the British tutors were in effect, re-enacting Socrates' self-ascribed role of midwife.

The Rhetorical 'Inducing' Strategies of Contemporary Academic Midwifery

The goals of the inducing process in the data discussed here, from contemporary higher education, are different from those of Socrates. There is no underlying epistemological assumption of finding 'unvarying and permanent principles' (Guthrie, 1961: 108), or knowledge about the eternal verities of goodness, truth, and beauty, as in Plato's philosophy. By the same token, nor is there any presumption of the ultimate wisdom of the tutor in the role of questioner, in the sense that Socrates was deemed by the oracle at Delphi to be the wisest man. The aims of the tutorial process are not concerned with acquiring knowledge of the essential nature of things, nor of dispelling preexisting claims to knowledge or understanding. Rather they reflect criteria of relevance and value to the academic practice of the disciplines concerned. In this case, those disciplines were the creative and performing practice disciplines of fine art, music, dance, drama and media. The criteria of relevance in these cases can be summarised as:

> The need for the student to demonstrate critical evaluation;
> The need for the student to achieve analytical clarity, in disciplinary terms, about what they are doing, what they have done, and what they want to attempt to do next;

The need for the student to determine the future direction of the work;
The need for the student to show commitment to the process of developing the work.

How the tutors attempt to induce their students to verbalise according to these four major criteria will be illustrated and discussed in the following sections.

The Intercultural Tutorial Data

The data I am drawing on here come from one-to-one tutorials between British tutors and Japanese students, along with some tutorials with British students in fine art. The Japanese students were all on bridging programmes to degrees at either undergraduate or postgraduate level in the creative and performing arts disciplines, and were all new to participation in British academic culture. At the same time, they were also students of EAP. The data was gathered by the author, and consists of 21 videotaped fine art tutorial sessions between three British tutors and 20 Japanese students and one British student; six audiotaped tutorials in music and dance between British tutors and Japanese students; and numerous notes made by the author during the observations of the tutorials in all disciplines. In some cases, the tutorials served jointly as end-of-course assessments in both the arts discipline and English language.

The length of the tutorial session varied from 15 to 45 minutes. The English proficiency of the Japanese students ranged from lower to upper intermediate level. The duration of their stay in England ranged from six months to two years. The physical presence of objects, such as paintings, sketch books, sculptures or installations in the case of fine art students, and models for stage design or videotaped drama or documentary productions in the case of media and drama students formed the basis of discussion in those tutorials, while recent performances on a musical instrument or in dance were the focus of tutorials in those disciplines. This meant that the production by the student within the disciplinary discourse was not only verbal, and that the tutors had available to them other modes of assessing (assuming that assessment is at least always an implicit part of such pedagogical interactions) the students. However, the availability of non-verbal disciplinary discourse serves in turn to foreground the intrinsically verbal mode of the tutorial as genre. It highlights the necessity of speech and indeed specific kinds of saying, (Hiraga & Turner, 1995; Turner & Hiraga, 1996) demanded by the tutorial as a specific kind of cultural performance.

The Tutorial as Genre

Given that it is an established event in the context of institutional academic culture, the academic tutorial may be viewed as a genre. As Swales notes, 'active discourse community members ... give genre names to classes of communicative events that they recognise as providing recurring rhetorical action' (Swales, 1990: 55). Recurring rhetorical action will be looked at here in the exchange types which serve to constitute more specifically the creative practice tutorial. While the specific content focused on differs, depending on whether the discipline is fine art, music, drama or dance, it was striking how similar the rhetorical action on the part of the tutors was in all of those creative and performing arts disciplines. In particular, they all deployed similar kinds of elicitation strategies. These revolved predominantly around what was the current state of the work or performance, how it had reached that state, what the issues were, and how it was going to be developed or taken forward. Such a developmental dynamic relating to process and progress in the student's work (Turner, 1996, 2001) is paralleled also in the momentum of the tutorial itself.

As might be expected, given the intrinsic power relationship of the institutional context, the overall dynamics of the creative and performing arts tutorials was controlled by the tutor. The tutor would make the opening and closing moves and initiate the topics for discussion, which were, however, motivated by the students' work or performance. The tutor-initiated exchange types could be seen in a simple tripartite beginning, middle and end phase structure. This structure could be followed through in the course of one tutorial event, beginning with what had been done since the last tutorial (or during a vacation); following through with probing the student on what they thought they had achieved and leading on to discussing what would be worked on next.

State-of-the-art Openings

The beginning phase of the tutorial, whereby the tutor would establish what kind of work the student was doing or what she/he was focusing on would include the following kinds of elicitations, which I call 'state-of-the-art' openings:

- What aspects of technique are you working on at the moment? (music)
- How did you make this piece? What is it made of?
- What is the material? (fine art)
- Tell me how you went about adapting the film? (media studies)

These broad-based openings offered room or discursive space for the student to elaborate on their own work or performance. They were not intended as factual information gathering questions, tout court. However, that was often how they were treated by the students. They would give simple responses such as:

- This work is collage.
- The film is based on three things.
- I like to play Beethoven.

These responses would not be elaborated on further. This left the tutor to probe further, to get behind the scenes as it were, to what was motivating the students to do what they were doing and how they were going about doing it. So, tutors would then ask such things as

- What are/were you trying to achieve?
- Do you think it's successful?
- How do you feel about that?

The state-of-the-art questions were intended as lead-ins to the issue of development. Behind their mainly factual façade, relating to actual practice in the respective disciplines, there was an implicit demand not only to describe but also to explain the significance of the work that was being, or had been done. However, very often this implicit question had to be made explicitly before the tutor got the kind of response required. The fact that the tutorials were intercultural was in itself a driver of opening up the implicit to the explicit, and thereby also revealing the import of the elicitation strategies.

The Developmental Dynamics

What is of overriding importance in the creative practice tutorials is the meaning or purpose of an activity and the reasons for doing it. Given this, the student must then be able to evaluate the work, whether that might be a performance or a painting, and to show an awareness of what kind of criteria might be relevant in doing so. These criteria relate to the disciplinary discourse and revolve around the analytical parameters of what make a particular performance or piece of work successful or not, what could be done better or done differently and why. The students therefore are expected to know how to evaluate what they have done, have some idea of strengths and weaknesses and have some idea of what to focus on next.

Dialectical Dynamics

One recurring exchange type related to the expression of doubts or worries about the direction of the work. The principle behind this exchange type appears to be to foster a cognitive dialectic whereby it is not only a clear idea of where the work is going next that can lead to development but also a sense of uncertainty or doubt about where to go or what to do next. In this latter case, the first step is to express those doubts as understanding them also provides a kind of clarity, which leads to a negatively based decision on what not to pursue.

The British fine art student in the following extract gives voice to this process with regard to his own work, where what he has discarded as a mode of working provides a kind of certainty as to what not to develop further, in the interests of development happening in a different way.

Excerpt 1

01 **British Tutor One:** Can we be clear on the things that you feel that you
02 have, em, discarded, or, even perhaps, put to one side? You've
03 mentioned one of them, you mentioned moving from the,-
04 **British Student One:** [Yeah]
05 **British Tutor One:** from, from the use of the circular device.
06 **British Student One:** Yes.
07 **British Tutor One:** Mm .. You seem not inclined to use that any more.
08 **British Student One:** Not just now, no. That kinda stems from when I was
09 trying to work with the image of pebbles dropping in the water and the kind
10 of rhythm that ensued from the circles forming out, and they're actually
11 forming something complete
12 **British Tutor One:** [Yeah, … yeah,]
13 **British Student One:** I like that idea but, .. I, that's why I gotta, it's kind of,
14 I'm trying to get clear in my mind exactly .. where I'm going and I feel that's
15 perhaps kind of going too fast ahead for me, in a way. I feel very unsure
16 as to which way I'm going just now.

Despite the fact that his state of mind about his work is one of uncertainty, this British student is nonetheless very clear about the underlying process of development that is involved. He responds immediately to the tutor's search for agreement on the state of play 'can we be clear now on..' and 'you seem not inclined to ...', elaborating on, and giving reasons as to why this is not the case.

The point of interest here is that the tutor's elicitation strategies were indirect. They were leading the student to make his own judgements, in Socratic terminology, to know the state or extent of his own ignorance, or in this case uncertainty. The tutor did not ask directly for example, whether the student thought 'using the circular device' was good or bad, nor did he proffer his own judgement on whether or not this was the case.

What the tutor's probing developed was, as in the purpose of the Socratic dialogue, the process of reaching agreement on what is known and what is not known. In this case, it was a question of the student knowing the state of play, of being clear on what was going on in his work, or even of what was not going on in his work, before further development could take place.

Inducing Dialectical Thinking

In the tutorial context discussed here, the dialectical process going on in the student's head, is mirrored, or in effect produced, by the process of dialogue with the tutor. It is the role of the tutor to facilitate the dialectical process of cognition in the student. On the one hand, the tutor role is invested in bringing the student to understand and to voice for him or herself what the issues are, what the current state of play is. On the other hand, the tutor steers the process forward. This works dialectically. The student has first to reject what is not working, to understand why this is the case, and ultimately to move on to consider what might work. It seems that the pedagogic role of the tutor is to induce the internal cognitive–creative dialectic between doubts and certainty, confusion and clarity that the student has to go through. The dialogic pedagogy in effect mirrors the dialectic process of cognition. In the pedagogic dialectic, the tutor's role is to induce clarification of what the problems are, 'Can we be clear on the things ...' as in extract one above. In this tutorial, the tutor moves on to give recommendations, in this case on the kinds of paper the student might consider working with, which point to future action that might help the student move forward. In other cases, the tutor recommends looking at the work of particular artists, usually in a linguistically indirect way, such as:

You might think about looking at the work of ...

Such indirectness of course has its own problems in intercultural tutorials, where the student might not actually recognise the advice as more like an injunction: go and look at the work of. ... Ultimately, there will be an expectation in future tutorials that the student has looked at the work of the specific artist mentioned and formed a view as to how this artist's work is relevant to the student's work, or not. Whether the consultation of the artist's work leads to inspiration and forward planning of the student's own work, or to a rejection of its relevance to the student does not matter. In either case, the process would be insightful. Such an opportunity however, is often missed when the student does not understand the implicit recommendation as of pedagogic value.

In other cases, in order to move the creative process forward, the tutor sometimes encapsulates for the student what the tutor sees as the issues and feeds that encapsulation back to the student. This is the case in the following excerpt. The number serves to differentiate the different participant tutors and students.

Excerpt 2

British Tutor One: Let me just recap. Perhaps the principle change in your thinking has been a shift from what you call hard shapes to soft shapes.

Japanese Student One: Yes. First I was drawing with a ruler but now I am drawing without anything. (videotaped fine art tutorial)

Such recapitulatory exchanges set the tone for an underlying understanding that what was being discussed was a process of ongoing development. This underlying developmental dynamics was evidenced also in the fact that what might be called 'the recapitulation exchange' could occur not only towards the end of the tutorial, where it could be seen as the turning point for how the work was to be taken forward, but also at the beginning, where the recap as it were, served to locate the state of development in a student's work from one tutorial to the next. For example, tutors would say such things as:

Remind me what we discussed last time,

or:

so, let's just recap; last time we talked about ..., and you were going to...

The Culturally Hidden Nature of Dialectical Development

The tutorial process itself, however, regarding both the role of the student and the underlying dialectical dynamics of development, may not seem very relevant or transparent to a student from a very different pedagogical culture, where assumptions about the thought processes involved may also be different. The difficulties involved here are illustrated in the intercultural tutorial discussed below.

In as much as the British student above is articulate about his uncertainty, despite the fact that this is not the most desirable state to be in for an artist and the development of his work, he seems to understand both the underlying dynamics of the tutorial process, and of the cognitive process, whereby he needs to develop the work. He says:

> I'm trying to get clear in my mind exactly .. where I'm going (lines 13–14)

He voices the temporary nature of his state:

> that's going too fast ahead for me ... I feel very unsure as to which way I'm going just now (lines 15–16).

In the following excerpt with a Japanese student, where the situation as regards the stage of the student's work is similar, the flow of the tutorial is very different.

Excerpt 3

British Tutor One: Well, what you're beginning to express now, I think, are ideas which are somewhat confused.

Japanese Student Two: Yeah.

British Tutor One: Slightly confused, about differences of, your interest.

Japanese Student Two: Yeah.

British Tutor One: Are there other things that you need to tell me about?

Japanese Student Two: Ah, yeah.

British Tutor One: Cause I need, I don't just need, I don't just want to know about things that you're certain of.. I need to know things about .. er, which you are uncertain. .. I'm not sure that I've explained that very well. Do you understand? ..

Japanese Student Two: Mm.

British Tutor One: I mean my function as a, as a teacher is to help clarify, to make clear, doubts and uncertainties. (videotaped fine art tutorial)

Inducing the Tutor: Resistance as Reverse Midwifery

In the above excerpt, apart from apparently agreeing with what the tutor says, the student does not help the dialogue to progress. She offers no elaboration of her confusion or what the constraints may be on the development of her work. This very interestingly seems to lead the tutor into inarticulacy. He feels he has not expressed himself very clearly. He then comments on his own role, and in so doing provides a rationale for his line of questioning, and indeed for the overall purpose of the tutorial.

This reflection also fortuitously offers a triangulation opportunity for the discourse analyst, confirming the interpretation of both what's going on in the tutorials more broadly, and the significant role played by the negative dialectics of doubt and uncertainty in particular. The tutor is in effect explicating the illocutionary force (Austin, 1955) of his questions.

There is a further ironic twist to this excerpt in that the student has in effect enacted a reverse midwifery process. In showing resistance or reluctance to voice what's going on in terms of how her work is progressing or not, the student is effectively 'inducing' the teacher into a clearer explication of his motives for asking the questions he is asking.

Inducing Critical Evaluation

The following series of excerpts, from one specific fine art tutorial with a different British tutor, is a particularly good example of the range and sequence of elicitations that the tutor makes in an attempt to 'induce' the student into making an evaluative judgement. The tutor enacts five different evaluation-inducing strategies in a crescendo of provocation culminating in a rather dramatic scenario, whereby the tutor asks the student to imagine which of her works she would put on a bonfire and which she would save. It is the persistence, and indeed imagination, that the tutor puts into the inducing strategies that reveal the importance of inducing, that is, that the judgements should come from the student rather than from the tutor.

The combined excerpts come after about half an hour of tutorial time, and it is clear to the observer that the tutor likes this student's work, probably another reason for his persistence. The work consists of 12 painted canvases depicting clouds and sky, which were based on views from the aeroplane that the student had found fascinating on her journey over from Japan.

Excerpt 4a

01	**British Tutor Two:** Which is the best one?
02	**Japanese Student Three:** Mm, I can't say that because,-
03	**British Tutor Two:** [Which] is the worst one?
04	**Japanese Student Three:** Em .. no, I like to say these are all together, it's
05	**British Tutor Two:** [Yeah.]
06	**Japanese Student Three:** one, -work.
07	**British Tutor Two:** [Yeah.]
08	**Japanese Student Three:** So, I don't mind if someone,-
09	**British Tutor Two:** [All right]
10	**Japanese Student Three:** look at priority on this one.

In this excerpt, the tutor has deployed two rhetorical strategies to elicit evaluation from the student. They are:

Rhetorical Inducing Strategy 1: a superlative evaluation, 'which is the best one?' (line 1)

Rhetorical Inducing Strategy 2: a superlative evaluation in dialectical opposition to the previous one 'which is the worst one' (line 3).

The student puts up some resistance to the fact that she's being asked to evaluate one canvas in particular, as she sees her work in holistic terms as one work. She implies that she does not mind if he makes a judgement as to one being better than another. However, as the immediately following excerpt shows, the tutor abruptly dismisses this reply and pursues the same line of questioning, this time deploying Rhetorical Inducing Strategy 3.

Rhetorical Inducing Strategy 3: a more narrowly focused closed question, based on the same dialectic of evaluative choice.

This time, however, the question relates back to a previous stage in the developmental process: 'are there any that are not here because they were no good?' (line 13)

Excerpt 4b

11	**British Tutor Two:** [OK, no no no, I, no, no, no, I'm not] asking
12	about me. I know which one I think's best

13   **Japanese Student Three:** [Mmmh]
14   **British Tutor Two:** But, but, are there any that you, that are not here
15   because they were no good?
16   **Japanese Student Three:** Pardon?
17   **British Tutor Two:** Are there any of these,-
18   **Japanese Student Three:** [Mm-m.]
19   **British Tutor Two:** which have not been put on the wall because
20   you did not think they were very good?

Here, the tutor makes explicit that he has his own judgement on which
one is best, but that is not the point. He tries very carefully to ask her to
spell out her process of choice making before the event of showing the
work she is showing. Nonetheless, he still fails to induce her to make the
kind of judgement he wants her to make. So, he tries again, this time
asking her more specifically about the number of canvases she has painted
altogether:

Excerpt 4c

22   **British Tutor Two:** No, no. Wait a minute. I don't think you've
      understood.
23   How many of these have you made?
24   **Japanese Student Three:** Er, just, em, before this, er, before .. this
      stage
25   of painting on the canvas, I made, er, lots of drawings.
26   **British Tutor Two:** Yes, but how many of these on canvas have you
27   made?
28   **Japanese Student Three:** .. Em .. Just .. these ..
29   **British Tutor Two:** So they're all here?
30   **Japanese Student Three:** [or,-] Yeah, all.
31   **British Tutor Two:** [So it's] a 100% success ?

The student is making a valiant attempt here to explicate the process she
has gone through, stating that she made lots of provisional drawings first,
a process that would be expected in the discipline. However, this still is
not what the tutor wants, so he deploys Rhetorical Inducing Strategy 4.

Rhetorical Inducing Strategy 4: Provocation

    The fourth rhetorical inducing strategy is a provocation: So it is a 100%
success? The student understands the provocation, but her uptakes to it
are defensive. She appears to think he is criticising her way of working
(line 24). She defends herself against the tutor's provocation by implying

that her paintings were not an immediate success (she had worked very hard on these pieces):

Excerpt 4d

32 **Japanese Student Three:** But, .. I actually eh, em, .. I've actually, em,
33 peeled a lots of paint off
34 **British Tutor Two:** [Yeah]
35 I, I, I, I, I'm not, I'm not trying to catch you [laughs]
36 Japanese Student Three: [laughs]

The student's defence is however, not what the tutor wanted. As he says, he was not trying to catch her out. Presumably this means in the context that he was not implying that she had done anything wrong, for which she would have needed to defend herself. He could tell how hard she had worked and this was evident earlier on in the tutorial when he had asked about her procedure for making the box-shaped canvases.

In defending herself in this way, the student is also positioning the tutor as evaluator. He has then to defend himself against that role, as he does when he says: I am not trying to catch you. What is interesting at this point of reciprocal defensiveness, which is also a point of speaking at cross purposes, is that it forces the tutor to finally provide a statement about the motivation for his questions.

Reverse Midwifery: Spelling Out the Rationale

In providing a metapragmatic statement, as he does in the following excerpt, the tutor is not only giving the reason for his persistent questioning, he is also spelling out the underlying developmental dynamics of creative practice, which was discussed above in terms of the tutorial as genre.

Excerpt 4e

37 **British Tutor Two:** I'm really trying to find out wh, what, how you can
38 distinguish between,
39 **Japanese Student Six:** [Mm -m.]
40 **British Tutor Two:** something which enables you to say, I, I, like this more
41 than that; this is the way forward, this is the way to go.

The tutor's fallback into explaining the motivation behind his utterances is yet another example of 'reverse midwifery', whereby the student ultimately 'induces' the tutor to give an explanation rather than the other way round as was intended. As tutors doubled their efforts to induce the expected uptakes to their questions or comments, in so far as they were not succeeding, the students were inducing them to state with greater clarity what they wanted. It could be said that in such instances the process of intercultural communication is in effect changing the dynamics of tutor–student interaction. The onus is on the tutor to perform, to explicate, to try out different moves, in order to move the tutorial process forward.

Rhetorical Inducing Strategy 5: Hypothetical Drama

The Socratic persistence of British Tutor Two is undiminished, however. He has not yet given up on the student making an analytic evaluation of her own work and after telling her that all of the paintings are good, but that 'some are better than others', that 'they're not all of the same value', he launches into a dramatic hypothetical scenario concerning which four she would choose if he were to throw eight of them on a bonfire.

The next excerpt goes on from line 51.

Excerpt 4f

51   **British Tutor Two:** .. Mm, if we were to say, I, I'm going to ask you to
52   choose four ..
53   **Japanese Student Three:** Mm-m.
54   **British Tutor Two:** Let's say. And I've got a big bonfire over here, I've got
55   a big fire, over here,-
56   **Japanese Student Three:** Mm, right.
57   **British Tutor Two:** Right. We've got 1, 2, 3, 4, 5, 6, 7, 8, 9, 10, 11, 12. We've got
58   twelve.
59   **Japanese Student Three:** Mm-m.
60   **British Tutor Two:** And I'm going to put eight of them on the bo, on the fire.
61   **Japanese Student Three:** Mm-m.
62   **British Tutor Two:** And save four.
63   **Japanese Student Three:** Mm-m.
64   **British Tutor Two:** Right, and you're going to be very sad.
65   **Japanese Student Three:** .. Mm.
66   **British Tutor Two:** Because your work is going on the fire.
67   Which four would we keep?
68   **Japanese Student Three:** Mm-m.

69   **British Tutor Two:** Which four? Show me.
70   **Japanese Student Three:** I cannot choose.
71   **British Tutor Two:** Yes you can. You must.
72   **Japanese Student Three:** Mmm. Why do you know, why do you
      want to
73   know that? Because, ..
74   **British Tutor Two:** [Because it will] tell me something.

The tutor persists in his strategy of provoking the student into choosing four paintings. The student continues to resist, it must be said, expertly matching his level of persistence, protesting that her work is 'part of the universe' that she is trying to show construction of the universe. Seventeen lines later, including hesitations, the tutor is still trying, but this time he also, once more, makes a clear pedagogic point. When the student still resists, he eventually reveals in more fundamental terms the rationale for his questioning. This encapsulates the rationale for student learning in fine art: the development of a critique.

The fact that this 'revelation' works as a kind of dramatic denouement in this tutorial, bears witness to the extent that the expectation of critique is taken for granted. The tutor does not really expect to have to spell it out. What it also reveals is the importance attached to the fact that it is the student who should be able to make the evaluation. As he said at an earlier stage, the tutor knows which ones he thinks are better, but that is not as important as the student being able to see for herself, or to make her own judgement, by understanding the visual criteria at stake.

Excerpt 4g

91   **British Tutor Two:** You have made each one.
92   **Japanese Student Three:** Mm.
93   **British Tutor Two:** Each one is like your baby. You've made each
       one,-
94   **Japanese Student Three:** Mm.
95   **British Tutor Two:** You know? But, but, but if you say, because I made
       it,-
96   it therefore is OK,-
97   **Japanese Student Three:** Mm-m.
98   **British Tutor Two:** You will never develop any .. critique.
99   **Japanese Student Three:** Critique?
100   **British Tutor Two:** Critique.
101   **Japanese Student Three:** Critique

The tutor now goes on to explain that the basis of the student's criticism at the moment is her own experience whereas she needs to be able to make an analytical understanding of her work, based on such criteria as for example, perspective, or painterly texture, the basis of her critique.

It cannot be said that this student was uncritical. In fact, in her resistance to making the choices that the tutor wanted her to make, she was in effect being critical. She was standing her own ground. However, what she was not responding to were the underlying analytical criteria of the discipline. As a student in the discipline, she was obliged to make those kinds of judgements.

It is possible that if the tutor had explicitly flagged the importance of the student making judgements and developing a critique of her work right at the beginning, he might have got the kinds of responses he required. However, that was not what his tutor subjectivity, as a Socratic midwife, was programmed to do.

Socrates and Meno

In the following extract from one of Plato's better known dialogues, the *Meno*, famous for the distinction it makes between knowledge and opinion, similar inducing strategies as revealed in the extract above may be seen. The extract is quoted from Guthrie (1961: 135):

Socrates: If someone knows the way to Larissa, or anywhere else you like, and then when he goes there and takes others with him he will be a good and capable guide, you would agree?

Meno: Of course

Socrates: But if a man judges correctly which is the road though he has never been there and doesn't know it, will he not also guide others aright?

Meno: Yes he will.

Socrates: And as long as he has a correct opinion on the points about which the other has knowledge, he will be just as good a guide, believing the truth but not knowing it.

Meno: Just as good.

Socrates: Therefore true opinion is as good a guide as knowledge for the purpose of acting rightly. That is, what we left out just now in our discussion of the nature of virtue, when we said that knowledge is the only guide to right action. There was also, it seems, true opinion.

Meno: It seems so.

Socrates: So right opinion is something no less useful than knowledge.
Meno: Except that the man with knowledge will always be successful, and the man with right opinion only sometimes.
Socrates: What? Will he not always be successful so long as he has the right opinion?
Meno: That must be so, I suppose. In that case, I wonder why knowledge should be so much more prized than right opinion, and indeed how there is any difference between them.
Socrates: Shall I tell you the reason for your surprise, or do you know it?
Meno: No tell me.
Socrates: It is because you have not observed the statues of Daedalus.

Socrates then goes on to explain the importance of 'tying down' claims to knowledge by analogy with the need to tie down the statues of Daedalus. These statues, by the famous sculptor Daedalus, look as if they are about to fly off, and therefore in order to secure their value, they would need to be tied down.

In this extract, Socrates uses examples of the hypothesis, and the provocation strategy, 'so right opinion is something no less useful than knowledge', in order to elicit agreement from Meno at each stage of the argumentation he is pursuing. While Meno initially agrees with the points Socrates makes, he gradually comes to ask the questions for himself which reveal the flaws in the argument. While the issues in my data are very different, the rhetorical, dialogic, process is very similar. There is no concern for an understanding of educational absolutes such as virtue for example, nor is it a question of revealing the extent of the student's ignorance, or that he sees the flaws in his argumentation. Nonetheless, the tutor's probing does mirror the purpose of the Socratic dialogue in that he is trying get the student to make the correct, or within the confines of the discipline, an appropriate, judgement.

Occidentalist Inducing Strategies Reiterated in Educationally Different Context

The suggestion that the tutors in the above extracts from my data were working according to a particular cognitive-rhetorical dynamic that has its roots in a specifically 'western' educational culture is reinforced when it is echoed in a very different national context, but with a colonial heritage of English-speaking education, namely South Africa. This was the case in Chick's study (Chick, 1985), where in one of his excerpts, there is a striking resemblance in the function and use of what I called the 'superlative evaluation' strategy, as deployed in Excerpt 4a of my data. This strategy, in Chick's example, asking a student to identify what he thought was the best answer he had written in an examination, occurred in a study which Chick calls 'the interactional accomplishment of discrimination'. The excerpt showed the interaction between a native English-speaking tutor and a Zulu student with EAL, studying in an English medium institution. The context for the tutorial is a post-examination discussion which students were asked to arrange after being told that they had not done so well, not because of ability or lack of preparation, but because they were 'unsure of the examiners' expectations' (Chick, 1985). The students were told that the discussions would focus on the extent to which expectations were shared. The discipline concerned here is applied linguistics and the students were postgraduates.

From Chick (1985: 320–321)

44   **T:** alright now perhaps you can tell me which of those er you thought … you
45   did best in … which you were happiest about
46   **S.** I I'm not sure but
47   **T.** yes
48   **S.** I think it number 5
49   **T:** number 5
50   **S:** (not clear)
51   **T:** alright … that that's right that that was the question that we thought
52   was your best question
53   **S:** m
54   **T:** alright … erm and then which of the two there
55   **S:** I … I think one and two are
56   which was equally difficult
57   **T:** equally difficult
58   **S:** yah
59   **T:** and
60   **S:** not actually difficult but I think er not prepared thoroughly or my
61   **S:** approach in answering was not quite … according to expected
62   **S:** standard.
63   **T:** er in the case of which one both of them
64   **S:** I think both.

In line 63, the tutor shows the same strategic dynamics as in my data, moving from the more open-ended, 'which is the best' to a more narrowly focused question 'which one?' 'or was it both?' The tutor in the South African example goes on to explain that the answer to one question was worse than the other and the conversation goes in to discussing why which question was chosen and how many questions had been prepared for. The tutor then goes on to probe how the student set about preparing for the examination, setting up a similar rhetorical dynamic to the probing for information on the student's drawing in Excerpt 4 above, and having similarly poor results. He asks:

Can I ask how you set about preparing that question? (line 85)

It seems that whether the 'western' and English-speaking tutor's questions are about finding out how a student has gone about preparing their art work or how they have tackled examination questions, there is a similar underlying dynamic. On the one hand, there is an expectation on the part of the tutor that the student will be pre-disposed to reflecting on and evaluating what they have done or how they have done what they have done, and on the other hand, that this self-reflexive process is a good method of furthering learning. When the student, usually from a genealogically different educational culture (but not necessarily so, as socialisation into educational norms is not the same for everyone), does not meet the tutor's taken-for-granted expectations, the reaction is seldom to question those deep-lying cultural assumptions.

While the social context of Chick's study is very different from the international education context of my data, the subject position of the institutionally more powerful participant, namely the tutor, stands out for its sameness. Despite speaking from within different disciplinary discourses, and in different geographic locations, each tutor takes up the occidentalist, educationist, subject position of Socratic midwife.

Genealogical Effects

From such a genealogical perspective, it is not surprising that Chick's article is entitled: 'the interactional accomplishment of discrimination'. In other words, even when the aim is well-meaning, namely to include 'others' in the educational process, when that process is being enacted from within deeply embedded cultural norms, the outcome is discriminatory because the 'other' is not working from within those same norms.

What is required here is something similar to what Leung (2005) in the context of communicative language teaching methodology talks of as:

a preparedness to interrogate the ethno-cultural and sociolinguistic basis of one's own judgments on one's own and others' preferred language forms and ways of using languages. (Leung, 2005: 130)

Whereas Leung uses the term 'ethno-cultural', my preference is for the term 'genealogical', as it foregrounds not only powerfully value-laden cultural construction, but also its continuing effects and largely unquestioned assumptions. Also, the focus here is on subject positions within an educationist discourse rather than on the individual ethno-cultural identity, or ethnoscapes (Appadurai, 1990) of the participants.

What is common to all the examples from the data presented here is that the tutors' utterances index in linguistic action the combined genealogical–cultural assumptions of the tutor's role as intellectual midwife and the student's role of giving birth to independent judgements and by doing so, showing independent motivation to learn. This does not mean that the tutors consciously see themselves as Socratic mentors. In the UK higher education context of my data, they did not, although when I suggested to one of them that there was a resonance with the Socratic dialogue, he agreed, and was not at all unhappy with the suggestion. These tutors were not educationists either, in the sense of belonging to the education faculty. They had their own academic disciplines. Their rhetorical strategies, however, revealed an 'inducing' mentality, reminiscent of Socrates in Plato's dialogues, implying a non-conscious genealogical inheritance. To put this in Foucauldian terms, what they reveal is a 'governmentality', the effect of an occidentalist power/knowledge.

Chapter 11

Resisting the Tao of Talk:
Verbalisation in Intercultural Context

Introduction

In the previous chapter, the focus was on the efforts British tutors made to induce critical judgement in their students' contribution to tutorial talk. I suggested this tutoring approach harked back to a kind of Socratic midwifery, a practice invested with the valorisation of the Socratic dialogue in the western intellectual tradition. At the same time, the Japanese students' resistance to their efforts induced what I called 'reverse midwifery', whereby the more powerful participant is led to account for their linguistic action, thereby enacting a kind of role reversal between tutor and student. In one exchange in particular, the tutor eventually voiced the rationale for his probing as the importance for the student (in this case, a fine art student) of developing a critique of her work. In this process, the role of verbalisation was particularly important.

In this chapter, I want to explore further the students' perceptions of the role of verbalisation, how they saw the need to talk about their work, and why they often appeared to put up resistance to it. This can largely be explained by the assumptions and expectations they bring with them from their educational background experiences and in particular, the culturally weighted difference attached to the role of silence, as opposed to that of talk, as well as the differing significance of the role, and perception, of listening.

Speaking Culturally in Pedagogic Contexts

The western cultural predisposition towards positively evaluating students who speak in pedagogical contexts was affirmed by Jaworski and Sachdev (2004) in their research into the role and perception of silence. They conducted a study of the references teachers wrote for pupils who were applying for university places in the United Kingdom. In their analysis of this genre, they highlighted the prominence given to talk as an indicator of merit in those potential students. Explicit evaluations of the students' communication skills privilege talk over silence. It seems that students who can speak well, whether in giving oral presentations, or expressing opinions and contributing to discussions in class, are assumed to be 'good' students who are likely to do well in their studies. Two contrasting examples of the evaluative tone in such references, one praising talk and the other presupposing the negative evaluation of silence will suffice here to exemplify their point:

(1)   He has made a number of excellent oral presentations confidently, and he makes valuable contributions to group discussions.
(2)   She has a quiet, thoughtful reserve about her but this should not be hastily interpreted. (Jaworski & Sachdev, 2004: 229)

It can generally be said, then, that in the pedagogical context of 'western', mainly Anglophone institutions, the expectation of verbalisation on the part of students is crucial to the mode of interaction, such that difficulties can arise when the expectation is not met. The communicative situation was indeed very difficult in my data, when the attempts made by the British tutors in the creative fields, to induce their Japanese students to talk about their work, met with very little success.

Learning through Speaking

Both these examples from Jaworski and Sachdev's study, and my data, indicate the wider educational significance that actually speaking, that is, verbalising or voicing what is understood, is deemed to have; see also the discussion in Kim and Markus (2002). The underlying presupposition seems to be that through voicing the state of play in one's learning, as it were, the learning process itself is taken further. This verbalising process, then, plays an integral role in the process of learning and understanding itself. The example par excellence of the process of learning through verbalisation is the Socratic dialogue. Socrates also explains the epistemological significance of saying or speaking, which he arrived at in his search for clear definitions of the virtues. Similarities were rejected and distinctions made because what could be *said* of one thing, for example, could not be said of another. Socrates' arrival at this dialectical method is described by Tarnas as follows:

> After having investigated every current system of thought from the scientific philosophies of nature to the subtle arguments of the Sophists, Socrates had concluded that all of them lacked sound critical

method. To clarify his own approach, he decided to concern himself not with facts but with *statements about facts* (my emphasis). (Tarnas, 1991: 36)

While the British lecturers in the intercultural tutorials illustrated in the previous chapter were enacting traces of the role of Socrates at the birth of the academy in the western intellectual tradition, by encouraging their students to voice their thoughts and ideas, their Japanese student inter-locutors, on the other hand, were distinctly not playing this dialectical game. Those students show how they are in effect resisting the hegemony of their 'western' educational contexts and bringing aspects of their own educational and pedagogical cultures to bear on their international educa-tional interactions. Insight into those aspects of what might be called Confucian resistance will be explored throughout this chapter in relation to the existing literature, a focus group with East Asian students on the same programme, but in a different year from the students in the tutorials analysed previously, and retrospective interviews, one year later, with some of those Japanese students whose tutorials were recorded.

Talking about Talking

In a focus group which the author held with a group of East Asian (mainly Japanese) students, who were on the same programme as the stu-dents whose tutorials were recorded, but in a different year, the students were quite vociferous in their condemnation of how much time was spent talking. In particular, they seemed to resent being forced to talk about their work. They wanted rather to be shown how to perfect it, how to improve their skills and techniques. One student also said that she felt she was being 'brainwashed' by talk. I interpreted this to mean both the fact that she was constantly being asked to talk about her work and the fact that her tutors were constantly talking to her. I did not realise the full significance of expectations formed in a very different pedagogic cultural context, until I had read more widely in the literature. It seems that what she and many of her fellow students were expecting was more of a 'somatic pedagogy' (Lebra, 1993), see the more detailed discussion in the following chapter, where the teacher's role is to act as an exemplar or model, and demon-strate for the students what they should do.

In the retrospective interviews also, the role of verbalisation came up constantly from different perspectives. Those interviews were conducted with seven of the Japanese students, in Japanese, one year after their video-taped tutorials had taken place[1]. The students watched the video of their own tutorial and were asked questions on what they thought was going on in them, more specifically on why they thought the tutors were asking the kinds of questions they did and why the students behaved as they did. All excerpts have been translated from the Japanese transcriptions.

Unfortunately, not all tutorial extracts in the previous chapter could be matched with retrospective interviews. Nonetheless, the interviews elicited telling examples of both the role of verbalisation as it was perceived by the students, and of the process of learning to work in and with an intercultural context. As the students were still students, having gone on to the first year of a BA or to an MA, the interviews benefited from their greater understanding of what the purpose of the tutorials was. They were able to look at themselves performing as they did a year ago and make comparisons with how they understood the process now. Comments on whether, and in which respects, their behaviour had changed, were particularly valuable. Again these related primarily to how they understood the role of verbalisation. A range of differing attitudes towards it was expressed, ranging from the positive through the ambivalent to the negative. The first two excerpts from different students show a realisation of the positive value of 'explaining' or talking about the work to reach a clearer understanding of it. These students may be seen as having adapted well to the western perspective predominant in their intercultural contexts.

Retrospective interviews; Excerpt 1:

At this time (of the videotaped tutorial), I did not realize my problems. ... I did not know what was my subject or my theme. But I was in the place that I had to explain the concept of my work, which made me think about my problems, or what I needed to do. So, my idea became clearer and clearer, and at the same time, my work was changing.

Retrospective interviews; Excerpt 2:

I think he wanted to know why I did it in that way. So, he was trying to help me to explain myself. You know at that time, it was quite difficult for me to establish a clear logic on my work. Also, it was English which was much more difficult. I usually try to make sense of it after I'm done. I do paintings just with intuitive feeling. I realized it was very important to express my vague feeling with words.

Another student referred to the role of the tutor in talking things through when the student felt blocked and didn't know how to take the work forward. He makes a comparison here with his experience of art education in Japan.

Retrospective interviews; Excerpt 3:

> I had experienced it many times, but getting into a slump is a bad thing in Japan. You may be able to talk to your teacher, but I did not. I thought getting into a slump is a bad thing and I thought that I had to solve the situation by myself. But here, when your tutor asks how you are doing, and you answer that you are not doing well honestly, he would set up a tutorial and talk with you about how to solve the problem.

The negative experience for this student in the Japanese context of what he calls a 'slump', whereby it's more a question of stoicism, of keeping going until he finds a way out of the problem by himself, contrasts with the potential of the experience as a necessary stage in the dialectical process of development. As was discussed in the previous chapter, a dialectic of development powers the genre of tutorial in creative practice disciplines.

In one of the retrospective interviews, where the student's understanding of this dynamic was being probed, the student makes it clear that she was in fact expecting a very different kind of tutorial interaction. This comes from an interview with the student in the tutorial where the tutor is trying to get her to tell him if there is anything she is unsure of, and ends up explaining why he is asking the question, I shall show the excerpt again, in order to contextualise her response.

British Tutor One:	Well, what you're beginning to express now, I think, are ideas which are somewhat confused.
Japanese Student Two:	Yeah.
British Tutor One:	Slightly confused, about differences of, your interest.
Japanese Student Two:	Yeah.
British Tutor One:	Are there other things that you need to tell me about?
Japanese Student Two:	Ah, yeah.
British Tutor One:	Cause I need, I don't just need, I don't just want to know about things that you're certain of.. I need to know things about .. er, which you are uncertain. .. I'm not sure that I've explained that very well. Do you understand? ..
Japanese Student Two:	Mm.
British Tutor One:	I mean my function as a, as a teacher is to help clarify, to make clear, doubts and uncertainties.

The source of difficulty for the student was in fact that she was expecting the tutor to play a very different role. She was expecting him to give
her explicit instructions on what to do. The student has been asked
whether, from her current perspective, she now realised what had been
going on.

Retrospective interviews; Extract 4:

I think he wanted to know about my current interests, or what I experienced during summer. Based on that, he wanted to know what I am
going to do in the new term, which was the last term for me. But I did
not have any idea about my work at that time. I just did what he told
me to do. I did not know the way of teaching art here. I feel like I
cannot work unless somebody gives me some assignment.

The last two lines are of particular significance. They show that while the
British tutor was putting a lot of effort into getting the student to say how
she felt, what she wanted to do, what she knew she did not want to do,
what the current ideas she was working with were, and so on, the student
was simply waiting to be told what to do. She needed to work in response
to a particular assignment and had not expected to create her own project
of work. This may be seen as an example of 'pragmatic transfer' (Kasper,
1992; Odlin, 1989), whereby the student had carried over expectations of
the nature of tutor–student interaction in a Japanese context into that of
her current British situation. She was struggling not only with the kinds of
things the British tutor was asking her but with the whole ethos of education and impetus for learning. She talks of her previous experience as an
art student in Japan, as follows:

Retrospective interviews; Extract 5:

I was going to an art college, and I was trained to have techniques to
draw some object within a certain time limit. We usually had some
motif like a person or object in front of us. This decreases our creativity, and I am having a hard time here. In Japan, students learn techniques. It seems like it is different art from that of England. They have
a certain stereotype about art in Japan, and there are things you have
to do in order to enter an art college. So, I got confused when I was
told to do what I wanted to do here.

She compared her experience as an art student in Japan, where she was
told what to do and trained in techniques for how to do it, with her

bewilderment in the British context of being left to come up with ideas on her own. This chimes very much with what learning psychologists have found when contrasting western and East Asian approaches to learning (Gardner, 1989; Biggs, 2005). As Biggs puts it:

> In the West, we believe in exploring first, then in the development of skill; the Chinese believe in skill development first, which typically involves repetitive, as opposed to rote learning, after which there is something to be creative with. (Biggs, 2005: 55)

Appreciating Educational Difference

It is not always the case that the intercultural experience leads to misunderstandings or confusions about teacher and student roles. The benefits of the dialectical process of developing his work have obviously been recognised by the student speaking in Excerpt 3 above. He saw that the process of talking through a negative experience with the tutor, what he called getting into a 'slump', could act as a catalyst in taking his work forward. This student was an MA student who had done his undergraduate studies in Japan. When asked if a similar process would happen in Japanese art education, he replied in the negative:

Retrospective interviews; Excerpt 6:

> Well, I do not think they would just ignore me. But I do not think they would do the same things as the adviser here. They would not willingly analyze or clarify problems for me.

He further observed that there was little need to explain the work that was done in the Japanese context, that it was more likely that the tutor evaluated a work according to his or her own taste. He shows his understanding of the UK teaching and learning context, as it relates to fine art education, by explaining it as follows:

Retrospective interviews; Excerpt 7:

> Here, the adviser guides you by considering the situation and the student objectively. They try to look at things from the student's perspective. Then they think how to develop more. I think this is the way to teach here.

This student is obviously well integrated into his current educational cultural context and understands very well the role of verbalisation and its relationship to developing or learning. However, not all students similarly appreciated this role, and put up some resistance for a variety of reasons.

On Preferring not to Speak

While the above student understood the dynamics of verbalising one's inner state in order to promote the development of the creative work, other students chose a different approach. One was to maintain a Japanese sense of stoicism, which the above student also implied in relation to how he would have reacted on getting into a 'slump' in the Japanese education context. Such stoicism was more explicitly voiced by the student in Excerpt 6. She would rather be stoical and deny that she is having problems (which in this case effectively means maintaining silence) than admit weakness to her tutor. This explanation arises when the Japanese interviewer probes why she did not just tell the tutor she was in difficulty:

Retrospective interviews; Excerpt 8:

Japanese Interviewer: Before he became like this [=persistent in asking], you could have told him, for example, that you were confused, or you had such and such problems, or you needed his help.

Japanese Student: I think I didn't want him to realize I am such a person. I still think so. I pretended to be a strong person. I did not want him to know my weak point.

Such an underlying attitude, where from her perspective, in not showing her weaknesses, she may be seen to be preserving her face as a student, the effect is completely counter-productive in the context of the British higher education tutorials. It is not just a question of the need for the student to say something for its own sake, the need for the student to outline her/his position in relation to the state of the work, in the case of fine art studio practice, or the learning process more broadly, is key to the interactional dynamics of the tutorial and to the rationale for the tutorial taking place at all. This makes the issue of resistance to verbalising problematic in the intercultural context, even though it is perfectly justifiable in the cultural context of the student's background language and educational culture.

In her exploration of why Japanese students remain silent in seminars in the Australian higher education context, Nakane (2006: 1817) found that 'politeness strategies and orientations seemed to have a very strong influence on the student's silence'. Referring to Brown and Levinson's theory of politeness (Brown & Levinson, 1987), she mentions three uses of silence that might apply when someone has been asked a question, namely:

An off-record strategy;

A pause for thinking time;

An inability to speak due to embarrassment.

Both the first and the third strategies may be seen as defensive in the context of Japanese students. The off-record strategy was illustrated by the student speaking in Excerpt 6, who does not want to show her weak point. While Nakane illustrates the off-record strategy with Japanese students who have not answered despite being nominated in a seminar situation, another student in her study exhibits the third strategy, while giving a similarly defensive explanation as to why she was silent in class. This student puts the issue as follows:

> How can I say something 'wrong' in Japan, saying something 'wrong' is well not quite bad, but somehow it's like shameful, if you say something wrong, you feel embarrassed, and that sort of thing I still have with me. So yeah I hate saying something wrong, in front of people. (Nakane, 2006: 1818)

In the first case, the student does not want to show her weakness, in the other, she is too embarrassed to say the wrong thing.

In a similar study investigating the reasons for the silence of Chinese students at a university in the United States, Liu (2002) identified patterns of behaviour which are appropriate in the Chinese background contexts of the students, but transfer negatively to their current North American contexts. The reasons the students gave for their silence included a sense of respect for the teacher and a fear of wasting other students' time if they made an inappropriate contribution. By the same token, they often felt that their North American counterparts were speaking for its own sake, and not necessarily making a relevant contribution to the debate. The Chinese students' silence, however, as with the Japanese students in Nakane's study was perceived as non-engagement with the class.

In yet another study on the reasons for East Asian students' silence in class participation, this time focusing on Korean students, Lee found that:

> [B]road sociocultural differences between Korean and US society regarding the value of public speaking, the roles dictated by gender and age, and role expectations in class between US and Korea were evident in the patterns of classroom participation. (Lee, 2009: 153)

She also determined the degree to which the students both accommodated to western practices and maintained their own sense of what was important. She states:

> the students constantly blended expectations from the two distinct discourse practices and frequently switched between viewing discussions as heuristic tools or evaluative processes. On the one hand, they seemed genuinely to believe that participation offered a valuable means of learning. Yet they also seemed to retain much of their expectations of the Korean classroom, as evident in their valuing the teacher's responses or comments over those of other students and in the belief that the instructor and students were responding not as co-contributors of meaning but as evaluators of their knowledge and ability. (Lee, 2009: 153)

Silence at Cross-Purposes

The problem for international education here is that the pragmatic transfer of East Asian attitudes to silence works negatively in the intercultural context of a western institution. Especially in the British tutorials described here, where the process of taking the tutorial forward depends on the student responding appropriately to the tutor's elicitations, staying silent in order to avoid embarrassment could be seen as working against the maintenance of rapport (Tannen, 1985; Spencer-Oatey, 2000) between the interlocutors. As Tannen (1985: 96) pointed out, silence can be either a marker of rapport (e.g. where knowledge is shared, or mutual familiarity pertains) or defensive. In a Japanese educational context, the likelihood is that a student's silent behaviour when asked a question would have marked an end to the interaction, with no threat to the face of either interlocutor perceived and rapport maintained. In the case of the retrospective interview where the student did not want to show her 'weak point', the student's stance may be seen as defensive, that is, defending her positive self-image as a Japanese student, who would not want to show ignorance or weakness.

This culturally specific defensive use of silence was illustrated by another student in her retrospective interview, but in this case, she was also relying on the tutor behaving in a more typically Japanese manner and ceasing to probe her further. She gives her explanation of the situation as follows:

Retrospective interviews; Excerpt 9:

I thought so [=that the tutor is waiting for me to say something] at this time. But I thought 'if I say this, he would ask me more questions, so let's not say anything'. I did not have enough English skills to answer him if he would ask me heavy questions. That's why I thought I should not talk.

This student was trying to be deliberately strategic in her use of silence. She thought that saying anything at all might lead to even more difficult questions. She mistakenly thought she could pre-empt this by remaining silent. As with some of the students in Nakane's and Liu's studies, she also gives lack of language proficiency as a reason for her silence.

It is well known that attitudes to silence in the Japanese cultural context are not negative, and that the maintenance of silence is rather seen in general terms as a good social attribute (Barnlund, 1989; Lebra, 1993; Loveday, 1986). Conversely, being seen to talk too much or talk unnecessarily is frowned upon. Indications of such an attitude were apparent also in some of the student's retrospective interviews.

OververbaIising

The issue of silence is tied up also with negative perceptions of verbalisation. This was seen particularly in the following student's interview where a contrastive perspective on pause length between speaking in the UK context and in Japan revealed a rather irritated response to talk:

Retrospective interviews; Excerpt 10:

People here do not wait for my response. They keep expressing what they have in their mind. I think that Japanese people think about what they say for a while before they actually say it.

The above situation may be related also to Nakane's second reason given for silence, namely thinking time. A second perspective on this, from another student, seems rather to berate the tutor for as it were, oververbalising. Their persistence in inducing a response from the student may have negative, rather than the desired, effects. As the student went on to say:

Retrospective interviews; Excerpt 11:

But when I am asked about something I am not sure, such as when my tutor asks me about my work, I cannot answer very well. In England, if a student does not talk, teacher tries to keep the conversation and talk. He talks about many things, from many perspectives, which causes my idea messier. Then, I lose confidence about my work. It happens sometimes.

A similar scenario in a British context, and working to the detriment of the students, was identified also in Japanese students' performance in the oral tests of the University of Cambridge Local Examinations Syndicate's (UCLES) English language proficiency tests. In her study of their generally underperforming scores, Norton (2001) described their difficulties as follows:

> Hesitancy and pauses of several seconds occur directly after examiner questions. Japanese students are often reticent when requested to elaborate upon their response. This prompts further intervention from the examiner who feels the necessity to clarify the task or encourage candidate participation. (Norton, 2001: 68)

This situation of performance in language tests virtually mimics the relationship between Japanese students and their British tutors in the intercultural tutorials described in the previous chapter.

The issue of what might be termed 'ververbalisation' and its relationship to pause length was voiced also by another student who put it into a contrastive cultural perspective. He states:

Retrospective interviews; Excerpt 12:

> I often have a long pause even when I am talking in Japanese. And I think English people always try to explain in detail about what they are talking about. ... Japanese usually become silent when, such as they are nervous. But I think when English people get nervous, they become more talkative than usual.

Japanese students in Nakane's study made similar comments regarding the ease with which their Australian peers were able to speak. The following quote is an example:

> I think they just put their thoughts into words and speak straight away. And they don't think they are silly. ... They think opinions are opinions, and it's a good thing to speak. (Nakane, 2006: 1818)

While silence is seen as the safer option for Japanese students on the whole, English native speakers, possibly because they are aware of the positive evaluation of making a contribution, may in fact achieve the opposite by, as it were, speaking themselves into trouble. We have the phrase in English, 'talking yourself out of something' where talking is intended to exculpate, but this can have the opposite effect. This resonates with the nervous talkativeness described in Excerpt 10, which may not be an appropriate form of talking, especially in the academic context.

Playing the Speaking Game

Whether or not all the students interviewed one year into their studies fully understood the rationale for their tutorial interactions, it is significant that most of them have nonetheless modified their behaviour in terms of making an effort to speak. They have perceived the importance of speaking, and do so for what seem to be politically pragmatic reasons. They have decided to work the system as it were. As one student put it:

Retrospective interviews; Excerpt 13:

I realized that if you didn't say anything, their [=tutors'] attitude would change, and they would not come to be so serious when talking to me.

This student has clearly recognised that what she says to a tutor is interrelated with what she gets back from them. She feels that the more she tells the tutor about her work, and how she is progressing, the more substantive feedback she is likely to get from them. She also fears her work will not be taken seriously if she does not speak about it. In other words, she has understood that the work does not speak for itself as it were, which is likely to have been the expectation in the Japanese context, where the tutor's role is to tell the student what to do and then to evaluate the work. This was exemplified in another retrospective interview where the student makes a comparison between the role of the tutor in the Japanese context and that in Britain. Of the role played by Japanese tutors in teaching art, which is primarily concerned with improving the students' techniques, he refers also to their related role of evaluating what the students have done. He says:

Retrospective interviews; Excerpt 14:

they are subjective, and their judgements rely on their taste.

In other words, the role of talking about or explaining the work from the student's perspective is not necessary in the Japanese context. An expectation of being graded nonetheless transfers to the British context, where it is conflated with the need to speak about the work. This leads to a fear of the effects of not speaking, as is apparent in the following excerpt from another student, who clearly continues to think in terms of immediate grading:

> **Retrospective interviews; Excerpt 15:**
>
> ... , so if I do not say anything, I will get a bad grade. So, I try to say as much as I can, even if I speak terrible English.

Here the inhibitive factor of language proficiency, mentioned also above, is overcome by the students' fear of what will happen if they do not speak. Speaking ungrammatically wins over not speaking at all. These students have identified speaking as a high stakes activity.

Complexities of Face in Pauses and Silence in Intercultural Tutorials

While tolerating silent pauses may be seen as a way of enabling thinking time, the following extract from an intercultural tutorial provides a complex twist to this. The extract comes from the original tutorial of the student speaking retrospectively in Excerpt 9 about keeping silent in order to avoid getting into deeper water as it were. Here it can be seen that the British tutor is really pressing the student to make some kind of statement regarding her work.

Videotaped Tutorial; Excerpt 5

British Tutor One:	How do you see your studio work developing? Tell me.
Japanese Student Five:	Em.. [6-second pause, student looks confused] .. this term?
British Tutor One:	this term [7-second pause]
Japanese Student Five:	I want to use colour. I'm not sure.
British Tutor One:	Have you been thinking about it? [Another 7 seconds]
British Tutor One:	Do you have any ideas? Are you waiting for me to say what to paint?

This extract brings up a number of different issues relating to intercultural pedagogy. On the one hand, the tutor cannot be accused of not giving the student enough thinking time, often felt to be a feature of neglect on the part of the native speaker when interacting with an L2 speaker. However, on the other hand, the number and length of the pauses in the extract in effect shifts the balance from their being facilitative to their being face-threatening. While the student has been trying to end the line of questioning by remaining silent, and thus, in terms of her own perception of things, save her positive face, the tutor's persistence becomes more like a threat, an 'answer or else'. This is particularly the effect of the third long pause. The tutor then does in fact indirectly reprimand the student for ostensibly waiting for him to tell her what to paint. He has understood that this expectation of direct instruction is often a transfer from teacher behaviour in the Japanese educational context, but he clearly expects her to adapt to the British context.

In this context, the tutor's persistence is justified in terms of the ratio- nale for the tutorial. As previously discussed, the tutorial is student cen- tred and develops on the basis of the student's interests, what he/she wants to do, or centres on the work that the student has already done, and how it might be developed. As there is no work to hand in this tutorial, which took place after the summer break, he needs the student to project forward to ideas she wants to develop. Her reluctance to verbalise – even if only to say that she has not thought about it – makes it difficult for the tutor, hence his repeated attempts to draw her out.

In the intercultural interaction of the above encounter, then, there are a number of culturally counterposing issues going on. There is the expec- tation of tutor–student roles, whereby the Japanese student is expecting/ hoping that the tutor will tell her what to do, while the onus in the British context is on the student to set the scene as it were by presenting her own ideas for discussion. In the terms of politeness theory, there is conflicting attendance to different aspects of face (Brown & Levinson, 1987). The student is attending to her positive face from a Japanese perspective (being a student who neither embarrasses herself nor her tutor by pro- fessing ignorance) whereas she should ideally be protecting herself against the threat to her negative face (a student in danger of being rep- rimanded) by giving a response appropriate to the British tutorial con- text. At the same time, her silence is a threat to the British tutor's positive face, as without her participation, his role as guide and commentator on her work is redundant.

Contemplating both Speech and Silence

Both of these issues, of tutor–student roles, and orientations towards face, compound in the culturally countervailing importance of verbalisa- tion and silence. However, the importance of verbalisation in the English- speaking cultural context, then, is not simply one that can be seen in the polarised terms of speaking or silence. As was illustrated in the case of the Japanese student speaking above in Excerpts 3, 6 and 7, he showed that he had understood the importance of verbalising his state of mind, in the interests of a process of development, that is, moving forward in his work. This means that it is not simply speaking per se that is important. He had accommodated to the underlying rationale for verbalising ideas, doubts, and so on, in the British educational context, without relinquishing his Japanese personality, as a non-talkative person. This student's ability to move between the two cultures and understand the prevailing differences between speaking and being silent in a purposive way was, however, quite distinct.

Preferring to Listen

Despite an awareness of the importance of speaking and the considerable amount of effort that went into doing so, some students were also aware of the tension that existed for them between speaking and listening. An illustration of this tension, and how it is related to background cultural assumptions about the role of the tutor, is given by the following student in her retrospective interview about her videotaped tutorial. She states:

Retrospective interviews; Excerpt 16:

I was very nervous about this tutorial. I thought about what I was going to say in the tutorial the night before. No idea came up; but there was something I wanted to talk about. When I was in the tutorial however, I felt like I had to listen to what my tutor said, just like every Japanese student does in Japan, you know, – to keep saying 'yes, yes.'

As well as showing the importance of agreeing with the tutor, or at least respectfully acknowledging what the tutor has said, this excerpt exemplifies an understanding of the 'listening mode' that Jin and Cortazzi (1998) also identified as the predominant attitude of Chinese students. In their study, which focused on cross-cultural contrasts in asking questions in classroom interaction, they emphasised that for Chinese students, listening came first. The issue of respect for the teachers was also prominent. Namely, it was important to listen to what the teacher had to say first before they themselves spoke. Jin and Cortazzi also make a distinction between the different types of questions that students typically ask. They talk about 'heuristic' and 'reflective' types of question asking. While the former sees questions as an integral way of finding things out, as part of the process of learning, the latter kind of question asking happens only after a certain amount of knowledge has already been learnt.

While both questioning modes may happen in both British and Chinese learning cultures, Jin and Cortazzi relate the former primarily to the skills-based learning which British teachers value and the latter to the knowledge-based learning which Chinese teachers value. As they put it:

> For the Chinese students one has to learn something and know something about a topic before one can ask, otherwise a question will look foolish. (Jin & Cortazzi, 1998: 51)

What westerners are prone to call 'rote learning' may be seen by Chinese as part of a longer educational progression in which memory comes first, to be followed later by understanding and questioning, either questioning to oneself or to teachers and fellow learners. In Chinese terms, a learner needs to know *before* asking. In British terms a learner comes to know *by* asking. The common misperception by westerners of Chinese students' learning as rote learning is taken to task by Biggs (2005). He makes a distinction between 'rote' learning and 'repetitive' learning. He states:

> Both rely on a rehearsal strategy, and it could well be that rehearsing precludes conscious thought of meaning in both cases. The difference lies in the learner's 'intentions' with respect to meaning. In rote learning, meaning has no place in the learner's intentions, in repetitive learning it has, at some point in the deployment of the learned material. (Biggs, 2005: 54)

Both aspects of learning talk, asking questions, as in Jin and Cortazzi's study, or explaining what's going on in your academic work, as in my study, are differently inflected in the cultural contexts of China, Japan, Korea and the United Kingdom and they also interact differently with what teachers expect to do and what they expect their students to do.

The Intercultural Complexities of Listening

An interesting insight into the intercultural complexities of listening behaviour as a pedagogic expectation comes from Suzanne Scollon's (Scollon, 1999: 13) outline of the differing perceptions of a 'western' and a Chinese lecturer, both lecturing in English, in Hong Kong. The listening pattern of the students, surely the default mode for a lecture, is interspersed with their talking to each other at the same time as the lecturer is speaking. As the lecture is in English and the talk between the students is in Chinese, it may be assumed that they are discussing the content of the lecture, perhaps clarifying things for each other. However, the 'western' lecturer is upset by this, and stops talking until silence is regained. By contrast, when a Chinese lecturer is speaking, he merely raises his own voice to be heard above the students' discussions. He may at some point request silence, but basically condones the students' behaviour. There are times then when a listening mode is preferred, from a western perspective. This is probably related to the pedagogic genre concerned, such as a lecture, but the cultural assumption that it is rude to speak across someone who holds the floor, may also have been behind why the British lecturer appeared offended and was herself silent until silence from the audience was regained.

The propensity of the Chinese students to talk in the lecture context, albeit in their own language, and with each other, contrasts markedly with the apparent resistance to talk in the context of a seminar in a western institution, or especially in a one-to-one with their tutor, as discussed above. In the Hong Kong context of Scollon's example, the students are arguably engaging in 'learning talk', but somewhat ironically, the western lecturer saw it as disruptive, and would presumably have preferred a fully engaged listening mode, presupposing silence.

Conclusion

There are clearly differences in how talk, silence and listening are evaluated and promoted in the respective cultural academic contexts. The educational role of verbalisation is distinct in western contexts, particularly English-speaking academic contexts, but issues of relevance and purpose play a strong role in the desirability of what is said. Talk for its own sake is seldom the best policy. However, this distinction between talk and relevant talk becomes even more complicated in intercultural communication contexts when the student interlocutors choose silence over talk, or listening and respect for their teachers over their individual contribution, for, as it were, the culturally wrong reasons.

The genealogical cultural roles of verbalisation have evolved differently. On the one hand, in the western context, we have the valorisation of the dialogic, and on the other hand, in the Confucian context, we have resistance to what I have called the 'tao' of talk. This spatial conceptualisation of the 'tao' or way of learning is foregrounded in East Asian cultures. This latter issue, exploring the Confucian genealogical heritage of spatial conceptualisations related to teaching and learning will be discussed further in the following chapter.

Note

1.   I would like to acknowledge my gratitude to Dr Masako Hiraga of Rikkyo University, Tokyo, for carrying out the retrospective interviews (discussions on the cultural relevance of the content), and arranging for their translation into English.

Chapter 12

The Way of Learning: The Spatial Relations of Learning and Teaching in the Confucian/Taoist Tradition

Introduction

This chapter explores some of the issues behind the tutor–student encounters already discussed, bringing to bear the interpretive potential of a Confucian or Taoist understanding of the educational process involved. Whereas the process of verbalisation has been seen as important in relation to learning in the western educational tradition, what I would like to foreground as being important in the Confucian/Taoist tradition is a more spatial conceptualisation of learning and teaching. Specifically, the word Tao, translates as 'way' and the Way is upheld as a major overarching principle in the Confucian tradition, sanctioning behaviour more generally.

The chapter focuses particularly on the contrasting perspective of the role of the tutor from that of the Socratic midwife. The Confucian mentor is an exemplar, providing a model for the students to follow and learn from, in their own individual journey of self-perfection. Concomitantly, then, good students are ideally 'followers' of the tutor.

Differing underlying conceptualisations of the process of development in learning, in western and East Asian contexts, as well as the significance of process itself, will also be addressed.

The Confucian Heritage in Educational Discourse

There is no shortage of literature in English on the Confucian tradition of teaching and learning. This topic arises easily in any discussion of the Confucian tradition because of the central importance of education in its precepts and practices. For example, Bond (1991), Chen (1990), Dawson (1981), de Bary (1983, 2007), de Bary (1989), Fitzgerald (2003), Fox (1994), Hall and Ames (1987), Young (1994), Scollon (1999) and Watkins and Biggs (2005) all give accounts, and this literature is often drawn on to explain differences in assumptions and expectations of student and teacher behaviour, particularly in the context of ELT. In addition, there are a number of edited collections where aspects of communication and features of language, which become prominent in east–west discourse, are discussed. These include Gudykunst (1993), Kincaid (1987), Samovar and Porter (1994), Smith (1987), Scollon and Scollon (1995) and Ting-Toomey (1994), among others. It is not the aim here to survey this extensive literature, but to acknowledge its existence and the range of variables that have already been isolated and contrastively discussed in different contexts. The particular focus here is restricted to the intercultural context of contemporary higher education in Anglophone institutions, and how particular aspects and conceptualisations of the role and function of the teacher and student in the Confucian tradition provide resources for understanding interaction in this context.

The Teacher as Model

In his discussion of the Neo-Confucian educator, Chu Tsi, who was working at the time of the Northern Sung dynasty in 12th century China, de Bary talks of the importance of actively developing innate potential. He states:

> The potential is innate but must be actively developed; the process is one of bringing out from within something that has its own life and luminosity rather than imprinting or imposing on it something from without. (de Bary & Chaffee, 1989: 195)

There is then a similar conceptual underpinning to the process of teaching and learning in both the Socratic and Confucian cultures. What differs is the understanding of how this is achieved. While the dialogic, the importance of verbalising, is prioritised in the Socratic way of learning, the process of developing learning according to Confucian principles is more sequential. As illustrated in the tutorial data I analysed, learning or developing understanding in one's discipline tends to move forward in a dialectical manner, clarifying ideas by understanding their polar opposites. What is important to learning in the Confucian way is following the 'Eight Steps'. According to de Bary (1989: 196), these consist of successive steps in self-cultivation and involve a range of cognitive, social and moral operations. The underlying principle is one of self-perfectibility and the ultimate goal one of self-perfection, as outlined also in (Lee, 2005; Li, 2009).

The teacher's role in helping the students develop their potential to be the best they can be is not so much one of midwifery, but rather one of providing a model. This was borne out in Jin and Cortazzi's (1998) study. After videoing a number of classes conducted by Chinese teachers, and subsequently interviewing the teachers on their methods, they pointed out the importance to the teachers of providing models. As they state:

> The teachers emphasized the role of models, that students should pay close attention to demonstrations and should imitate, recite and learn models by heart. (1998: 39)

They go on:

> The teacher, as a model, should be a worthy example of morality and of mastery, that is one who has mastered the subject taught. (1998: 39)

The significance of providing a model in Confucian influenced education suggests a different kind of pedagogy altogether from what is routine in western institutional contexts. Such an understanding could easily set up expectations on the part of students for their teachers to provide some kind of authoritative stimulus first, before the students begin to learn, and could therefore account for the perceived reluctance of East Asian students in particular to proffer ideas or opinions in more open-ended discussion or learning formats as might be found in western contexts. On the other hand, this perception of reluctance may have led to the overdetermined labeling of East Asian students as passive, and prepared only to 'listen and obey'. For example, in a questionnaire study, Littlewood (2000) found that his student informants did not always agree with such a positioning. Cheng was also adamant that the assumption of reticence on the part of Chinese students was a western misperception (Cheng, 2000). There is nonetheless a case for the perception of Asian students as resistant to speaking in certain ways. As already discussed, proffering their own judgements and evaluations was often a source of difficulty for the Japanese creative and performing arts students, who were studying at a British institution. Placing their reluctance in relation to their expectations of a model or more direct instruction from their tutors, as those Japanese students themselves expressed it in their retrospective interviews, is not the same as labeling them as 'passive', however. This comes rather from the expectation, or at least desire, in the western cultural context of a more proactive verbalising stance on the part of the student. As discussed in Chapter 8, in relation to the issue of stereotypes and othering, such ethnocentric value systems easily project their negatively evaluated opposites on to behaviour that does not conform to expectations or desires.

The importance of the model in a somatic pedagogy

The importance of models is invoked also in Lebra's (1993) contrastive discussion of the idea of self and communication in Japan and the United States. Here, she talks of the importance of 'bodily' communication, and exemplifies this by reference to the classical performing arts of *noh* drama, and *kabuki*, Japanese dance. What is particularly significant about these performing arts is that they are based on *kata* or 'fixed forms of aesthetic expression'. The Japanese word 'kata' is also often translated as 'model' and is widely recognised in the following maxim for the learning process:

> Kata kara hait-te, kata o deru model from enter-GER, model ACC exit
> To enter by imitating the model, and exit out of the model. (Turner & Hiraga, 2003: 166)

Taking up Kasulis's (1990) formulation of 'somatic enactment', Lebra (1993) sees this process of how *kata* are learnt as a 'somatic' pedagogy. While Kasulis used the term in relation to religious rituals, the formulation nonetheless has resonance in more general teaching and learning contexts. It is perhaps also symptomatic of a cultural ethos, whereby a more holistic understanding of life and living is assumed, that aspects of educational and religious contexts more easily transfer or correspond than in the west. Lebra gives her description of somatic pedagogy as follows and makes at the same time a telling contrastive distinction with the verbal pedagogy associated in western educational contexts:

> In somatic pedagogy, *kata* is taught and learned through modelling and imitating in a teacher–pupil dyadic contact instead of verbal instructions and communication. (Lebra, 1993: 78)

This contrast between somatic and verbal pedagogy indicates a major distinction in approaches to learning and helps to explain why misunderstandings and confusions arise in intercultural contexts, especially when situated in western institutions, where the role of talk and assumptions arising from the willingness to talk are so crucial.

Spatial Relations in the Etymological Semantics of Chinese Characters

As Hiraga (1998) has shown in her etymological analysis of Japanese 'kanji' or the Chinese characters used in Japanese, the educational methodology of 'following the master' is also embedded semantically in vocabulary relating to teaching and learning. Through her analysis of the original meanings embodied in the Chinese characters, the literal concept of 'following' can be discerned. For example, the most common Japanese word for a teacher is *sensei*. *Sen* in *sensei* originally conveyed the sense of 'one pair of feet going before another', or 'to make an advance before others'. On the other hand, the Japanese words for a pupil, *seito*, and for a student, *gakuto*, both have the Chinese character, *to*, which etymologically means 'to step and walk along a path'. Hence, the teacher and the pupil/student are represented metaphorically as the one leading the other, as they walk along a path. Within the same semantic field, the phrase, *mana-bi-no michi*, which means 'study', or 'learning', breaks down in terms of its Japanese grammatical structure as follows:

learning-GENITIVE road,

and so means literally, 'path of learning'. The verb involved is *michibiku*, meaning 'to lead', and so the phrase manifests concisely, the underlying cognitive conceptualisation of following or being led along a path. In terms of its etymological derivation in Chinese characters, however, the concrete image of *michibiku* is 'to let someone pass through by holding or pulling his/her hands'. This image not only reinforces the leading and following relationship between teacher and student, it also gives a very strong sense of attachment. Such an image of concrete attachment, one could also say 'somatic' attachment, emphasises the importance of the teaching and learning bond that is forged between teacher and student. This is often conceptualised as a metaphorical extension of the hierarchical kinship ties that exist between parent and child. The 'rules' for teacher–student communication may therefore be seen as commensurate with those of parent–child (or father–son) communication, mentioned as one of the five important relationships in the Confucian book of rites.

A further corollary of the concrete image of the student closely following the teacher is the symbolic value of showing obedience. The verb *shita-gau* in Japanese means both 'to follow' and 'to obey'. The issue of obedience is one which figures prominently in discussions of East Asian students in western contexts and which, because of the negative connotations of passivity and submissiveness in the western educational context, brings with it a predisposition to evaluate negatively the learning behaviour of those students. It was this predisposition that Littlewood critiqued on the basis of his study mentioned above. However, as can be seen in the association of meanings in the Chinese characters, the conceptualisation of 'obey' does not connote passivity, but rather an active 'following' as constitutive of a diligent student. Here again we have an example of where deeply embedded cultural conceptualisations, where they relate to the context of learning, can set up diametrically opposed assumptions in the inter-cultural context.

Dialogic or Spatial Relations: Contrasting Epistemologies of Teaching and Learning

Strongly related to the semantics of leading and following is the notion of the path or 'way' between and beyond them, the basis on which the process operates. The notion of 'tao' and its associated philosophy of Taoism, also strongly linked with Confucianism, although emerging in a later historical period, means 'way' and is cognate with the Japanese 'doo'. This conceptualisation forms the common suffix in the traditional Japanese arts of performing the tea ceremony, doing flower arrangement, music, poetry, calligraphy, painting and the martial arts. The names for some of these highly valued cultural disciplines are as follows: *sadoo* (tea ceremony), *kadoo* (flower arrangement), *budoo* (martial arts) and *shodoo* (calligraphy). Here, the spatial metaphor of the way or path may be seen to point to an epistemological contrast with the speech orientation of the suffix 'logy', which is often used in the naming of academic disciplines in English, such as biology, psychology and sociology, not to mention the theoretical concept of epistemology itself.

In ancient Greek, *logos* meant 'speech', as well as 'reason' and 'logic', and is considered key to the western way of thinking. It is the motivation for Derrida's concept of 'logocentrism' and following on from this, feminist critiques of 'phallogocentrism'. The empirical manifestation of the centrality of speech is seen in the importance of dialogic interaction, not least in teaching and learning. The primacy of verbal reasoning then, along with the importance of verbal interaction in teaching and learning form a distinct conceptual contrast with following a path or the way. Each conceptualisation is embedded, and indeed embodied, in culturally inherited educational methodologies.

In her contrast of Socratic and Confucian principles, Scollon (1999) notes that while Socrates pursues a line of questions, Confucius never asks questions, or if he does, he answers them himself. Usually it is the case that his students ask the questions. Interestingly, from my point of view here of foregrounding the prominence of spatial conceptualisations of the relationship between learning and teaching, the example she gives is one where one of Confucius's students, Tzu-chang has asked about 'going forward without obstruction', in other words, keeping the 'way' of learning clear. The answer given in the analects is as follows:

> If in word you are conscientious and trustworthy and in deed single-minded and reverent, then even in the lands of the Barbarians you will go forward without obstruction. But if you fail to be conscientious and trustworthy in word or to be singleminded or reverent in deed, then can you be sure of going forward without obstruction even in your own neighbourhood? When you stand you should have this ideal in front of you, and when you are in your carriage you should see it leaning against the handle-bar. Only then are you sure to go forward without obstruction. (From *Analects* XV.6, cited in Scollon (1999: 19) from Lau (1983: 149–150)

Here a linear, straightforward, spatial dynamic is clear.

The role of the teacher as an exemplary model also links in to this underlying spatial conceptualisation of literally following a path. In helping the learner to keep the end goal in sight and not be distracted or 'obstructed', the teacher shows the way. The expectation is that students will 'follow' their teachers, and the associated moral expectation is that the teachers embody an exemplary model of human behaviour.

Following the Way of the Teacher

The 'way' in which to learn the traditional Japanese arts is known as the *shu ha ri* methodology, which translates as 'keep' 'break' and 'leave' in English; see also (Turner, 2001; Turner & Hiraga, 2003). The first step is to follow ('keep') the style of the master by imitating, repeating and practising what he/she has done. When the student has finished the long process of such imitative learning and has passed the test to become a junior master, then he/she is allowed to transform ('break') the style by introducing modifications. Only a few students can succeed in reaching the last stage in which he/she is allowed to 'leave' the former master to create a style of his/her own.

With reference to the approach of Chinese educators to the teaching of art and music, Biggs' (2005) description of their underlying principles shows a similar understanding. He puts it in contrastive terms to western priorities, emphasising the importance of developing skills and creating a beautiful product:

> Chinese educators also believe that art should be both beautiful and morally good; the idea of one right way pervades teaching. Thus skill

is developed first, in pursuit of the 'right way'; teaching is 'by holding the hand', not simply to direct, but to create the beautiful. The end is a product, not a process; in China both music and art teaching are performance-oriented. (Biggs, 2005: 55)

In another discussion of conceptualisations of self and creativity in relation to the Confucian learning process in general, that is, not restricted to art education, Lan (2002) echoes this understanding of principle and practice. He states:

Learning process is social (in Confucian tradition). By observing, mimicking, reflecting upon ritualistic communication behaviours, we gradually become more and more participating members of our cultural/discursive communities. As cultural ideals which embody the Tao become natural to us, we interpret these cultural norms for each given situation, thus becoming creative ourselves. (Lan, 2002: 71)

While the concept of creativity is valued in both the western and the Confucian educational cultural heritages, then, both how it is conceived of and the process by which it is achieved are different. The Confucian emphasis on the creative potential of learning through models contrasts somewhat negatively with the perception of mimicry and copying in the west, where such a process is seen as somewhat stultifying. However, the process does not end there. It merely provides a strong foundation on which to build or creatively 'leave'. Not only is the understanding of models different in the Confucian tradition, how they are used in teaching and learning is different. Such a dynamic of differing understandings of the process of creativity seems to be at play in the excerpt from the intercultural tutorial discussed in the following section.

Different Lines of Development: Dialectical or Incremental

The underlying conceptualisation of the path or the way is explicitly brought to bear in the topic of discussion in the following excerpt from a fine art tutorial. The British tutor, the third that I have brought into play in the intercultural tutorials, is outlining a recurring issue in her work with Japanese students, which she sees as a major difference in approach to the development of ideas. This fine art lecturer is speaking from a knowledge of Japan, having won a Japan Foundation scholarship to work there, researching the aesthetics of Japanese gardens. These aesthetics influence the artist/lecturer's own work in painting.

The specific creativity/learning issue being discussed in the tutorial is that of conceptualising a finished object before the process of making it has begun. This was a recurring topic in the fine art tutorials I observed, and not restricted to this example. In this example, however, the concern is outlined in detail.

Tutorial Excerpt 5

British Tutor Three: All, all I'm trying to say, at the moment, is that I wonder if there is somehow in the expectation, somehow in the way you're taught more generally, in any subject, that you learn to go from here to here via certain steps, and you reach here, and you don't really, you're not expected to question why it is you're getting there. You're taught to follow a path so, let's say, you're taught the technique of oil painting, and you're taught that there are certain things that you do in oil paintings, that there's a certain aim or goal, a certain result that is expected from oil painting and you are not taught, you're not made to think about the fact that you could go over there with it, that oil painting doesn't have to be like this. It could be something else. So it's quite a narrow path. This is oil painting, this is brush and ink painting, this is ceramics, ah, this, this is silkscreen painting.

Japanese Student Five: Yeah, so it's completely divided.

British Tutor Three: Yeah. Whereas here, you know, you've got the idea and we ... you're expected to think about what is the most relevant, appropriate media or material for that idea. And you're expected or encouraged, to try things out.

Japanese Student Five: from my experience .

British Tutor Three: until you find what's just the right thing to fit that idea.

Japanese Student Five: Yes.

British Tutor Three: So that's quite a big difference isn't it?

Working with preconceived ideas, as it was called by several tutors, implies a 'path' methodology, where all the steps are mapped out in advance, and making the work simply becomes a procedure of following them. Such a procedure of course complies with the *shu ha ri* dynamics of the student following in the footsteps of a master, as discussed above, albeit without the master in actual attendance. The 'master' in this context is the idea in the student's head. Earlier on in this discussion, the student had stated that she had come to Britain as a postgraduate student in order to develop her ideas as an artist, in a way that would not have been possible at art schools in Japan. However, what the tutor shows is that even in the development of ideas, there can be a different approach at work. Development may be conceptualised in terms of the achievement of a desired result or as an integral part of the process of making art itself. The tutor is emphasising the importance of process, of trying things out, of being able to discard ideas in order to move forward with what works better. It seems however, that the student has by contrast been following the principles of the *shu ha ri* learning process. This requires perspicuity of observation, and thoroughness and determination in carrying out whatever process or procedure is necessary to achieve the desired object or outcome. The adherence to such principles is in contradistinction to the contemporary practice of British art education, which values rather the individual exploration of ideas, the development of which cannot be mapped out in advance. As illustrated in previous chapters, I have characterised this western cultural preference as a concern for a more dialectical engagement with ideas.

The Product/Process Distinction

The product/process distinction, which was made clear in the tutorial excerpt above, is itself a key parameter of cultural difference in contrastive studies of teaching and learning between western and East Asian contexts. A similar emphasis on the importance of process in American art education was made by Biggs, in contradistinction to the importance placed on product in Chinese art education, as was cited above. He states:

> American education is more concerned with the process than with the product; exploring and creating are seen as more important than honing the specific skills needed to achieve a particular artistic product of an acceptable and recognised standard. (Biggs, 2005: 55)

This contrast in emphasis arose also as a point of confusion for international students studying the creative arts at the University of the Arts London. In a report on their experiences, Sovic (2008) quotes the following Taiwanese student, who states the issue succinctly:

> It is slightly different from what I expected. ... Unlike Taiwan, here in the UK I have learned what they are really concerned about is more

students' learning process, and less learning outcomes. My tutors here seem to me to be very concerned about where my ideas come from, how I develop and what research I initiate with my ideas. It is essential that the formation of ideas, conducting research and completion of my final piece of work are integrated throughout the whole process, even if the work itself is not very attractive. I am still trying to accommodate this major difference in relation to the teaching and learning approach here. (Sovic, 2008: 12)

Sovic further makes the point that students 'can fail if they do not understand that tutors expect to see evidence of the design process when assessing the work' and mentions the case of a student who had failed her first year through not realising this.

The importance of process as part of the western cultural dynamics of learning and assessment is not restricted to practice in the creative arts. It works generally as an approach to learning in higher education, across the disciplines. For example, it is important also in the negotiation of thesis writing with a supervisor. In her discussion of this in relation to Korean engineering students in the United Kingdom, Yoo points to how it differs from what might be expected in Korea:

> For PhD candidates, supervision, as the major practice in the UK education system, was not seen as just directing or guiding students in the directions which supervisors want; supervision was considered to be a process of interaction between students and supervisors including negotiation, debate, answering and explaining. (Yoo, 2008: 191)

The expectation of more direct guidance from a supervisor, including being told what to read, or in the case of scientific experiments, what to do, complies with the Confucian 'following' mode. However, it conflicts with the more dialectical process of presenting a draft for discussion, developing it further as a result of clarifications and/or the identification of potential further areas to investigate. Misunderstanding of the role of the supervisor and student in this regard is a common occurrence, whatever the discipline, and features frequently in the higher education press, for example Johnson *et al.* (2000) and Kim (2007). Whether it is a case of showing evidence of the process of designing or drafting, or of developing one's thinking through the process of exchanging ideas and gaining clarification and insights, the dynamics of process, and indeed predominantly dialectical process, is itself essential in the western educational context, and is ultimately infinite.

Intercultural Inversion: Leading the British Tutor to Follow the Way

In this section, I give an example of 'intercultural inversion', whereby the intercultural context, in throwing up differing expectations of behaviour actually leads to a change in behaviour, in this case, of the British tutor. The situation was that a group of students had persuaded the course tutor to give a slide show of his own work. He duly prepared such a show, which he presented along with appropriate art historical references and commentary. The 'show' was incorporated into an end-of-year party, and was much appreciated by the students. Although I did not see the significance of this event at the time, the students had in effect turned their own culturally informed expectations of the tutor–student relationship into a new event in the course curriculum. This became clear to me a year later with a different cohort of students, when in a focus group discussion on the cultural differences that the students experienced, a recurring theme was the fact that they never saw any of their tutors' work. They even seemed to berate their tutors for it and contrasted them unfavourably with instructors in Japan who 'led the students to absorb what they (the instructors) were doing and showing'. This very telling formulation exhibits strongly the kind of 'somatic' enactment demanded by the understanding of the teacher as model.

While the British lecturer was actually rather flattered to have had the request to show his work, the performative on the part of the students was less one of compliment, and more one of coercion, or at least one of gentle persuasion. In effect, the students had led the tutor to perform a role of demonstrating or showing as befits the Japanese cultural (and indeed, Confucian) role of tutor, thereby enacting a kind of intercultural transfer: a British tutor plays the role of a Japanese tutor in a British context. As with the case of what I called 'reverse midwifery' discussed in Chapter 10, whereby the students 'induced' the tutor into the explicating and elaborating role expected of them, here, the students have effected a reversal in the institutional power relationship by implicitly imposing their own agenda on the tutor, and making the tutor act according to their own expectations of the tutor role. Instead of the tutor leading the students, it was rather a case of the students leading the tutor. The event could even be seen as one of the students putting their tutor to the test! Whilst the occasion was a celebratory one rather than strictly speaking a pedagogical one, it nonetheless suggests that here a new 'intercultural' genre had been born, adjusting the British context to the expectations of Japanese students.

Conclusion

The investment of value over time in educational practices of following the model, listening, what might be called proactive speaking and proactive silence, has led to different effects in genealogically different cultural contexts. What might be valued positively in one cultural, and associated linguistic, context might rather be rated negatively in another. It is this value-laden nature of teaching and learning behaviour which can lead to apparently diametric opposition when the value systems meet, as they do in intercultural contexts. Specifically, the underlying assumptions and expectations of the differing cultural constructions of teaching and learning may conflict or at least disrupt in some way, the expectations embedded in the host institution, in which the intercultural communication takes place. What has been shown in this chapter is how a Confucian interpretive framework can be brought to bear on both explaining some instances of differing value systems in conflict in western institutional contexts and on highlighting the richness of intercultural interaction that is currently going on in those institutional contexts. This intercultural interaction is not only of interpretive interest, however. It is in itself playing a part in the fairly recent global cultural construction of the international university. Some examples of its impact have been played out in this chapter. The next chapter provides another example of the transformative effects of the Confucian impact on the intercultural dynamics.

Chapter 13
The Discursive Dance of the Intercultural

Introduction

In this chapter, I focus on one particular intercultural tutorial or advisory session encounter, which, by virtue of the number of cultural variables it brings into play, merits closer scrutiny and the spelling out of the individual issues. I do not have a transcript of the tutorial itself, it was outlined to me,[1] and I have 'dramatised' it, as it were, in a number of scenes, which in themselves compress and illustrate the kinds of feelings and approaches, a kind of 'everyman' international student is likely to have and to take in similar, everyday and routine contexts of the study experience. They concern the frequently recurring issue of what kinds of advice or guidance a student can expect from a British tutor, and how to go about getting it. Taken together as a series of interlinked steps of problem solving, the 'scenes' comprise a vignette of considerable intercultural complexity. The significance of the issues and educational background assumptions identified will be discussed after presenting an outline of how the tutorial encounter was staged.

A Tutorial Vignette

Scene I: Being Stuck A Japanese student is having difficulty making a start on her MA dissertation.

Scene II: Getting Help
                 She enlists the help of a Japanese PhD student she knows at the same institution.
                 The PhD student arranges a meeting with the MA course convenor

Scene III: Action

The PhD student accompanies the MA student to the meeting.

Scene IV: The Meeting with the Course Convenor
The PhD student acts as the mediator for the MA student and explains the situation.

Scene V: Not Getting the 'Right'/Expected Help.
The student has expected/still expects specific guidance, on reading, organisation, possibly even to be given a specific topic for the dissertation.
The tutor starts to explain how to structure a dissertation, talking about giving an introduction, developing the body of the text, and providing a conclusion.

Scene VI: Paying No Attention
The student pays no attention to what the course convenor is saying, believing she knows about issues of structuring the text already, and thinking to herself: Why is he telling me this?

Scene VII: Mediation
The MA student tells the PhD student in Japanese that she is interested in gender, and mentions the kind of data she is thinking of gathering;
The PhD student translates and relays this to the course convenor;
The course convenor suggests some background reading and how to go about data collection.

Scene VIII: I'm not Telling YOU – Issues of Loyalty
Thinking she will facilitate the process of drafting and receiving feedback, which she understands as being necessary and useful, the PhD student now asks the MA student in English when she will submit her first draft.
However, the MA student will not commit to a date. The PhD student interprets this non-committal approach as being a result of the fact that the course convenor is not actually the supervisor of her dissertation. She therefore feels under no obligation to negotiate this with anybody else. To do so could even be seen as a betrayal of a sense of loyalty to the actual supervisor.

Scene IX: Exhortation and Closure
The course convenor tells the student to get on with the introduction and literature review, and thereby ends the meeting.

The Intercultural Interplay of Inferences and Relevance with Regard to the Tutor Role

There are a number of differing intercultural issues here, which I will introduce from the perspective of the MA student. The first is the expectation of tutor roles. In the particular case under discussion here, the student feels under pressure to make a start on her MA dissertation, and has had no specific guidance from her supervisor on what she should do. When she contacted the Japanese PhD student for help, her actual supervisor was not available and so the appointment was made with the MA programme convenor.

As indicated in the quote from the Korean PhD student in engineering, as well as in evidence from the literature, as discussed in the previous chapter, the default expectation on the part of East Asian students seems to be one of direct guidance from the supervisor on what is to be done. From discussions with many such students on this issue, it seems that requests for help from students may be as open-ended as 'what should I read for the literature review?' and the expectation is that they will be told. In other cases, students have put off contacting their supervisors about the problems they are having, and the longer the period of time becomes, the more difficult it gets to make contact. In some of those cases, students have returned home without completing their PhD studies.

A Chinese student records the following specific instance in her own PhD, in which she tracked the experiences of four Chinese students throughout their year of MA study. In this instance, the expectation of direct guidance, or as it was more specifically, direct explanation, was not met. It came from one student in particular who expressed his frustration at not being able to get his tutor to answer his queries directly. As the student puts it, rather succinctly, with a good philosophical understanding of the cultural differences:

> I tried to make a couple of appointments with him, as I didn't quite understand what he had said in the lecture. I know I can't generalise, but every time I went to meet my tutor, I had some specific problems to solve. However, somehow, he led you into sort of general discussion. For example, 'what's your idea' or 'how do you think of it'. He seemed to respect your thinking a lot and tried to resolve the problem through the exchange of questions. Tutors here like debating with you. The problem is at the end of the day my questions still remain unanswered. This dialogic way may not be suitable for Chinese students. We hope the tutor will give more advice and guidance. (Ding, 2008: 159)

This student had obviously encountered yet another 'Socratic midwife'. While he understood the 'respect' for independent student thinking on the part of the tutor, he nonetheless simply wanted the tutor to be more direct about things, to give explicit explanations, rather than continually attempt to elicit from the student what he thought. The result in this case was that the student eventually gave up seeking out tutorials at all. This was surely not the intended outcome on the part of the tutor, and seems generally undesirable in educational terms.

What is often behind an apparent reluctance on the part of British tutors to give direct guidance is the desire not to 'spoonfeed'. The negative notion of spoonfeeding is a recurring one in informal discourse on the educational process, particularly at the level of higher education. Often the refrain, applying to all students, not only international ones, is that 'they get too much spoonfeeding in school'. The assumption is that this is debilitating, depriving the student of the opportunity to think for himself/herself.

This value of independent thinking is at the heart of the Socratic dialogue. It recurs repeatedly in western educational discourse, and lies behind many institutional practices. For example, in their work on the academic advisory session in a North American context, where graduate students choose their course options, Bardovi-Harlig and Hartford (1990, 1993, 1996) pointed to the value placed on those students who 'showed initiative' and made suggestions as to what courses they would like to take, as opposed to those who merely exercised 'compliance' and waited for their advisors to suggest courses. International students from different cultural traditions were often in this latter camp, no doubt unaware of the workings of the underlying value system. As such, attitudes towards independent thinking are culturally value-laden, and can lead to misinterpreting student behaviour which does not appear to comply with its always present assumptions.

In the extract above, from the Chinese student who gave up on seeking out tutorials, there is a sense not so much of wanting to be told what to do, but rather of an unrequited desire for shared scholarship. This suggests a need for greater awareness on the part of western educated scholars to be somewhat more flexible in the exercise of their pedagogic practices. Ultimately, such tutors would save themselves time and give their students greater satisfaction if they put aside their prejudices about 'spoonfeeding' their students, and made some adjustments for differences in cultural expectations of the tutor role.

Age-related Communication and Peer Mentoring

The second issue exemplified in the above vignette is the significance of age relationships in Confucian cultures. The sensitivity of such relationships is starkly illustrated in Coulmas's (1992) example of an employee who kills his colleague because of what he sees as the colleague's inappropriate use of a form of address. The age relationship is both lexicalised and indicated grammatically in the use of specific words and word endings. In this case, the address form used by the victim was as if to a junior member of staff, but although the insulted colleague was indeed newer to the company, he was in fact older in age, and merited therefore a different, more polite, form of address.

Fortunately, while age-related differences also play a role in educational contexts, and may be disruptive in intercultural contexts, they are unlikely to be taken to the above extreme. Nonetheless, an age-relationship difference of only one year changes the way students address each other and can change the form of lexicalisation used. This means that here also the age relationship is highly sensitive. 'Junior' students are unlikely to speak up in front of 'seniors.' This can lead to a situation of negative transfer in the intercultural educational context, especially in relation to the group dynamics of seminar participation.

It would seem that the everyday Korean value of Chaemyon which Lee describes as 'face-saving with respect to one's status' (Lee, 2009: 143) works in a similar way to socially acceptable age-related behaviour in the Japanese context. Keeping Chaemyon is particularly important among men and 'is preserved and nurtured through a hierarchical social order that requires deference of the younger to the older' (Lee, 2009: 143). This was borne out in the behaviour of the two male participants in her study, who had also experienced 'hierarchical military practices' and seemed more hesitant to speak up in the class than the female Korean students, despite the fact that they were doctoral students and had been in the United States for a longer period of time. Lee also asserts the pervasive nature of Chaemyon in Korean society, whereby younger people remain silent while older people talk, even when there is disagreement about what is being said.

Familiarity with the social appropriateness of such silent behaviour and the tensions that can arise if the age (and therefore status) of other students is not known, easily transfers to international educational contexts. Although in the British institutional context, all students are in the same boat as it were, regardless of age, 'juniors' from the same linguistic culture often do not wish to speak in deference to 'seniors'. The seminar leader is likely to be oblivious to the existence of such age relations and may mentally label students as uncommunicative or non-participatory.

As awareness of differently motivated behaviour has increased, especially in ELT contexts, strategies for dealing with it are more widely available. They include promoting a more comfortable ambience for promoting talk, as well as being more explicit about the reasons why talk is expected. At the same time, there is a more widespread sense of injunction on teachers to avoid knee jerk reactions to their students' behaviour, which see them as lacking in competence. This is what Leki calls 'narrow thinking' (Leki, 2001).

The mediation in the tutorial vignette is the result of the age and social status relationship difference between the MA student and the PhD student. These relationships between senior and junior students are known in Japanese as *sempai-kohai* relationships. In such a relationship, the more senior student will 'take care of' (the phrase most often used when directly translated from the Japanese) a more junior student. Such senior/junior relationships are encouraged, in Korean and Chinese educational contexts also, from the early stages of schooling onwards.

While what is called peer mentoring is becoming more common in British institutions, where perhaps second- or third-year students provide support for first-year students, and there are therefore superficial similarities in the process, they are qualitatively and socially very different relationships. It is also unlikely that such mentoring in the British context would extend to organising a meeting for another student with his/her course convenor. There is also a certain formality, or expected propriety or Confucian *li* about the senior/junior relationship that gives it cultural significance in the British context, and differentiates it substantially from the issue of peer mentoring.

What is of particular interest here is not so much how the students address each other or relate to each other, but the fact that an East Asian cultural mode of interaction has been inserted into a British institutional event. These students have successfully transferred a practice of support from their own background cultural context.

Intracultural Mediation in Intercultural Perspective

The third issue I want to discuss in relation to the above vignette is one relating to the cultural value placed on the process of mediation itself. In her discussion of the importance in Japanese social behaviour of defending face, Lebra (1976) listed mediated communication, or asking someone else to transmit some kind of awkward message, as one of the ways of doing this. It would seem then that the MA student mentioned above, like some of the students discussed previously, did not want to admit that she was having difficulty, and so enlisted the help of a more experienced student. From this perspective, she was saving face. When interpreted from the British side, however, from the perspective of the MA course convenor, it is possible that the perceived necessity for a mediator reflected badly on the student. The course convenor may have seen this as an example of a weak student, someone who seemed intellectually weak, in so far as she was unable to take the initiative and begin to work independently on her research, as well as being linguistically weak in that she was incapable of explaining her problems in English, on her own. This is yet another example of the 'two-faced' nature of intercultural communication, where saving face in one cultural context means in effect 'losing face' in another.

Hidden Loyalties

The fourth issue of interest in the vignette is the most hidden one. I would not have discerned it without the interpretive help of the Japanese PhD student. It concerns the bond of loyalty that the student perceives to exist between her and her thesis supervisor. As mentioned in the discussion on the Confucian tradition of teaching and learning, and especially in terms of the importance of the five types of communication, there are expectations of mutual responsibility between tutor and student, and therefore also certain rules of propriety which apply in what gets communicated to whom, and who does not need to be told.

The fact that an international student may invest a degree of 'loyalty' in a supervisor, or possibly anyone with responsibility for marking work, such that she/he becomes the sole person whose advice is respected, may elude a British tutor. The corresponding expectations that a student has as a result, of a tutor looking out for that student's welfare, and taking a special interest, are likely also to be disappointed. In discussions I have had with students about what they felt made a good tutor, words from a generally affective discourse were common. For example, one student talked about the importance of tutors being 'kind-hearted', and another talked of the importance of being able to 'trust' her tutor. It seems that, especially at postgraduate level, the interpersonal dimension of tutor–student relations are quite different in East Asian contexts in general, approximating more to the parent–child relationship than the more distant, professional, and possibly, in some contexts, simply administrative role that a British tutor perceives her/himself as having.

Hierarchical Communication and the 'Humble' Student

If the above vignette illustrated some of the issues emerging from age-related communication, which may be seen as one form of hierarchical communication, another is the qualitative difference in how the student communicates with the teacher. This is also dependent on the 'following' mode discussed in the previous chapter, but can be manifested in what from a western perspective are unexpected ways. In the kind of hierarchical communication that is appropriate between tutor and student, the East Asian student may be constrained to diminish or keep humble his/her own contribution. Evidence of this kind of behaviour was found to be at the source of why Japanese students did not give detailed elaborations in response to elicitations from their tutors (Turner & Hiraga, 1996). In response to a discourse completion task prompt, where students have been asked to imagine they are in a tutorial situation, where they are receiving feedback from an essay they have written, and the tutor has said:

Tutor: Are you familiar with the work of X? [where X can be any scholar relevant to the discipline of the student]

One Japanese student, in Japan, has written the following reply to this stimulus, in English:

Japanese Student: Yes, a little.

In a follow-up interview on the responses (conducted by the present author), it became clear that the above student had interpreted the prompt as a suggestion for further reading rather than an elicitation aimed at getting the student to state what she knew of the author and whether or not it was relevant to incorporate some of the ideas in her essay. The stimulus prompt is ambiguous in that regard. However, what was more interesting was how the student explained why she had limited herself to the minimum in her response. This is shown in the extract which follows:

Interview Extract

Interviewer [I]:   So you think the tutor is making a suggestion rather than testing your knowledge. What would you do?

Japanese Student [JS]:   I would find X's book after the class, I always do that.

I: Your actual response is very short. A little. Is there a reason for that?

JS: It depends on the X, but maybe I want more or some brief information from my teacher even if I know more [than] a little.

I: Right. Yeh. So, it's .. Is that because you don't want to take too long a turn before the tutor. Why don't you give the information that you know already, now.

JS: Maybe I think my understanding .. the way of understanding is not so good or is not so … in the right way .. not right but in a good way, so maybe I want to hear my teacher's suggestion first. It sometimes happens for example, in the music class, I have played the flute since I was six years old and my teacher always asks me how long did you practise this piece, and I practise every day, I practise six hours every day but I said I played a little or I tried my best .. but. … That kind of thing this means … a little means.

I: So you're being kind of .. deliberately modest.

JS: Yeh.

What is crucial here is that the student feels she should take her cue from the tutor. This further exemplifies the importance of the role of the tutor as model, as discussed in the previous chapter. The student waits to hear 'more or some brief information' from her teacher before giving her own response. In her example of how she responds to her music teacher, she also adverts to a deliberate 'humbling' of her own efforts. She minimises the amount of practice she has put in. This would seem to be a social correlate of the grammatical 'humble' form identified by the linguist Martin in relation to the Japanese and Korean languages (Martin, 1964). He was referring to what he called 'the axis of reference', whereby speech in Japanese and Korean is divided into humble and neutral forms. This axis was differentiated from a second one, which he termed the axis of address, which was divided into plain, polite and honorific. The 'humble' form is always applied in relation to the speaker of him or herself and not to the addressee. The student above is therefore 'self-humbling' not only in relation to how she converses with her tutor, but also in her attitude to the field of reference, in this case, talking about the amount of work she has done. The cultural and social expectations of this 'good' student behaviour, whereby the student minimises her/his own efforts, further enhance the role of the teacher as being one of authority and taking the lead in any interaction. This in effect militates against what is commonly preferred in 'western' educational contexts of 'student-centred' teaching, but it's not simply a question of a cultural preference for teacher-centred teaching. Perhaps the most crucial value at play here is the Confucian one of self-perfectibility, and the role of humility in this process. As Li puts it:

> Humility is regarded not as a personal weakness but as a personal strength because humble individuals are willing to self-examine, admit their inadequacies, and practice self-improvement. Humility

also leads one to want to learn from anyone. Therefore respect and humility go hand in hand. (Li, 2009: 56)

Putting the operation of the value of humility in contrastive perspective Li also points up how it is often misunderstood in western contexts. She states:

The deference that Asian learners show to teachers does not stem from their fear or blind acceptance of authority but from their deep sense of humility. (Li, 2009: 56)

There is then a whole system of mutual reciprocity of linguistic behaviour, a set of *li* or rites of propriety, which conduce to promote what might be seen from a western perspective as teacher-centredness. However, this belies the underlying reality of pro-active student learning.

Transformative Aspects of the Intercultural Performative

What I have done in both this chapter and the previous one is illustrate how some of the underlying assumptions in the Confucian mode of teaching and learning are highlighted in the intercultural context of interacting in a western educational context, where differing assumptions come into play. It is important to emphasise, however, that it is not only a question of raising awareness of the differing perspectives and expectations of students from genealogically different educational cultures, the intercultural dynamic itself is having an effect on pedagogic interactions and pedagogic practices in higher education in the English-speaking world. In other words, the performance of the intercultural is transformative. Routine tutorial encounters, such as asking for advice, can have enfolded into them, a Confucian enactment of senior student–junior student relationships. This enactment in turn contains within it a face-saving practice, whose social function would only be recognised in its original cultural context, and not the one to which it has transferred.

Similar transformative/performative effects were seen in the case of what I called 'reverse midwifery', whereby the inducing role of the tutor, the institutionally more powerful participant, was effectively taken over by those students who resisted the tutors' Socratic strategies, and thereby positioned the tutors in the role of students giving reasons for their actions. Furthermore, in the case of the pedagogical event, whereby a British fine art tutor was positioned as a model teacher in Confucian cultural terms, and made to show his own work, a new intercultural genre was performed.

The more such spaces of resistance open up, however small, and the more 'petits recits' of the cultural 'other' are heard, in everyday tutor–student interaction, the more performative and transformative they become.

The terms 'home' or 'source' and 'target' language from foreign language education no longer suffice to frame the process of intercultural communication in the intercultural context of international higher education. The intercultural, where a melange of interacting variables from different cultural styles and value systems of communication is possible, is in effect setting its own course of action. Both the traditional Socratic and Confucian norms of pedagogic interaction, often taken for granted in their own contexts, and hierarchised in the western context of international education, are being performatively transformed. Despite the institutionally embedded power relationship, which privileges the tutor, the tutorial encounter is a contested site, an unstable ground, where the footfalls are unpredictable.

Note

1. I am grateful to Ayako Shibata for recounting and discussing this event with me.

Chapter 14
The Critical Rhetoric of Being Critical

Introduction

The contrasting educational ideologies I have elaborated in the preceding chapters are the result of deeply embedded cultural value systems which have produced preferred modes of tutor–student interaction. These modes in turn reproduce the respective norms and values in continuing tutor–student interaction. In the current global context of expanding international education, however, such an assumption of ongoing reproduction is not so viable. To take one, perhaps the prototypical intercultural dyad, at least in western educational institutions, the subject position of the tutor is rooted genealogically in a pedagogic discourse going back to Socrates, and the subject position of the student is rooted in the Confucian tradition. As was demonstrated in the previous chapters, these differently constructed subject positions often confronted mismatched expectations of communication style in their interlocutor. This was particularly the case in the intercultural tutorials discussed in Chapter 10. Here, the conventional academic genre, 'tutorial' set up a subject position for the student as critical analyst.

Being critical is historically embedded in western educational culture as a positive value. This requires familiarity with the rhetoricity of being critical. The rhetoricity of being critical relates to its embodiment in discursive text and its enactment in pedagogic interaction. As is thematic in this book, and is developed in further sections of this chapter, such rhetoricity is an effect of the deepseated cultural embedding of ways of using language and interacting with others in debate that is grounded in the western intellectual tradition.

The value of being critical has also led to the notion itself having rhetorical effects, such that the use of the word 'critical' can be a hotly contested site of intellectual power struggles. Some of these struggles in the field of language studies will be looked at, as well as how being critical features in relation to the ontology of the university, in the work of the philosopher of higher education, Ronald Barnett.

Critical Students

The ways in which language is used to enact critical practice is a site of struggle for many international students in western institutions of higher education, not least those with a Confucian educational heritage. This stems, on the one hand, from the value system giving the notion of 'being critical' a strong rhetorical force in the western academic system, and, on the other hand, from their lack of familiarity with the rhetoricity of being critical. For example, the kinds of questions the British tutors asked in Chapter 10 stood out because the Japanese students in the inter-cultural tutorials often appeared to have difficulty answering them. It seemed that the major difficulty was that these students, new to British academic culture, did not expect their tutors to be asking the kinds of questions they did. If anything, they expected a role reversal whereby rather than having to evaluate their own work, the tutors should be eval-uating the students' work and giving advice and instruction on how to improve it.

Such contrasting expectations of the respective roles of tutors and stu-dents give intercultural tutorials between British tutors and East Asian students, newly arrived in Britain, the potential to become comedy sketches. On the one hand, the tutor is desperately trying to elicit some kind of critical comment from the student, while, on the other hand, the student is ardently awaiting words of wisdom from the tutor. There is indeed an (unwitting) comedic element to the tutorial Excerpts 4a to e in Chapter 10, as the tutor persists in deploying ever more innovative strate-gies, culminating in a hypothetical threat to put her paintings on a bonfire, so that she might be forced to select four works and thereby demonstrate some degree of critical evaluation. The student meanwhile continues to resist his ever more hyperbolic exhortations.

What these excerpts showed is that despite deploying five different inducing strategies altogether, all of which failed to give the British tutor what he wanted, exercising critique is not a simple, transparent proce-dure. The problem in the tutorials discussed may have been the indirect-ness of the tutor's questions. His ulterior motive was to induce the student's critique, but this was not foregrounded explicitly until he had tried several different ways of doing it indirectly.

This indirectness in the tutors' utterances intended to elicit critical commentary serves to highlight the importance and taken-for-grantedness of a culture of critique in the academic context. As such, expecting critique from indirect elicitation is an example of a process of naturalisation. The naturalisation of discursive practices and how this reinforces hegemony is a point made forcefully by Fairclough (1995). As he states:

> A particular set of discourse conventions (e.g. for conducting medical consultations, or media interviews, or for writing crime reports in newspapers) implicitly embodies certain ideologies – particular knowledge and beliefs, particular 'positions' for the type of social subjects that participate in that practice, (e.g. doctors, patients, interviewees, newspaper readers), and particular relationships between categories of participants. (Fairclough, 1995: 94)

While the injunction to be critical may be implicit, it is a major criterion for academic success in both written work and spoken contexts. This means that any apparent resistance on the part of students to performing as critical analysts gets them labelled 'uncritical', a strongly negative evaluation. Such labelling is not restricted to students from very different linguistic and cultural backgrounds, however. The tension exists also for British students, as was pointed up by Kress and Fowler (1979) in their discussion of the ambiguous role a student finds her or himself in, when applying for a place at university. On the one hand, the student needs to be:

> polite, unrebellious, modest, while on the other hand, and at the same time, s/he needs to show 'adequate confidence and independence of opinion'. (Kress & Fowler, 1979: 75)

Nonetheless, the cultural embeddedness of the expectation of 'independence of opinion' often reveals itself most clearly in the bewilderment of students who are not aware of this value system. This means that they are frequently labelled 'uncritical', for example, when their written work is found to be too descriptive, see for example, Ballard and Clanchy (1991); Johns (1991); and English (1999), or when they fail to provide spoken critical commentary in tutorials.

Uncritical Students?

A good example of where a student's lack of familiarity with the required rhetoricity of being critical results in a negative evaluation of their work comes from (Ballard, 1996). The example relates to a Japanese student who was asked by his politics lecturer to give his opinion about the fact that there were two conflicting interpretations of the reasons for the Great Depression. The student replied:

> 'But I do not have an opinion – I am a student.' (Ballard, 1996: 155)

The student was bewildered by the fact that he had got a low mark for his essay and equally bewildered by the tutor's question. In his essay, 'he had merely written parallel ideas of the lives and accounts of each scholar without making any critical analysis or reaching an evaluation of the merits of their respective theories in relation to the Great Depression' (Ballard, 1996: 163). The student's position was that it was not his role, as a student, to criticise or evaluate the views of eminent scholars or to tell his reader (his lecturer) what to think. Moreover, as he saw it, the purpose of a comparison is to achieve some opening for harmony between opposing views, not to pit them against each other. This neatly points up an important tension between the value systems of being critical and seeking harmony, of giving independent opinions or what from a Japanese perspective might be seen as maintaining *enryo*, or refraining from voicing an opinion. While this student was therefore being a 'good' student in the terms of a culture where *enryo* was valued, this was not the case in his Australian institutional context. The important point to make here is that this student's poor performance in his essay was as a result of unfamiliarity with both a different cultural value system and the rhetorical instantiation of criticism, but not of being a weak student.

Being Critical but not Exercising Critique

The issue of whether or not a student is critical does not rest solely upon whether she/he has an opinion or not, however. This is part of, but not the whole story, as another look at an excerpt from a fine art tutorial in the United Kingdom will illustrate.

Going back to the tutorial Excerpt 4c in Chapter 10, where the Japanese student is resisting the British tutor's best efforts to engender her critique of her own work, it cannot actually be said of this student that she is 'uncritical', even within the 'western' academic context. It may well be said of her from the perspective of the East Asian academic context, on the other hand, that she is not a typical 'good' student, as she does not demurely show obedience to the tutor, and not express her own opinion.

She is in fact quite adamant that her 12 canvases exhibit one work and therefore she cannot differentiate between them:

26 **BT:** Yes, but how many of these on canvas have you made?
27 **JS:** " .. Em . . Just .. these ..
28 **BT:** So they're all here?
29 **JS:** [or, -] Yeah, all.
30 **BT:** [So it's] a 100% success?
31 **JS:** .. But, .. I actually eh, em, .. I've actually, em, peeled a
32   lots of paint off
33 **BT:** [Yeah]
34   I, I, I, I, I'm not, I'm not trying to catch you. [laughs]
35 **JS:** [laughs]
36 **BT:** I'm really trying to find out wh, what, how you can distinguish
37   between,-
38 **JS:** [Mm -m.]
39 **BT:** something which enables you to say, I, I, like this more than
40   that; this is the way forward, this is the way to go.

The student's uptakes to this line of questioning by the tutor are defensive. In other words, she is defending her position against what she feels is her tutor's criticism (i.e. negative opinion) of her work. In this respect, she is being critical, in the sense of not simply passively accepting what the tutor says. She stoutly defends her own practice, responding to what she thinks he is criticising, that she has not done enough work on the paintings. However, as he shows in line 34, this was not his point. He was not criticising her but rather inducing her to critique her own work.

The issue is that her standpoint needs to be developed within the analytical parameters of the discipline. Exercising critique is therefore something more than being 'critical', which can amount to little more than disagreeing. The student is critically defending, but not critically examining within the prevailing parameters of the specific discipline. In this context, she needs to look at her work as paintings and not just as *her* work into which she's put a lot of effort, and which she possibly has to defend against the tutor's opinion.

At stake here is a rhetorical move beyond simply giving or defending an opinion. This rhetorical move is ultimately one of justification, that is, making a comment and backing it up against the criteria that have been established in the disciplinary context.

Justifying Rhetoric; Justified Critique

There will obviously be differences in the criteria underlying judgements that can be made in different disciplines. In the fine art tutorial excerpt above, for example, these might relate to the texture of the paint, the quality of the brushstrokes, the approach to perspective, and many other things. The existence of such differences in relevant criteria has led to claims that critical thinking is different in different disciplines. My contention is, however, that the conjunct cognitive/rhetorical moves of claim or comment and justification are generic. They do not embody in its entirety what constitutes critical thinking, but are required in the intellectual cultural practice of critique. The kinds of content allowable or relevant will vary according to discipline, but the juxtaposition of the rhetorical moves, *claim*, however hedged it may be, plus *justification*, whether it directly supports the claim or delimits its scope or applicability in some way, is germane to the process of both constructing and identifying an argument. These rhetorical conjunct strategies are well known to teachers of EAP, and other teachers of academic writing. They are therefore taught particularly in the context of academic writing as well as in that of giving seminar presentations. However, what tends not to be known, even by EAP teachers themselves, is that these conjunct strategies have a long genealogical heritage.

Being Critical in Genealogical Perspective

The prototype for the process of making a critical judgement may be seen in Plato's distinction between opinion and knowledge and the relationship between them as one of movement towards certainty and stability. In Plato's dialogue 'The Meno', Socrates explains the distinction between knowledge and right opinion by developing the analogy with tethering or keeping in one place, the statues of Daedalus. Daedalus, in Greek mythology, was a sculptor who was famous for creating statues that looked as if they were moving. Plato's dialogue runs as follows:

> True opinions are a fine thing and do all sorts of good so long as they stay in their place; but they will not stay long. They run until you tether them by working out the reason. That process, my dear Meno, is recollection, as we agreed earlier. Once they are tied down, they become knowledge, and are stable. That is why knowledge is something more valuable than right opinion. What distinguishes one from the other is the tether. (Plato, 1956: 154)

In other words, knowledge of anything is tied down by the ability to give a reason for what we know. As the 20th century moral philosopher Hare states in relation to Plato's understanding and promotion of the ancient Greek notion of *logos*:

> the demand for a reckoning of the reason, or account of the explanation or definition of the cause or explicit answer to the *question "why?"* (no one translation is adequate) is Socrates' and Plato's most central and seminal idea. (Hare, 1991: 24)

While Plato's epistemology of 'working out the reason' by 'recollection' from pre-existing absolute knowledge, stored in the soul, as it were, is of course no longer viable, the cognitive process of 'working out the reason', and the rhetorical process of delivering it in terms of claim and justification, remains a prevalent demand in academic culture, wherever there is a case to construct an argument. Moreover, this is the case, even though the European Enlightenment assumption that the truth is out there, waiting to be discovered, is no longer routinely taken for granted, especially in the humanities and social sciences. To cast the issue in a Foucauldian idiom, what we have are 'regimes of truth' prevailing in discursive practices. From this perspective, there will be different criteria, more or less consensual, within different disciplinary or sub-disciplinary discourses, against which positions taken up can be evaluated.

Maintaining a Platonic idiom, we can still talk in terms of proffering an opinion, but instead of making a distinction between opinion and knowledge, we can make a distinction between giving an opinion and giving a knowledgeable opinion, in the context of critique. The latter would include a justification for the opinion, based on relevant criteria. While such rhetorical conjunct moves as claim plus justification, or evidence for claim, are routine, and teaching them could be seen as pragmatic, or uncritically teaching the conventions, see the discussion between Allison and Pennycook below, they are also the effects of power, of a genealogically embedded cultural value system, and as such cannot simply be de-inscribed, or written out of cultural history. This does not mean that they necessarily continue to be widespread. The performative process of intercultural communication in increasingly internationalised universities may well result in their becoming gradually less common. What is perhaps the most important point is that placing those rhetorical strategies in their genealogical context emphasises their cultural embeddedness as opposed to their exemplifying any abstract cognitive process, which is universally 'good'. It is the common assumption of such a consensus that is the source of much of the difficulty in the debates around being critical, as discussed further below.

Globalisation and the Culture of Critique

The development of critical thinking is not restricted to Britain, nor to education in the English language. 'Being critical' has gone global as an educational issue. For example, at the time of the sarin gas attacks on the Tokyo subway in the late 1990s, and the discovery that the leaders of the perpetrators were from one of the most prestigious universities in Japan, there was much talk of changing the education system to one where students were taught to be 'critical' rather than simply passive learners amassing knowledge for its own sake, without placing it in social contexts or making connections with other areas of knowledge. Such an education for becoming critical is linked also with creativity and the perception that whereas the education system in Japan and Singapore, for example, is associated with high achievement in maths and science, they are not noted for their strengths in innovation. A critical thinking culture has become a valuable educational product, therefore, one which many Asian education ministries are keen to import from the 'west'. The Singaporean government, for example, launched what was called a 'Thinking Schools, Learning Nation' policy in 1998 (Ministry of Education, 1998), designed to be the blueprint for schools in the 21st century. What might be seen as a commodity approach to policy, whereby a critical culture, or 'critical thinking' is bought in as it were, has in its turn brought notes of criticism to the debate as to how this curriculum should be delivered. Koh (2002), for example, critiques the prevalent tendency to teach critical skills as a package, and advocates a critical literacy approach, which helps students negotiate 'the language of business contracts and policy documents' that shape what Gee *et al.* have termed 'the New Work Order' (Gee *et al.*, 1996). Otherwise, critical thinking skills programmes operate in a vacuum. What is interesting to note here is that the label 'critical' itself has not been dispensed with. It has retained its value. The contention relates to what it is applied to, or associated with. The rhetorical exchange value of the critical is highly contested and fiercely fought over as will be seen further below.

The 'Critical' as Rhetorical Force

Quite apart from the rhetoricity of being critical, that is the longstanding rhetorical strategies embedded in exercising critique, the abstract notion of being critical in itself exerts enormous power and generates copious amounts of critique and counter-critique in contemporary higher education. I would like to suggest that it has 'honorific' status. An 'honorific' is a grammatical term in languages, such as Japanese, where 'vertical'

(Nakane, 1970) forms of communication are the norm. The honorific form is used when addressing a superior in a particular context. I'm borrowing that term here as a metaphor for the intellectual and rhetorical power that the word both yields and wields.

Within academic disciplines, for example, the word 'critical' is itself the prized badge of academic prestige and the locus of 'turf' wars on the academic terrain. This can be seen in research methodologies or interpretive approaches where fierce debates rage around the appropriation of the word 'critical' to preface an approach. The issues at stake may concern what is 'merely' descriptive as opposed to 'critical' or the fact that scientific objectivity is claimed without regard for the social context of the data and its effects. One particular debate pitted the pragmatic against the critical. This was in relation to approaches to ELT, especially EAP. The debate was published in the journal *English for Specific Purposes*. In his 1996 article in that journal, Allison joins a debate which had begun in Santos's (1992) article in the *Journal of Second Language Writing* on the difference in approach to teaching in L1 and L2 composition classes, whereby the approach to L1 was often explicitly ideological, but that to L2 was always pragmatic. Taking their cue from this article, Benesch's (1993) article in *TESOL Quarterly* on 'the politics of pragmatism' in ESL teaching and Pennycook's (1994a) article in *Applied Linguistics* on 'incommensurable discourses' followed up and expanded the debate in a critique of pragmatism. Allison takes issue with those accounts, particularly in relation to the teaching of EAP. He specifically challenges 'the validity of accounts that portray EAP pragmatism as a unified ideology offering support to the status quo of existing power relations in education and society' (Allison, 1996: 98–99). In an explicit rejoinder to what he saw as Allison's 'defence' of pragmatism, Pennycook (1997) elaborated on a distinction between 'vulgar' and 'critical' pragmatism, originally made by Cherryholmes (1988). Key to his critique was what he saw as the ready availability to EAP practitioners and theorists of a pragmatist discourse, which made it easy for them not to ask 'broader political and cultural questions' (Pennycook, 1997: 254). Quoting partly from Cherryholmes, Pennycook characterised vulgar pragmatism as 'valuing functional efficiency premised on unreflective acceptance of explicit and implicit standards, conventions, rules and discourse-practices that we find around us' (Cherryholmes, 1988: 151; Pennycook, 1997: 256). Such 'unreflective acceptance' was aided and abetted as it were by what Pennycook had also previously critiqued as the 'discourses of neutrality' (Pennycook, 1994b) surrounding the English language in particular, but relating also to language use more generally, so that 'conventions' were seen as fixed and not questioned.

The journal editors invited Allison to respond further and in that response, he indicated that given the choice between vulgar and critical pragmatism, the critical version was more appealing. As he put it:

> Once one accepts a choice between vulgar and critical pragmatism, there is no contest. (Allison, 1998: 313)

While he goes on to dispute the basis on which such a putative choice might be made, the above comment illustrates the point I am making here about the honorific nature of, or the cultural value attached to, the word 'critical'. The label 'vulgar' is of course negatively weighted, but nonetheless, the notion of a 'critical' approach is attractive in any field of enquiry and therefore in itself, regardless of substantive content, wields considerable rhetorical force.

This debate resonated further as a later article, also published in *English for Specific Purposes*, performed a kind of balancing act, putting forward the notion of 'critical pragmatism' (Harwood & Hadley, 2004) as an approach to teaching EAP. In this article, Harwood and Hadley bring a corpus-based methodology to bear on how a 'critical pragmatic' approach might be pedagogically implemented. This focused on the use of personal pronouns and possessive adjectives in academic writing, building awareness of how this process differed in different disciplines and what effect the use of these linguistic features had in their textual contexts. They illustrated this point by showing that while for some, the use of 'we' for single-authored papers was 'outrageously pedantic', their corpus data showed that it was the 'personal pronoun of choice for computer scientists and physicists writing single-authored papers' (Harwood & Hadley, 2004: 360). Their approach seeks to help students make informed or 'critical' choices in their use of linguistic features, and at the same time, garners the rhetorical choice of the honorific 'critical' for their own benefit. This middle way between a pragmatic and a critical approach is also a further instantiation of a dialectical manoeuvre, the cognitive/conceptual/rhetorical trope par excellence of the western intellectual cultural tradition.

Critically Examining the Use of the Word 'Critical'

Remaining within the broad field of language studies, another debate, where claiming or debunking 'the critical' in the analysis and interpretation of language use, was clearly itself a critical issue, was waged in the journal *Language and Literature*. This debate centred on the differences between discourse analysis and critical discourse analysis. Here, the word 'critical' raised Widdowson's critical hackles (Widdowson, 1995). The editors invited Fairclough to respond to the article (Fairclough, 1996), and in the tripartite nature of such journal debates, Widdowson wrote a further 'reply to Fairclough' (Widdowson, 1996) article. This rather fierce debate included arguments inveighing against the emperor's new clothes, accusations of political bias, of creating new definitions, or claiming the critical ground for oneself. A later article on the same subject, but without the agonistic duelling, in that it was written by a third party (Toolan, 1997) seemed to offer a sense of dialectical closure. In this article, Toolan made the point that:

> claims to scientific objectivity are no less rhetorical than claims to be genuinely critical. (Toolan, 1997: 87)

The voice of equanimity in this formulation both acknowledges the rhetorical forces at play, and at the same time, takes the rhetorical sting out of the word 'critical'.

Agonism and/or Critique

The fact that academic journals routinely encourage the exercise of critique and counter critique is in itself evidence of the cultural value invested in it. However, how the game has come to be played as it were has also raised critical voices. Tannen (1998) in particular critiques an all too ready agonism in contemporary culture. Her critique is not only addressed to the academic context, but to the fact that oppositional debates are mounted almost for their own sake, as this grabs the attention of readers or audiences. Showing the embeddedness of debate in western culture, going back to the ancient Greeks, Tannen's own advocacy is for dialogue rather than debate for its own sake. Such advocacy is in turn also evidence of a deeply rooted value system in the western intellectual tradition.

Critical Polysemy

These two contexts also point up the polysemy in the word 'critical'. In the agonistic context, the word prevails in its more emotive sense of disagreement or opposition, whereas in the context of engaging in dialogue, to be critical is both more cognitively demanding and rhetorically complex, as shown above in the tutorial extract, as well as in accounts of what it means to be critical, such as the rather unwieldy one given by Allison as follows:

> This has to do with examining assumptions, motives and consequences carefully, and with looking for inconsistencies and seeking to

understand if not resolve them, without being tied to (or alienated from) other more specific sets of sociopolitical concerns and practices as a required frame of reference for any speculative or investigative enquiry. (Allison, 1998: 313)

A discussion-based approach to critical thinking is what Gieve (1998) also describes in the context of his Malaysian students undertaking BEd TEFL degrees in the United Kingdom. As he puts it, what they received was:

a style of teaching that persistently asked them to examine the reasons for their actions, their beliefs, and their knowledge claims, requiring them to defend themselves and question themselves, their peers, their teachers, experts, and authoritative texts, both in class and in writing. (Gieve, 1998: 126)

This formulation is reminiscent of Hare's account of Plato's account of *logos*, given above. Gieve also emphasises the integral nature of critical thinking to pedagogic practice in higher education. This is opposed to any separate teaching of critical thinking skills and reinforces the point that critical thinking is an issue of cultural difference. As he states of his Malaysian students: 'critical thinking was the most striking demand made on them' (Gieve, 1998: 126).

Harwood and Hadley's (2004) case for a critical pragmatic approach, mentioned above, also drew on Lillis's (1999) description of what students' saw as an 'institutional practice of mystery', which this book also foregrounds as indicative of the need to investigate how the values of academic culture, and in particular its ways of using language, have arisen. For Harwood and Hadley, the phrase helps them construct their critical–pragmatic approach as one of 'demystification'. This adds yet another semantic frisson to the scope of the word 'critical'.

The difference in meanings of the word critical also came up from the perspective of a Japanese student in her retrospective interview on her British tutorial experience.:

I: stands for interviewer and
S: for student:
I: You said there are differences in the word "criticise" between Japanese and English. What do you mean by that?
S: In my opinion, criticising in the sense of Japanese is very one-way. You cannot get any returns. But in English, it is very interactive. You can get go and back.
I: I agree with you. They can argue, but we can't.

S: I do not like that part of our world. And I think I will be able to create something to change it. It is not good in Japan to speak out. I felt it strongly after I came back from London. That is not just my opinion, but a complaint. I got used to expressing myself while I stayed in London.

Here, the student seems to be comparing the use of criticism as reproach (a one-way communication) and criticism as discussion, which she sees as relevant in the British context and which she would like to be appropriate in the Japanese context.

Critically Differing Pedagogical Cultures

Such is the semantic flexibility of the honorific term 'critical', that it could also be appropriated to describe the mode of learning more familiar to East Asian students. Given the etymological source of the word 'critical' in the ancient Greek word *krites* meaning 'judge' (Onions, 1966), it is perhaps not surprising that it is used predominantly in the sense of a questioning and judging attitude in the western academic context. However, the word may be used also in a positive sense to convey the sense of precision, or close examination, which is necessary when astutely observing and following the teacher, which tends to be the case in Confucian influenced traditions (see the discussion in Chapter 12). To put it succinctly, we might discern in the differing expectations of the student role in the two differing genealogies of educational culture discussed in the preceding chapters, a 'critically speaking' (and writing) student and a 'critically observing' student. In the first case, a critical approach is to take apart, as in analyse distinctions and comparisons, verbally. In the other case, it is to observe and examine closely and seek to master a practice or body of knowledge. The value judgement, 'critical' or 'uncritical', need not then be a dividing line between the two educational cultures. However, it is the discursive practice of making and evaluating judgements, the prototype case of being critical, that is culturally contentious, as is discussed further below.

Questioning Critical Culture

The quote from the Japanese student in her retrospective interview above, where she shows her desire to be able to express herself in the same way as she has learnt to do in the cut and thrust of discussion in the United Kingdom, is exactly the kind of attitude that leads Greenholtz (2003) to question the relevance of teaching critical skills to such students. He points to the case of Japanese students returning to Japan after a year abroad stay in Canada. He states:

> I have seen students who have exiled themselves from the Japanese system because they have bought into the superiority of the Socratic approach and the individualist model. They mope around their home campus bewildered and bitter that their newly found ability to criticise and question is not considered praiseworthy in Japan. (Greenholtz, 2003: 128–129)

There is an increasing awareness among TESOL practitioners generally that 'being critical' is culturally relative, and has led to calls not to teach it to all students, for example, Atkinson (1997) and Fox (1994), on the grounds that it is not always beneficial to them. In yet another example of a 'critical' debate, several issues of the journal *TESOL Quarterly* gave space to commentary and counter-commentary on the issue of teaching critical thinking in ELT (Atkinson, 1997; Gieve, 1998; Benesch, 1999). The discussion points included the question of whether critical thinking was a decontextualised higher-order cognitive skill or a social practice, whether L2 students from cultural backgrounds where critical thinking was not the main focus of teaching and learning should be taught critical thinking at all, and whether it was a monologic or dialogic process in the Habermasian mode of communicative action.

Reformulating the Basis for a Critical Culture

In the above debate, Gieve, in particular, argues strongly for a position on critical thinking that relates to the Habermasian theory of communicative action, by emphasising the dialogic dynamics of their various interactions and the potential for subjecting them to all three types of Habermas's validity claims (Habermas, 1984), not just claims to truth underlying statements, but ethical claims to normative rightness inherent in actions and human relationships and claims to sincerity or truthfulness made by speakers, in the course of critical reflection. This view, which may be seen as a strong version of being in favour of being critical, chimes very much with the philosopher of higher education, Barnett's (1997) scheme of criticality and critical being, which also draws on Habermas's theory. Barnett has devoted a whole book to the issue of what he terms 'criticality' (Barnett, 1997).

The Higher Education Business of being Critical

In the title of his book *Higher Education: A Critical Business*, Barnett (1997) neatly encapsulates the current ambiguity of both the term 'critical', and the purpose of higher education in general. The evolution of the university into a business turns 'being critical' into one of its most cherished products, and it is ubiquitous in the specification of learning outcomes. At the same time, higher education is a 'critical' business in much the same way as a patient can suffer from a 'critical' illness. Its survival is on the line. The turn to managing higher education as a business, improving the factory line production of critical thinkers, as it were, has put the traditional ethos of higher education and criticality on the line. Barnett's main message, however, relates to enhancing the role of higher education in developing the 'critical person'. This is done in a spirit of critique of the more superficial lip-service that is paid to 'being critical'. Barnett recuperates a sense of the old liberal notions of higher education and at the same time takes forward the Enlightenment project of emancipation, drawing on Habermas's philosophically, politically and ethically based outline of a 'communicative rationality' (Habermas, 1984, 1989). Habermas argues for a communicative rationality in preference to the means-ends, rational purposive or instrumental, rationality, which he sees as predominating in contemporary society.

Barnett discerns four levels of criticality, putting the older, perhaps tainted version of 'critical skills' on the lower rung of his vertical system (Barnett, 1997: 75). As indicated in an earlier book on higher education (Entwistle, 1984), higher education lecturers' perceptions of what study in their discipline promoted, converged on the development of critical skills. It seems that every academic discipline wants its students to develop critical skills, to be able to critically analyse or evaluate certain issues germane to the field. However, under the influence of prevailing quality assurance regimes, the word 'critical' and its various collocates are likely to be detailed as a specific learning outcome in many different fields of study. This perspective has also led to technologising of 'critical skills' and the creation of programmes of skills development abstracted from their contexts of application, hence the tainted image, and the placing of critical skills on the lowest level of Barnett's scheme of criticality.

At Level 2, Barnett places 'reflexivity', that is reflection on one's own understanding; at Level 3 is 'a refashioning of traditions' and at Level 4 comes 'transformatory critique' or a re-framing of knowledge. However, what Barnett is crucially (or even critically) concerned with is not the domain of knowledge within which these levels are ascertained, but how they transfer beyond the academy to the domains of self and world. If criticality is constrained within the academy, then 'we shall reinforce the truncated sense of critical being that we have today in higher education' (Barnett, 1997: 76). In the domain of the world, those four levels of criticality translate as at Level 1, problem-solving or means-end instrumentalism; at

Level 2, reflective practice (adaptability, flexibility); at Level 3, mutual understanding and development of traditions; and at Level 4, critique-in-action (collective reconstruction). Barnett suggests that what criticality requires as action in the world is a critical 'disposition'. Such a disposition or 'critical spirit' is:

> not to be caught by talk of skills; by images of mere behavioural accomplishment, of techniques to get by with. Fundamentally it is about the kinds of people, of persons, that we are trying in higher education to help to bring about. (Barnett, 1997: 87)

As for critical self-reflection, Barnett is similarly scathing of what currently transpires (Barnett, 1997: 101):

> Higher levels of self-reflection, implied by notions of *Bildung* and even liberal education, let alone emancipation and self- empowerment, are not seriously on this agenda [the fulfilment of extramural agendas].

Four levels of criticality identified for self-reflection are self-monitoring to given standards and norms; self-reflection (reflection on one's own projects); development of self within traditions; and reconstruction of self. Barnett's ultimate project is what he calls a 'curriculum for critical being'. Critical being is where the three kinds of criticality, critical reason, critical self-reflection and critical action, come together.

Strikingly, Barnett's example of the highest level of criticality, of the critical person, acting in some way to transform society is of a young Chinese student standing in front of a line of tanks in Tienanmen Square. Such ultimate critical action is of course open to anyone anywhere in the world, and in terms of confronting state violence, is not new historically. In this way, however, he implicitly references the global applicability of criticality or critical being. While Barnett still situates the source of developing critical being in higher education, the rapidly internationalising context of contemporary higher education makes such a universalising discourse problematic. Barnett's critique of the superficial treatment of 'being critical' and his hierarchical structuring of levels of attainment for criticality, ending with the ontological notion of critical being, serve not least to underpin the importance of a notion of 'the critical' in the western intellectual tradition. By effectively positioning anyone in the world within this occidentalist educational ideal of criticality, what Barnett leaves out of account is the way in which language is used to enact this criticality, its rhetoricity, and to understand the notion of critical being. Furthermore, despite the fact that Chinese culture also spawns critical beings (as seen in the image of the student in front of the tank), it, along with other cultures, does not have a genealogically rooted intellectual culture of discursive critique, which has evolved to maintain the value of 'the critical'.

Critique: An Occidentalist Aporia?

Given not only the ideological embedding of a culture of critique in the western academic tradition, but also the fact that 'critique' is the mode of opposing a dominant way of doing things, there arises the vexed question of how we can go about critiquing critique, or whether we should. As Appadurai states in the context of a related cultural keyword, namely 'research':

> It is so much part of the ground on which we stand and the air we breathe that it resists conscious scrutiny. (Appadurai, 2001: 10)

In the context of globalisation, and the currently undisputed dominance of the 'western' academy, Appadurai makes the distinction between 'weak internationalisation' and 'strong internationalisation'. By 'weak internationalisation' he understands a situation whereby the community of researchers 'take the elements that constitute the hidden armature of our research ethic as given and unquestionable and proceed to look around for those who join us'. By contrast, 'strong internationalisation' is 'to imagine and invite a conversation about research in which ... the very elements of this ethic could be subjects of debate'. This latter option, he further states (Appadurai, 2001: 16):

> Is the surer way to create communities and conventions of research in which membership does not require unquestioned prior adherence to a quite specific research ethic. (Appadurai, 2001: 16)

The question is: is the culture of critique a 'quite specific research ethic' to which 'unquestioned prior adherence' is required? Appadurai's 'strong' procedure in 'inviting conversation' once more reiterates the trope of dialogue, and ultimately may not be that different from Tannen's preference for dialogue over agonism, or Habermas's 'communicative action', on which Barnett, speaking for the context of higher education as a whole, and Gieve, speaking in the context of TESOL, premised their arguments for the value of criticism. What we have here is an occidentalist aporia.

Performative Prospects

Barnett's is ultimately a top-down vision of what the enterprise of higher education should be about. It contrasts with an evolving picture of

what the international university is/does, from a rather bottom-up perspective of performativity, as witnessed in aspects of the intercultural
dynamics discussed and illustrated throughout this book. At the basis of
the dynamics of intercultural communication lies a paradox. On the one
hand, it is the intercultural interactions that bring into the spotlight the
continuing power/knowledge effects of both the assumptions of a Socratic
dialogue as the prototypical template for tutor–student interaction in a
western institution, and the Confucian dynamics of following the tutor/
master in, often silent, observance. On the other hand, it is the intercultural dynamics itself, its own performative effects, that are in fact destabi-
lising, and possibly dislodging the respective hegemonies of the intellectual
traditions. The performative dimension also foregrounds the ongoing creation of different kinds of student and tutor subjectivity, which the experience and enactment of contemporary international education is perforce
producing. By suggesting that intercultural interaction is helping to produce new kinds of subjectivity for contemporary international higher education, however, this is not simply to assume that participation in
international education of itself creates an internationalised subjectivity.
Such experiences may even reinforce a particularly ethnocentric perspective, or reinforce preconceived stereotypes as some studies of the perceptions of students on 'year-abroad' programmes have shown, for example,
Coleman (2001). Similarly, the aspiration towards having internationally
educated subjects, which may be espoused in the various internationalisation strategies of universities and governments around the globe, does not
simply make it happen.

To the extent that the prevailing hegemony of western institutional
practices is resisted, one critical question is: will the pedagogical delivery
of a culture of critique be sustained, might it crumble under critiques of its
hegemony or might it transform itself in the process of intercultural performance? Perhaps the only viable strategy is to keep it 'sous rature'
(under erasure) as Derrida puts it, a strategy that Hall also uses for what
he calls 'thinking at the limit' in postcoloniality (Hall, 1996), and see what
emerges.

The contemporary encounters of British tutors and East Asian students
illuminate differing genealogical practices of tutor and student subject formation whose intercultural encounters in the current moment of globalis-
ing education are themselves creating a pedagogic borderland, possibly a
'third space' (Bhabha, 1990, 1994; Kramsch, 1998), although for me, this
concept still has a sense of boundaries and enclosure. With the idea of
performativity, there need be no goal of a merged or hybrid intercultural
space, which accommodates the expectations on both sides, nor need there

be a wish for an ideal consensus on how best to interact, as may be inferred in the idealising tenor of hope for intercultural communication in much of the literature, for example, Young (1996). The scope here is modest. The ongoing performative of the intercultural is itself a dynamic of change in contemporary international higher education. It occurs in micro-level exchanges and behaviours between tutors and students. It is nonetheless a mark of resistance against the hegemony of taken-for-granted practice. As Zylinska has put it in relation to performativity theory in general:

> Distinctions between 'theory' and 'practice', 'ethics' and 'politics', 'value' and 'fact', or putting it crudely, between 'thinking about how things should be' and 'doing something about it', collapse when we analyse them through the notion of performativity, which – by describing the status quo – simultaneously establishes a certain reality. This process is, 'theoretically' at least, interminable. (Zylinska, 2005: 5)

While processes of globalisation at large, and the internationalisation of higher education in particular, continue, pedagogic practices can perhaps best be seen as performatively emergent.

References

Aitchison, C. and Lee, A. (2006) Research writing: Problems and pedagogies. *Teaching in Higher Education* 11 (3), 265–278.

Allison, D. (1996) Pragmatist discourse and English for academic purposes. *English for Specific Purposes* 15 (2), 85–103.

Allison, D. (1998) Research and discussion note. Response to Pennycook: Whether, why and how. *English for Specific Purposes* 17 (3), 313–316.

Althusser, L. (1971) Ideology and ideological state apparatuses. In *Lenin and Philosophy and Other Essays*. London: New Left Books.

Andrews, R. (1995) *Teaching and Learning Argument*. London: Cassell Education.

Appadurai, A. (1990) Disjuncture and difference in the global cultural economy. In M. Featherstone (ed.) *Global Culture: Nationalism, Globalisation and Modernity*. London: Sage.

Appadurai, A. (1996) *Modernity at Large: Cultural Dimensions of Globalization*. Minneapolis: University of Minnesota Press.

Appadurai, A. (ed.) (2001) *Globalization*. Durham and London: Duke University Press.

Ashcroft, B., Griffiths, G. and Tiffin, H. (2002) *The Empire Writes Back: Theory and Practice in Post-Colonial Literatures*. London: Routledge.

Atkinson, D. (1997) A critical approach to critical thinking in TESOL. *TESOL Quarterly* 31 (1), 71–94.

Austin, J.L. (1955) *How to do Things with Words*. Oxford: Oxford University Press.

Baker, G.P. and Hacker, P.M.S. (1984) *Language, Sense and Nonsense*. Oxford: Basil Blackwell.

Bakhtin, M. (1981) *The Dialogical Imagination*. Austin: University of Texas Press.

Bakhtin, M. (1986) *Speech Genres and Other Late Essays*. Austin: University of Texas Press.

Ballard, B. (1996) Through language to learning: Preparing overseas students for study in Western universities. In H. Coleman (ed.) *Society and the Language Classroom*. Cambridge: Cambridge University Press.

Ballard, B. and Clanchy, J. (1991) Assessment by misconception: Cultural influences and intellectual traditions. In L. Hamp-Lyons (ed.) *Assessing Second Language Writing in Academic Contexts*. Norwood, NJ: Ablex.

Bardovi-Harlig, K. and Hartford, B.S. (1990) Congruence in native and nonnative conversations: Status balance in the academic advising session. *Language Learning* 40, 467–501.

Bardovi-Harlig, K. and Hartford, B.S. (1993) Learning the rules of academic talk: A longitudinal study of pragmatic development. *Studies in Second Language Acquisition* 15, 279–304.

Bardovi-Harlig, K. and Hartford, B.S. (1996) Input in an institutional setting. *Studies in Second Language Acquisition* 18, 171–188.

Barnett, R.A. (1985) Higher education: Legitimation crisis. *Studies in Higher Education* 10, 241–255.

Barnett, R.A. (1990) *The Idea of Higher Education.* Buckingham: Society for Research into Higher Education & Open University Press.

Barnett, R.A. (1997) *Higher Education: A Critical Business.* Buckingham: Society for Research into Higher Education and Open University Press.

Barnett, R.A. (2000) *Realizing the University in an Age of Supercomplexity.* Buckingham: Society for Research into Higher Education & Open University Press.

Barnett, R.A. (2003) *Beyond All Reason. Living with Ideology in the University.* Buckingham: Society for Research into Higher Education & Open University Press.

Barnlund, D.C. (1989) *Communicative Styles of Japanese and Americans: Images and Realities.* Belmont, CA: Wadsworth Publishing Company.

Barthes, R. (1990) *S/Z.* Oxford: Basil Blackwell.

Barthes, R. (1993) *Mythologies.* London: Vintage Books.

Bartholomae, D. (1985) Inventing the university. In M. Rose (ed.) *When a Writer Can't Write: Studies in Writer's Block and Other Composing Process Problems.* New York: Guildford Press.

Bauman, Z. (2000) *Liquid Modernity.* Cambridge: Polity.

Bauman, Z. (2003) *Liquid Love: On the Frailty of Human Bonds.* Cambridge: Polity Press.

Bauman, Z. (2005) *Liquid Life.* Cambridge: Polity Press.

Bazerman, C. (1988) *Shaping Written Knowledge.* Madison: University of Wisconsin Press.

Belcher, D. and Braine, G. (ed.) (1995) *Academic Writing in a Second Language: Essays on Research and Pedagogy.* Norwood, NJ: Ablex.

Bell, V. (ed.) (1999) *Performativity and Belonging.* London: Thousand Oaks and New Delhi: Sage.

Bellah, R., Madsen, R., Sullivan, W., Swidler, A. and Tipton, S. (1985) *Habits of the Heart: Individualism and Commitment in American Life.* New York, NY: Harper & Row.

Benesch, S. (1993) ESL, ideology and the politics of pragmatism. *TESOL Quarterly* 27, 705–717.

Benesch, S. (1999) Thinking critically, thinking dialogically. *TESOL Quarterly* 33, 573–580.

Benesch, S. (2001) *Critical English for Academic Purposes. Theory, Politics, and Practice.* Mahwah, NJ: Lawrence Erlbaum Associates.

Berger, P.L., Berger, B. and Kellner, H. (1973) *The Homeless Mind: Modernisation and Consciousness.* New York, NY: Random House.

Berkenkotter, C. and Huckin, T. (1995) *Genre Knowledge in Disciplinary Communication.* Hillsdale, NJ and Hove: Lawrence Erlbaum Associates.

Bernstein, B.B. (1990) *The Structuring of Pedagogic Discourse (Class, Codes and Control).* London: Routledge.

Bernstein, R.J. (1986) *Philosophical Profiles. Essays in a Pragmatic Mode.* Cambridge: Polity Press.

Best, S. and Kellner, D. (1991) *Postmodern Theory: Critical Interrogations*. Basingstoke and London: Macmillan Education Ltd.

Bex, T. (1999) Representations of English in twentieth century Britain: Fowler, Gowers and Partridge. In T. Bex and R.J. Watts (eds) *Standard English. The Widening Debate*. London and New York: Routledge.

Bex, T. and Watts, R.J. (1999) *Standard English: The Widening Debate*. London: Routledge.

Bhabha, H.K. (ed.) (1990) *Nation and Narration*. London and New York: Routledge.

Bhabha, H.K. (1994) *The Location of Culture*. London: Routledge.

Biggs, J. (2005) Western misperceptions of the Confucian-heritage learning culture. In D. Watkins and J. Biggs (eds) *The Chinese Learner: Cultural, Psychological and Contextual Influences*. Hong Kong: Comparative Education Research Centre. The University of Hong Kong.

Billig, M. (1987) *Arguing and Thinking: A Rhetorical Approach to Social Psychology*. Cambridge: Cambridge University Press.

Birch, D. (1989) *Language, Literature, and Critical Practice: Ways of Analyzing Texts*. London: Routledge.

Bizzell, P. and Herzberg, B. (eds) (1990) *The Rhetorical Tradition*. Boston: Bedford Books.

Bizzell, P., Schroeder, C. and Fox, H. (eds) (2002) *Alternative Discourses in the Academy*. Portsmouth, NH: Boynton/Cook, Heinemann.

Blum-Kulka, S., House, J. and Kasper, G. (1989) *Cross-Cultural Pragmatics: Apology and Request*. Norwood, NJ: Ablex.

Bond, M.H. (1991) *Beyond the Chinese Face: Insights from Psychology*. Hong Kong: Oxford University Press.

Bond, M.H., Zegarac, V. and Spencer-Oatey, H. (2000) Culture as an explanatory variable: Problems and possibilities. In H. Spencer-Oatey (ed.) *Culturally Speaking. Managing Rapport through Talk across Cultures*. London, New York: Continuum.

Bourdieu, P. (1977) *Outline of a Theory of Practice*. Cambridge: Cambridge University Press.

Bourdieu, P. (1984) *Distinction: A Social Critique of the Judgement of Taste*. London: Routledge and Kegan Paul.

Bourdieu, P. (1988) *Homo Academicus*. Cambridge: Polity Press.

Bourdieu, P. (1992) *Language and Symbolic Power*. Cambridge, MA: Harvard University Press.

Bourdieu, P. and Passeron, J.C. (1977) *Reproduction in Education, Society and Culture*. London, Beverly Hills: Sage Publications.

Brereton, J.C. (1995) *The Origins of Composition Studies in the American College, 1875–1925. A Documentary History*. Pittsburgh: University of Pittsburgh Press.

Brown, P. and Levinson, S. (1987) *Politeness: Some Universals in Language Usage*. Cambridge: Cambridge University Press.

Burgen, A. (ed.) (1996) *Goals and Purposes of Higher Education in the 21st Century*. London: Jessica Kingsley.

Butler, J. (1997) *Excitable Speech: A Politics of the Performative*. New York and London: Routledge.

Butler, J. (2006) *Gender Trouble: Feminism and the Subversion of Identity*. New York, London: Routledge.

Buttjes, D. and Byram, M. (eds) (1990) *Mediating Languages and Cultures: Towards an Intercultural Theory of Foreign Language Education.* Clevedon: Multilingual Matters.

Byram, M. (1997a) Cultural studies and foreign language teaching. In S. Bassnett (ed.) *Studying British Cultures.* London & New York: Routledge.

Byram, M. (1997b) *Teaching and Assessing Intercultural Communicative Competence.* Clevedon: Multilingual Matters.

Byram, M. (ed.) (2004) *Routledge Encyclopedia of Language and Learning.* London: Routledge.

Byram, M. and Grundy, P. (eds) (2003) *Context and Culture in Language Teaching and Learning.* Clevedon: Multilingual Matters.

Byram, M. and Morgan, C. (eds) (1994) *Teaching-and-Learning Language-and-Culture.* Clevedon: Multilingual Matters.

Cameron, D. (1995) *Verbal Hygiene.* London: Routledge.

Cameron, D. (2001) *Working with Spoken Discourse.* London: Sage.

Canagarajah, A.S. (1999) *Resisting Linguistic Imperialism in English Teaching.* Oxford: Oxford University Press.

Canagarajah, A.S. (2002a) *A Geopolitics of Academic Writing.* Pittsburgh: University of Pittsburgh Press.

Canagarajah, A.S. (2002b) *Critical Academic Writing and Multilingual Students.* Ann Arbor, MI: University of Michigan Press.

Canagarajah, A.S. (2004) Subversive identities, pedagogical safe houses, and critical learning. In B. Norton and K. Toohey (eds) *Critical Pedagogies and Language Learning.* Cambridge: Cambridge University Press.

Canagarajah, S. (2006) Negotiating the local in English as a Lingua Franca. *Annual Review of Applied Linguistics* 26, 197–218.

Candlin, C. and Hyland, K. (1999) *Writing: Texts, Processes and Practices.* London: Longman.

Carson, J.G., Chase, N., Gibson, S. and Hargrove, M. (1992) Literacy demands of the undergraduate curriculum. *Reading Research and Instruction* 31, 25–50.

Carter, R. (1997) *Investigating English Discourse. Language, Literacy and Literature.* London and New York: Routledge.

Carter, R. and Nash, W. (1990) *Seeing Through Language.* London: Basil Blackwell.

Carter, S-A. (1998) *Access to Success Literacy in Academic Contexts.* South Africa: Juta Academic.

Carter, S-A. (2000) *Stolen Language? Plagiarism in Writing.* London: Pearson Education Limited.

Celce-Murcia, M. (ed.) (2001) *Teaching English as a Second or Foreign Language.* Boston: Heinle & Heinle.

Chen, J. (1990) *Confucius as a Teacher.* Beijing: Foreign Language Press.

Cheng, X. (2000) Asian students' reticence revisited. *System* 28, 435–446.

Cherryholmes, C. (1988) *Power and Criticism: Poststructural Investigations in Education.* New York: New York Teachers College Press.

Chick, J.K. (1985) The interactional accomplishment of discrimination in South Africa. *Language in Society* 14, 299–326.

Code, L (1995) *Rhetorical Spaces.* London: Routledge.

Colebrook, C. (1999) A grammar of becoming: Strategy, subjectivism, and style. In E. Grosz (ed.) *Becomings Explorations in Time, Memory, and Futures.* Ithaca and London: Cornell University Press.

Coleman, J. (2001) Language learner attitudes and student residence abroad: New quantitative and qualitative insights. In D. Killick, M. Parry and A. Phipps (eds) *Mapping the Territory: The Poetics and Praxis of Languages and Intercultural Communication*. Glasgow: Glasgow University Publications in French and German.

Connors, R.J. (1990) Overwork/underpay: Labor and status of composition teachers since 1880. *Rhetoric Review* 9, 108–125.

Corbett, J. (2003) *An Intercultural Approach to English Language Teaching*. Clevedon: Multilingual Matters.

Cottingham, J. (1988) *The Rationalists*. Oxford, New York: Oxford University Press.

Coulmas, F. (1981) *Conversational Routine. Explorations in Standardized Communication Situations and Prepatterned Speech*. Berlin: Mouton.

Coulmas, F. (1992) Linguistic etiquette in Japanese society. In R.J. Watts, S. Ide and K. Ehlich (eds) *Politeness in Language. Studies in its History, Theory and Practice*. Berlin: Mouton de Gruyter.

Coupland, N. (2000) Sociolinguistic prevarication about 'standard English'. *Journal of Sociolinguistics* 4 (4), 622–634.

Cox, B. (1991) *Cox on Cox: An English Curriculum for the 1990s*. London: Hodder and Stoughton.

Crosbie, V. (2005) Future directions for modern languages in the higher education landscape: An interview with Alison Phipps and Mike Gonzalez. *Language and Intercultural Communication* 5 (3 & 4), 294–303.

Crowley, T. (1989) *The Politics of Discourse: The Standard Language Question in British Cultural Debates*. London: Macmillan.

Crowley, T. (1991) *Proper English? Readings in Language, History and Cultural Identity*. London and New York: Routledge.

Culler, J. (1982) *On Deconstruction: Theory and Criticism after Structuralism*. Ithaca, NY: Cornell University Press.

Davidson, C. and Tomic, A. (1999) Inventing academic literacy: An American perspective. In C. Jones, J. Turner and B. Street (eds) *Students Writing in the University: Cultural and Epistemological Issues*. Amsterdam: John Benjamins.

Davies, S., Swinburne, D. and Williams, G. (eds) (2006) *Writing Matters*. London: The Royal Literary Fund.

Dawson, R. (1981) *Confucius*. Oxford: Oxford University Press.

De Bary, W.T. (1983) *The Liberal Tradition in China*. Hong Kong: The Chinese University of Hong Kong Press.

De Bary, W.T. (1989) Chu Hsi's aims as an educator. In W.T. De Bary and J.W. Chaffee (eds). *Neo-Confucian Education: The Formative Stage*. Berkeley; London: University of California Press, 183–218.

De Bary, W.T. (2007) *Confucian Tradition and Global Education*. New York, NY: Columbia University Press.

Dearing, R (1997) *Higher Education in the Learning Society*. Leeds: National Committee of Inquiry into Higher Education.

Deleuze, G. and Guattari, F. (1983) *Anti-Oedipus*. Minneapolis, MN: University of Minnesota Press.

Derrida, J. (1974) *Of Grammatology*. Baltimore, MD: The Johns Hopkins University Press.

Derrida, J. (1977) Signature event context. *Glyph* 1, 172–197.

Derrida, J. (1978) *Writing and Difference.* London: Routledge and Kegan Paul.

Derrida, J. (1981) *Dissemination.* London: Athlone Press.

Ding, H. (2008) Living through ambiguity. Unpublished PhD thesis. Goldsmiths, University of London.

Doi, T. (1973) *The Anatomy of Dependence.* Tokyo: Kodansha International.

Doi, T. (1981) *The Anatomy of Dependence.* Tokyo: Kodansha International.

Dreyfus, H.L. and Rabinow, P. (eds) (1982) *Michel Foucault: Beyond Structuralism and Hermeneutics.* Chicago: The Harvester Press Ltd.

Dudley-Evans, T. and St. John, M.J. (1998) *Developments in English for Specific Purposes A Multidisciplinary Approach.* Cambridge: Cambridge University Press.

English, F. (1999) What do students really say in their essays? Towards a descriptive framework for analysing student writing. In C. Jones, J. Turner and B. Street (eds) *Students Writing in the University.* Amsterdam: John Benjamins.

Entwistle, N. (1984) Contrasting perspectives on learning. In F. Marton, D. Housell, and N. Entwistle (eds) *The Experience of Learning.* Edinburgh: Scottish Academic Press.

Eriksson, G. (1980) The botanical success of Linnaeus. The aspect of organisation and publicity. In G. Broberg (ed.) *Linnaeus: Progress and Prospects.* Pittsburgh & Stockholm: Linnaean Research.

Fairclough, N. (1995) *Critical Discourse Analysis.* London and New York: Longman.

Fairclough, N. (1996) A reply to Henry Widdowson's 'discourse analysis: A critical view. *Language and Literature* 5 (1), 49–56.

Filmer, P., Jenks, C., Seale, C. and Walsh, D. (1998) Developments in social theory. In C. Seale (ed.) *Researching Society and Culture.* London: Sage.

Fitzgerald, H. (2003) *How Different Are We? Spoken Discourse in Intercultural Communication.* Clevedon: Multilingual Matters.

Flowerdew, J. and Peacock, M. (eds) (2001) *Research Perspectives on English for Academic Purposes.* Cambridge: Cambridge University Press.

Fortier, A-M. (1999) Re-membering places and the performance of belonging(s). In V. Bell (ed.) *Performativity and Belonging.* London: Sage.

Foucault, M. (1970) *The Order of Things.* London: Tavistock Publications.

Foucault, M. (1973a) *Madness and Civilisation.* New York, NY: Vintage Books.

Foucault, M. (1973b) *The Archaeology of Medical Perception.* New York, NY: Vintage Books.

Foucault, M. (1973c) *The Birth of the Clinic.* London: Tavistock.

Foucault, M. (1977) *Discipline and Punish: The Birth of the Prison.* Harmondsworth: Penguin.

Foucault, M. (1978) *The History of Sexuality, Volume 1: An Introduction.* New York, NY: Pantheon.

Foucault, M. (1980) *Power/Knowledge: Selected Interviews and Other Writings 1972–1977.* Brighton: Harvester.

Foucault, M. (1982) The subject and power. In H.L. a. R. Dreyfus, Paul (ed.) *Michel Foucault: Beyond Structuralism and Hermeneutics.* Chicago: The Harvester Press Ltd.

Foucault, M. (1991) Politics and the study of discourse. In G. Burchell, C. Gordon and P. Miller (eds) *The Foucault Effect Studies in Governmentality.* London: Harvester Wheatsheaf.

Fowler, H.W. (1926) *A Dictionary of Modern English Usage.* Oxford: Oxford University Press.

Fowler, R., Hodge, R., Kress, G. and Trew, T. (1979) *Language and Control.* London: Routledge & Kegan-Paul.

Fox, H. (1994) *Listening to the World: Cultural Issues in Academic Writing.* Urbana IL: National Council of Teachers of English.

Gadamer, H-G. (1975 & 1988) *Truth and Method.* London: Sheed & Ward.

Gardner, H. (1989) *To Open Minds.* New York, NY: Basic Books.

Gee, J.P. (1990) *Social Linguistics and Literacies: Ideology in Discourses.* London: Falmer Press.

Gee, J.P. (1996) *Social Linguistics and Literacies. Ideology in Discourses.* London: Falmer Press.

Gee, J.P. (2000) The New Literacy Studies; from "socially situated" to the work of the social. In D. Barton, M. Hamilton and R. Ivanic (eds) *Situated Literacies: Reading and Writing in Context.* London: Routledge.

Gee, J.P., Hull, G. and Lankshear, C. (1996) *The New Work Order: Behind the Language of the New Capitalism.* St Leonard's, Australia: Allen & Unwin.

Gieve, S. (1998) Comments on Dwight Atkinson's "A critical approach to critical thinking in TESOL." A Reader Reacts ... In The Forum. *TESOL Quarterly* 32, 123–129.

Giroux, H.A. (1992) *Border Crossings. Cultural Workers and the Politics of Education.* New York: Routledge.

Good, G. (1988) *The Observing Self: Rediscovering the Essay.* New York: Routledge.

Gowers, E. (1954) *The Complete Plain Words.* Oxford: Oxford University Press.

Graddol, D. (2001) English in the future. In A. Burns and C. Coffin (eds) *Analysing English in a Global Context.* London: Routledge.

Greenholtz, J. (2003) Socratic teachers and Confucian learners: Examining the benefits and pitfalls of a year abroad. *Language and Intercultural Communication* 3 (2), 122–130.

Grice, H.P. (1975) Logic and conversation. In P. Cole and J.L. Morgan (eds) *Syntax and Semantics, Vol. 3. Speech Acts* (pp. 41–58). New York, London: Academic Press.

Gudykunst, W.B. (ed.) (1993) *Communication in Japan and the United States.* New York: State University of New York.

Guilherme, M. (2002) *Critical Citizens for an Intercultural World: Foreign Language Education as Cultural Politics.* Clevedon: Multilingual Matters.

Guilherme, M. (2007) English as a global language and education for cosmopolitan citizenship. *Language and Intercultural Communication* 7, 72–90.

Gumperz, J. and Levinson, S. (1991) Rethinking linguistic relativity. *Current Anthropology* 32 (5), 613–623.

Guthrie, W.K.C. (1961) *Plato. Protagoras and Meno.* London: The Penguin Classics.

Habermas, J. (1984) *Theory of Communicative Action.* Cambridge: Polity.

Habermas, J. (1989) *The Theory of Communicative Action.* Cambridge: Polity.

Haggis, T. (2006) Pedagogies for diversity: Retaining critical challenge amidst fears of 'dumbing down'. *Studies in Higher Education* 31 (5), 521–535.

Hall, D. and Ames, R.T. (1987) *Thinking through Confucius.* Albany: State University of New York Press.

Hall, S. (1992) The west and the rest: Discourse and power. In S. Hall and B. Gieben (eds) *Formations of Modernity.* Oxford: Polity Press in Association with the Open University.

Hall, S. (1996) 'When was the post-colonial'? Thinking at the limit. In I. Chambers and L. Curti (eds) *The Post-Colonial Question Common Skies, Divided Horizons.* London: Routledge.

Halliday, M.A.K. (1978) *Language as Social Semiotic.* London: Edward Arnold.

Halliday, M.A.K. (1994) The construction of knowledge and value in the grammar of scientific discourse, with reference to Charles Darwin's *The Origin of Species.* In M. Coulthard (ed.) *Advances in Written Text Analysis.* London: Routledge.

Hare, R.M. (1991) *Plato' in Founders of Thought.* Oxford: Oxford University Press.

Harwood, N. and Hadley, G. (2004) Demystifying institutional practices: Critical pragmatism and the teaching of academic writing. *English for Specific Purposes* 23, 355–377.

Henriques, J., Hollway, W., Urwin, C., Venn, C. and Walkerdine, V. (1984) *Changing the Subject.* New York, NY: Methuen.

Hensher, P. (2006) The awful truth about our universities. *The Independent*, 23 March.

Hinkel, E. (ed.) (1999a) *Culture in Second Language Teaching and Learning.* Cambridge: Cambridge University Press.

Hinkel, E. (1999b) Objectivity and credibility in L1 and L2 academic writing. In E. Hinkel (ed.) *Culture in Second Language Teaching and Learning.* Cambridge: Cambridge University Press.

Hiraga, M.K. (1998) Japanese metaphors for learning. *Intercultural Communication Studies* VII (2), 7–22.

Hiraga, M.K. and Turner, J. (1995) What to say next? The sociopragmatic problem of elaboration for Japanese students of English in academic contexts. *JACET Journal* 10, 13–30.

Hobbes, T. (1985 [1651]) *Leviathan.* London: Penguin Classics.

Hobsbaum, P. (1984) Standards of written expression among undergraduates. In R. Williams, J. Swales and K. John (eds) *Common Ground: Shared Interests in ESP and Communication Studies.* Oxford: Pergamon, in association with the British Council.

Hodge, R. and Kress, G. (1988) *Social Semiotics.* Oxford: Polity Press.

Hofstede, G. (1980) *Culture's Consequences.* Newbury Park, CA: Sage.

Holbrook, S.E. (1991) Women's work: The feminizing of composition. *Rhetoric Review* 9, 201–229.

Holliday, A. (2009) The role of culture in English language education: Key challenges. *Language and Intercultural Communication* 9 (3), 144–155.

Holmes, P. (2006) Problematising intercultural communication competence in the pluricultural classroom: Chinese students in a New Zealand University. *Language and Intercultural Communication* 6 (1), 18–34.

Holquist, M. (1990) *Dialogism Bakhtin and his World.* London: Routledge.

House, J. (2006) Unity in diversity: English as a Lingua Franca for Europe. In C. Leung and J. Jenkins (eds) *Reconfiguring Europe The Contribution of Applied Linguistics.* London: British Association for Applied Linguistics in association with Equinox.

Hyland, K. (1994) Hedging in academic writing and EAP textbooks. *English for Specific Purposes* 13 (3), 239–256.

Hyland, K. (2000) *Disciplinary Discourses: Social Interactions in Academic Writing.* Essex: Pearson Education Ltd.

Ivanic, R. (1998) *Writing and Identity. The Discoursal Construction of Identity in Academic Writing*. Amsterdam: John Benjamins.

Ivanic, R. (2004) Discourses of writing and learning to write. *Language and Education* 18 (3), 220–245.

Jack, G. (2004) Language(s), intercultural communication and the machinations of global capital: Towards a dialectical critique. *Language and Intercultural Communication* 4 (3), 121–133.

Jardine, L. (1999) *Ingenious Pursuits. Building the Scientific Revolution*. London: Abacus.

Jaworski, A. and Sachdev, I. (2004) Teachers' beliefs about students' talk and silence. In A. Jaworski, N. Coupland and D. Galasinski (eds) *Metalanguage: Social and Ideological Perspectives*. Berlin: Mouton de Gruyter.

Jenkins, J. (2000) *The Phonology of English as an International Language. New Models, New Norms, New Goals*. Oxford: Oxford University Press.

Jenkins, J. (2006) Current perspectives on teaching world Englishes and English as a Lingua Franca. *TESOL Quarterly* 40 (1), 157–181.

Jin, L. and Cortazzi, M. (1998) Expectations and questions in intercultural classrooms. *Intercultural Communication Studies* VII (2), 37–62.

Johns, A. (1997) *Text, Role, and Context. Developing Academic Literacies*. Cambridge: Cambridge University Press.

Johns, A.M. (1991) Faculty assessment of ESL student literacy skills: Implications for writing assessment. In L. Hamp-Lyons (ed.) *Assessing Second Language Writing in Academic Contexts*. Norwood, NJ: Ablex.

Johnson, L., Lee, A. and Green, B. (2000) The PhD and the autonomous self: Gender, rationality and postgraduate pedagogy. *Studies in Higher Education* 25 (2), 135–147.

Johnson, S. (1755) *A Dictionary of the English Language*. London: Richard Bentley.

Jones, C., Turner, J. and Street, B. (ed.) (1999) *Students Writing in the University: Cultural and Epistemological Issues*. Amsterdam: John Benjamins.

Kachru, B. (1985) Standards, codification and sociolinguistic realism: The English language in the outer circle. In R. Quirk and H.G. Widdowson (eds) *English in the World: Teaching and Learning the Language and Literatures*. Cambridge: Cambridge University Press.

Kachru, B.B. (1988) ESP and non-native varieties of English: Toward a shift in paradigm. In D. a. B. Chamberlain, Robert (ed.) *ESP in the Classroom: Practice and Evaluation*. Hong Kong: Modern English Publications in association with The British Council.

Kachru, B. (ed.) (1992a) *The Other Tongue: English Across Cultures*. Urbana, IL: University of Illinois Press.

Kachru, B.B. (1992b) World Englishes: Approaches, issues and resources. *Language Teaching* 25, 1–14.

Kachru, Y. (1997) Cultural meaning and contrastive rhetoric in English education. *World Englishes* 16 (3), 337–350.

Kasper, G. (1992) Pragmatic transfer. *Second Language Research* 8 (3), 203–231.

Kasulis, T.P. (1990) Intimacy: A general orientation in Japanese religious values. *Philosophy East and West* 40, 434–439.

Kim, H.S. and Markus, H.R. (2002) Freedom of speech and freedom of silence: An analysis of talking as a cultural practice. In R. Shweder, M. Minow and

H.R. Markus (eds) *Engaging Cultural Differences: The Multicultural Challenge in Liberal Democracies*. New York, NY: Russell Sage Foundation.

Kim, Y. (2007) Difficulties in quality doctoral academic advising: Experiences of Korean students. *Journal of Research in International Education* 6, 171–193.

Kincaid, D.L. (ed.) (1987) *Communication Theory: Eastern and Western Perspectives*. New York, NY: Academic Press.

Kirkpatrick, A. (1995) Chinese rhetoric: Methods of argument. *Multilingua* 14 (3), 271–295.

Kirkpatrick, A. (2007) *World Englishes: Implications for International Communication and English Language Teaching*. Cambridge: Cambridge University Press.

Knorr-Cetina, K.D. (1981) *The Manufacture of Knowledge*. Oxford: Pergamon.

Koh, A. (2002) Towards a critical pedagogy: Creating 'thinking skills' in Singapore. *Journal of Curriculum Studies* 34 (3), 255–264.

Kramsch, C. (1993) *Context and Culture in Language Teaching*. Oxford: Oxford University Press.

Kramsch, C. (1998) *Language and Culture*. Oxford: Oxford University Press.

Kress, G. and Fowler, R. (1979) Interviews. In R. Fowler, R. Hodge, G. Kress and T. Trew (eds) *Language and Control* (pp. 63–80). London: Routledge & Kegan-Paul.

Kress, G. and van Leeuwen, T. (2001) *Multimodal Discourse: The Modes and Media of Contemporary Communication*. London: Arnold.

Kubota, R. (1999) Japanese culture constructed by discourses: Implications for applied linguistics research and ELT. *TESOL Quarterly* 33 (1), 9–35.

Lacan, J. (1977) *Écrits: A Selection*. London: Tavistock.

Ladyman, J. (2005) The happy logic of a just feast. *Times Higher Education Supplement*, 18th April, p. 28.

Lakoff, G. and Johnson, M. (1980) *Metaphors We Live By*. Chicago: University of Chicago Press.

Lan, H. (2002) Contrastive rhetoric. A must in cross-cultural inquiries. In P. Bizzell, C. Schroeder and H. Fox (eds) *Alternative Discourses in the Academy*. Portsmouth, NH: Boynton/Cook, Heinemann.

Langer, J.A. (2007) *How Writing Shapes Thinking: A Study of Teaching and Learning*. Colorado State University: WAC Clearinghouse.

Lanham, R.A. (1983) *Literacy and the Survival of Humanism*. New Haven, CT: Yale University Press.

Lave, J. and Wenger, E. (1991) *Situated Learning: Legitimate Peripheral Participation*. New York, NY: Cambridge University Press.

Law, N.W.Y., Yuen, A.H.K., Chan, C.K.K., Yuen, J.K.L., Pan, N.F.C., Lai, M. and Lee, V.S.L. (2009) New experiences, new epistemology, and the pressures of change: The Chinese learner in transition. In C.K.K. Chan and N. Rao (eds) *Revisiting the Chinese Learner*. Comparative Education Research Centre, The University of Hong Kong, Hong Kong: Springer.

Lea, M. (2004) Academic literacies: A pedagogy for course design. *Studies in Higher Education* 23 (2), 157–172.

Lea, M. and Street, B. (1997) *Perspectives on Academic Literacies: An Institutional Approach*. Swindon: Economic and Social Research Council.

Lea, M. and Street, B. (1998) Student writing and staff feedback in higher education: An academic literacies approach. *Studies in Higher Education* 23 (2), 157–172.

Lea, M. and Street, B. (1999) Writing as academic literacies: Understanding textual practices in higher education. In C.N. Candlin and K. Hyland (eds) *Writing: Texts, Processes and Practices*. London: Longman.

Lebra, T.S. (1976) *Japanese Patterns of Behaviour*. Honolulu, HI: The University Press of Hawaii.

Lebra, T.S. (1993) Culture, self and communication in Japan and the United States. In W.B. Gudykunst (ed.) *Communication in Japan and the United States*. New York, Albany: State University of New York.

Lee, G. (2009) Speaking up: Six Korean students' oral participation in class discussions in US graduate seminars. *English for Specific Purposes* 28, 142–156.

Lee, W.O. (2005) The cultural context for Chinese learners: Conceptions of learning in the Confucian tradition. In D. Watkins and J. Biggs (eds) *The Chinese Learner: Cultural, Psychological and Contextual Influences*. Comparative Education Research Centre, University of Hong Kong and The Australian Council for Educational Research Ltd.

Leech, G. and Thomas, J. (1990) Language, meaning and context: Pragmatics. In N. E. Collinge (ed.) *An Encyclopaedia of Language*. London: Routledge.

Leith, D. (1983) *A Social Hisoty of English*. London: Routledge.

Leki, I. (2001) A narrow thinking system: Nonnative-English speaking students in group projects across the curriculum. *TESOL Quarterly* 35, 39–67.

Leung, C. (2005) Convivial communication: Recontextualising communicative competence. *International Journal of Applied Linguistics* 15, 119–144.

Li, J. (2009) Learning to self-perfect: Chinese beliefs about learning. In C.K.K. Chan and N. Rao (eds) *Revisiting the Chinese Learner Changing Contexts, Changing Education*. Comparative Education Research Centre, the University of Hong Kong, Hong Kong: Springer.

Lillis, T. (1999) Whose 'common sense'? Essayist literacy and the institutional practice of mystery. In C. Jones, J. Turner and B. Street (eds) *Students Writing in the University: Cultural and Epistemological Issues*. Amsterdam: John Benjamins.

Lillis, T. (2001) *Student Writing. Access, Regulation, Desire*. London: Routledge.

Lillis, T. and Scott, M. (2007) Defining academic literacies research: Issues of epistemology, ideology and strategy. *Journal of Applied Linguistics* 4 (1), 5–32.

Lillis, T. and Turner, J. (2001) Student writing in higher education: Contemporary confusion, traditional concerns. *Teaching in Higher Education* 6 (1), 57–68.

Littlewood, W. (2000) Do Asian students really want to listen and obey? *ELT Journal* 54 (1), 31–36.

Liu, J. (2002) Negotiating silence in American classrooms: Three Chinese cases. *Language and Intercultural Communication* 2 (1), 37–54.

Locke, J. (1975 [1689]) *An Essay Concerning Human Understanding*. Oxford: Clarendon Press.

Loveday, L. (1986) *Explorations in Japanese Sociolinguistics*. Amsterdam: John Benjamins.

Lyotard, J.F. (1984) *The Postmodern Condition*. Minneapolis, MN: University of Minnesota Press.

MacDonald, S.P. (1994) *Professional Academic Writing in the Humanities and Social Sciences*. Carbondale and Edwardsville, IL: Southern Illinois University Press.

Mao, L. (2005) Rhetorical Borderlands: Chinese American rhetoric in the making. *College Composition and Communication* 56 (3), 426–469.

Martin, S.E. (1964) Speech levels in Japan and Korea. In D. Hymes (ed.) *Language in Culture and Society.* New York, NY: Harper & Row.

Marton, F., Hounsell, D. and Entwistle, N. (1984) *The Experience of Learning.* Edinburgh: Scottish Academic Press.

Mauranen, A. (1993) *Cultural Differences in Academic Rhetoric: A Textlinguistic Study.* Bern: Peter Lang.

Maxwell, J.C. (1881) *An Elementary Treatise on Electricity.* Oxford: Clarendon.

McNaughton, W. (1974) *The Confucian Vision.* Ann Arbor, MI: University of Michigan Press.

Miller, S. (1991) *Textual Carnivals: The Politics of Composition.* Carbondale, IL: Southern Illinois University Press.

Ministry of Education (1998) *Thinking Schools, Learning Nation.* Ministry of Education, Singapore.

Mitchell, S. and Evison, A. (2006) Exploiting the potential of writing for educational change at Queen Mary, University of London. In L. Ganobcsik-Williams (ed.) *Teaching Academic Writing in UK Higher Education: Theories, Practices and Models.* Basingstoke, Hampshire: Palgrave Macmillan.

Myers, G. (1996) Strategic vagueness in academic writing. In E. Ventola and Mauranen, A. (eds) *Academic Writing: Intercultural and Textual Issues.* Amsterdam: John Benjamins.

Myerson, G. (1994) *Rhetoric, Reason, and Society. Rationality as Dialogue.* London: Sage.

Nagel, T. (1986) *The View from Nowhere.* Oxford: Oxford University Press.

Nakane, C. (1970) *Japanese Society.* Berkeley: University of California Press.

Nakane, I. (2006) Silence and politeness in intercultural communication in university seminars. *Journal of Pragmatics* 38, 1811–1835.

Nash, W. (1990) Introduction: The stuff these people write. In W. Nash (ed.) *The Writing Scholar. Studies in Academic Discourse.* Newbury Park, CA: Sage.

Newton, I. (1730 [1704]) *Opticks: or a Treatise of the Reflections, Refractions, Inflections and Colours of Light* (4th Edn). London: Printed for William Innys at the West-End of St Paul's.

Nietzsche, F. (1956) *The Genealogy of Morals.* New York, NY: Anchor Books.

Norris, C. (1982) *Deconstruction: Theory and Practice.* London: Methuen.

Norris, C. (1987) *Derrida.* London: Fontana Press.

Norton, L.S. (1990) Essay writing: what really counts. *Higher Education* 20, 441–442.

Norton, B. (2000) *Identity and Language Learning: Gender, Ethnicity and Educational Change.* London: Longman.

Norton, J. (2001) The impact of cultural communication style upon oral proficiency interviews. In D. Killick, M. Parry and A. Phipps (eds) *Poetics and Praxis of Languages and Intercultural Communication.* Glasgow: University of Glasgow.

Nuffield Review. (2006) Higher education focus groups preliminary report. *The Nuffield Review of 14–19, Education and Training.* Oxford: University of Oxford.

Nunan, D. (1998) *Second Language Teaching and Learning.* Boston: Heinle & Heinle.

O'Regan, J.P. and Macdonald, M.N. (2007) Cultural relativism and the discourse of intercultural communication: Aporias of praxis in the intercultural public sphere. *Language and Intercultural Communication* 7 (4), 267–278.

Obelkevich, J. (1987) Proverbs and social history. In P. Burke and R. Porter (eds) *The Social History of Language.* Cambridge: Cambridge University Press.

Odlin, T. (1989) *Language Transfer. Cross-linguistic Influence in Language Learning.* Cambridge: Cambridge University Press.

Onions, C.T. (ed.) (1966) *The Oxford Dictionary of English Etymology.* Oxford: Clarendon Press.

Orr, S. and Blythman, M. (1999) Have you got ten minutes? Can you just sort my dissertation out? In P. Thompson (ed.) *Academic Writing Development in Higher Education.* The University of Reading: Centre for Applied Language Studies.

Palfreyman, D. (ed.) (2001) *The Oxford Tutorial: 'Thanks, you taught me how to think'.* Oxford: OxCheps.

Partridge, E.H. (1947) *Usage and Abusage: A Guide to Good English.* London: Hamish Hamilton.

Pennycook, A. (1994a) Incommensurable discourses? *Applied Linguistics* 15 (2), 115–138.

Pennycook, A. (1994b) *The Cultural Politics of English as an International Language.* London: Longman.

Pennycook, A. (1996) Borrowing others' words: Text, ownership, memory, and plagiarism. *TESOL Quarterly* 30 (2), 201–230.

Pennycook, A. (1997) Vulgar pragmatism, critical pragmatism, and EAP. *English for Specific Purposes* 16 (4), 253–269.

Pennycook, A. (2007) *Global Englishes and Transcultural Flows.* London: Routledge.

Perelman, C. (1981) *The Realm of Rhetoric.* Notre Dame: University of Notre Dame Press.

Phillipson, R. (1992) *Linguistic Imperialism.* Oxford: Oxford University Press.

Phipps, A. (2003) Languages, identities, agencies: Intercultural lessons from Harry Potter. *Language and Intercultural Communication* 3 (1), 6–19.

Phipps, A. (2006) *Learning the Arts of Linguistic Survival.* Clevedon: Multilingual Matters.

Phipps, A. and Gonzalez, M. (2004) *Modern Languages. Learning & Teaching in an Intercultural Field.* London: Sage.

Piltz, A. (1981) *The World of Medieval Learning.* Oxford: Basil Blackwell.

Plato (1956) *Protagoras and Meno.* London: The Penguin Classics.

Plato (1961) *Collected Dialogues.* E. Hamilton and H. Cairns (eds) Princeton: Princeton University Press.

Plato (1973) *Theaetetus.* Oxford: Clarendon Press.

Polanyi, M. (1966) *The Tacit Dimension.* New York, NY: Doubleday.

Pratt, M.L. (1992) *Imperial Eyes. Travel Writing and Transculturation.* London: Routledge.

Putnam, R. (1995) Bowling alone: America's declining social capital. *Journal of Democracy* 6 (1), 65–78.

Quirk, R. and Widdowson, H. (eds) (1985) *English in the World. Teaching and Learning the Languages and the Literatures.* Cambridge: Cambridge University Press.

Reddy, M.J. (1979) The conduit metaphor – A case of conflict in our language about language. In A. Ortony (ed.) *Metaphor and Thought.* Cambridge: Cambridge University Press.

Risager, K. (2006) *Language and Culture: Global Flows and Local Complexity.* Clevedon: Multilingual Matters.

Risager, K. (2007) *Language and Culture Pedagogy: From a National to a Transnational Paradigm.* Clevedon: Multilingual Matters.

Robinson, R. (1953) *Plato's Earlier Dialectic.* Oxford: Clarendon Press.

Rorty, R. (1979) *Philosophy and the Mirror of Nature.* Princeton, NJ: Princeton University Press.

Rorty, R. (1989) *Contingency, Irony, and Solidarity.* Cambridge: Cambridge University Press.

Rose, N. (1989) *Governing the Soul: The Shaping of the Private Self.* London: Routledge.

Rose, N. (1999) *Powers of Freedom: Reframing Political Thought.* Cambridge: Cambridge University Press.

Russell, B. (1918) The philosophy of logical atomism. In D. Pears (ed.) *The Philosophy of Logical Atomism.* IL: La Salle. London: Allen and Unwin.

Russell, D. (1991) *Writing in the Academic Disciplines, 1870–1990. A Curricular History.* Carbondale, IL: Southern Illinois Press.

Said, E.W. (2003) *Orientalism.* London: Penguin.

Samovar, L. and Porter, R. (eds) (1994) *Intercultural Communication: A Reader.* Belmont, CA: Wadsworth.

Santos, T. (1992) Ideology in composition: L1 and ESL. *Journal of Second Language Writing* 1 (1), 1–15.

Savignon, S.J. (2007) Beyond communicative language teaching: What's ahead? *Journal of Pragmatics* 39, 207–220.

Schon, D.A. (1991) *The Reflective Practitioner: How Professionals Think in Action.* Aldershot: Avebury.

Schon, D.A. (1987) *Educating the Reflective Practitioner: Toward a New Design for Teaching and Learning in the Professions.* San Francisco: Jossey-Bass.

Scollon, R. and Scollon, S.W. (1981) *Narrative, Literacy and Face in Interethnic Communication.* Norwood, NJ: Ablex.

Scollon, R. and Scollon, S.W. (1994) Face parameters in East–West discourse. In S. Ting-Toomey (ed.) *The Challenge of Facework: Crosscultural and Interpersonal Issues.* New York, NY: State University of New York Press.

Scollon, R. and Scollon, S.W. (1995) *Intercultural Communication.* Oxford: Blackwell.

Scollon, S.W. (1999) Not to waste words or students: Confucian and Socratic discourse in the tertiary classroom. In E. Hinkel (ed.) *Culture in Second Language Teaching and Learning.* Cambridge: Cambridge University Press.

Scott, M. (2003) Proofreading or what you will. *Learning Matters.* Institute of Education, University of London, Newsletter, 12, 7–8.

Scott, P. (1995) *The Meanings of Mass Higher Education.* Buckingham: SRHE/Open University Press.

Seidlhofer, B. (2002) Habeas corpus and divide et impera: 'Global English' and applied linguistics. In K.S. Miller and P. Thompson (eds) *Unity and Diversity in Language Use.* London: British Association for Applied Linguistics in association with Continuum.

Shapin, S. (1984) Pump and circumstance: Robert Boyle's literary technology. *Social Studies of Science* 14, 481–520.

Shapiro, M. (1997) Bowling blind: Post-liberal civil society and the worlds of neo-Tocquevillean social theory. *Theory and Event* 1 (1).

Silverman, K. (1983) *The Subject of Semiotics.* Oxford: Oxford University Press.

Singleton, J. (1991) The spirit of gambaru. In B. Finkelstein, A. Imamura and J. Tobin (eds) *Transcending Stereotypes: Discovering Japanese Culture and Education.* Yarmouth, ME: Intercultural Press.

Smith, L.E. (1987) *Discourse Across Cultures: Strategies in World Englishes*. London: Prentice-Hall.

Smith, R.J. (1983) *Japanese Society: Tradition, Self and the Social Order*. Cambridge: Cambridge University Press.

Sovic, S. (2008) *Creative Learning in Practice*. University of the Arts, London: Centre for Excellence in Teaching and Learning.

Spencer-Oatey, H. (ed.) (2000) *Culturally Speaking: Managing Rapport through Talk across Cultures*. New York, NY: Continuum.

Spencer-Oatey, H. (1996) Reconsidering power and distance. *Journal of Pragmatics*, 26, 1–24.

Sprat, T. (1958 [1667]) *History of the Royal Society*. Saint Louis, MO: Washington University Studies.

Steiner, G. (1961) The retreat from the word. *Language and Silence: Essays 1958–66*. London: Faber & Faber.

Street, B. (1993) Culture is a verb: Anthropological aspects of language and cultural process. In D. Graddol, L. Thompson and M. Byram (eds) *Language and Culture*. Clevedon: British Association for Applied Linguistics in association with Multilingual Matters.

Street, B.V. (1984) *Literacy in Theory and Practice*. Cambridge: Cambridge University Press.

Strenski, E. (1988) Writing across the curriculum at research universities. In S.H. McLeod (ed.) *Strengthening Programs for Writing across the Curriculum*. San Francisco, CA: Jossey Bass.

Swales, J. (1985) *Episodes in ESP*. Oxford: Pergamon Institute of English.

Swales, J. (1990) *Genre Analysis: English in Academic and Research Settings*. Cambridge: Cambridge University Press.

Swift, J. (1957) *Proposal for Correcting the English Tongue Polite Conversation*, etc. Oxford: Blackwell.

Tannen, D. (1985) Silence: Anything but. In M. Saville-Troike and D. Tannen (eds) *Perspectives on Silence*. Norwood, NJ: Ablex.

Tannen, D. (1998) *The Argument Culture: Moving from Debate to Dialogue*. New York, NY: Ballantine.

Tapper, T. and Palfreyman, D. (2000) *Oxford and the Decline of the Collegiate Tradition*. London: Woburn.

Tarnas, R. (1991) *The Passion of the Western Mind*. New York, NY: Ballantine Books.

Thaiss, C. and Zawacki, T.M. (eds) (2002) *Engaged Writers Dynamic Disciplines*. Portsmouth, NH: Boynton/Cook.

Thomas, J. (1983) Cross-cultural pragmatic failure. *Applied Linguistics* 4, 91–112.

Thomas, J. (1995) *Meaning in Interaction. An Introduction to Pragmatics*. London: Longman.

Thompson, P. (1999) Exploring the contexts of writing: interviews with PhD supervisors. In P. Thompson (ed.) *Academic Writing Development in Higher Education: Perspectives, Explorations and Approaches*. Reading, MA: Centre for Applied Language Studies, University of Reading.

Thonus, T. (1999) Dominance in academic writing tutorials: Gender, language proficiency, and the offering of suggestions. *Discourse and Society* 10 (2), 225–248.

Threadgold, T. (1997) *Feminist Poetics*. London: Routledge.

Ting-Toomey, S. (ed.) (1994) *The Challenge of Facework: Crosscultural and Interpersonal Issues*. New York, NY: University of New York Press.

Tocqueville, A. d. (1969) *Democracy in America*. Garden City, NY: Anchor.
Toolan, M. (1997) What is critical discourse analysis and why are people saying such terrible things about it? *Language and Literature* 6 (2), 83–103.
Trow, M. (2005) Reflections on the transition from elite to mass to universal access: Forms and phases of higher education in modern societies since WWII. In P. Altbach (ed.) *International Handbook of Higher Education*. Norwell, MA: Kluwer.
Tudor, A. (1999) *Decoding Culture*. London: Sage.
Tudor, I. (2001) *The Dynamics of the Language Classroom*. Cambridge: Cambridge University Press.
Turner, J. (1992) *IATEFL Annual Conference Report*. Cardiff: IATEFL.
Turner, J. (1996) Cultural values in genre skills: The case of the fine art tutorial. In M. Hewings and A. Dudley-Evans (eds) *Evaluation and Course Design in EAP*. London: Prentice-Hall Macmillan in association with The British Council.
Turner, J. (1999a) Academic literacy and the discourse of transparency. In C. Jones, J. Turner and B. Street (eds) *Students Writing in the University: Cultural and Epistemological Issues*. Amsterdam: John Benjamins.
Turner, J. (1999b) Academic writing development in higher education: Changing the discourse. In P. Thompson (ed.) *Academic Writing Development in Higher Education: Perspectives, Explorations and Approaches*. Reading, MA: Centre for Applied Language Studies, University of Reading.
Turner, J. (1999c) Problematising the language problem. In H. Bool and P. Luford (eds) *Academic Standards and Expectations. The Role of EAP*. Nottingham: Nottingham University Press.
Turner, J. (2001) Finding out or following through: Tropes of learning in cross-cultural perspective. In M.P. David Killick and A. Phipps (eds), *Poetics and Praxis of Languages and Intercultural Communication*. Glasgow: University of Glasgow, French and German Publications.
Turner, J. (2003) Writing a PhD in the contemporary humanities. *Hong Kong Journal of Applied Linguistics* 8 (2), 4–53.
Turner, J. (2004) Language as academic purpose. *Journal of English for Academic Purposes* 3 (2), 95–109.
Turner, J. and Hiraga, M.K. (1996) Elaborating elaboration in academic tutorials: Changing cultural assumptions. In H. Coleman and L. Cameron (eds) *Change and Language*. Clevedon: British Association for Applied Linguistics in association with Multilingual Matters Ltd.
Turner, J. and Hiraga, M.K. (2003) Misunderstanding teaching and learning. In J. House, G. Kasper and S. Ross (eds) *Misunderstanding in Social Life. Discourse Approaches to Problematic Talk*. London: Longman.
Utley, A. (1998) It's official: Grammar's gone downhill. *Times Higher Education Supplement*, 13th February 1998, London.
Valdes, J.M. (ed.) (1986) *Culture Bound. Bridging the Cultural Gap in Language Teaching*. Cambridge: Cambridge University Press.
van Peer, W. (1990) Writing as an institutional practice. In W. Nash (ed.) *The Writing Scholar. Studies in Academic Discourse*. Newbury Park: Sage.
Venn, C. (1984) The subject of psychology. In J. Henriques, W. Hollway, C. Urwin, C. Venn and V. Walkerdine (Eds) *Changing the Subject*. New York, NY: Methuen.
Venn, C. (2000) *Occidentalism. Modernity and Subjectivity*. London: Sage.
Voloshinov, V.N. (1973) *Marxism and the Philosophy of Language*. New York, NY: Seminar Press.

Wallace, M.J. (1991) *Training Foreign Language Teachers: A Reflective Approach.* Cambridge: Cambridge University Press.

Watkins, D. and Biggs, J. (eds) (2005) *The Chinese Learner: Cultural, Psychological and Contextual Influences.* Comparative Education Research Centre. University of Hong Kong and The Australian Council for Educational Research Ltd, Hong Kong.

Watt, I. (2000) *The Rise of the Novel.* London: Pimlico.

Weedon, C. (1987) *Feminist Practice and Poststructuralist Theory.* Oxford: Blackwell.

Whitehead, A.N. (1979 [1929]) *Process and Reality.* New York: Free Press.

Widdowson, H. (1995) Discourse analysis: A critical view. *Language and Literature* 4 (3), 157–172.

Widdowson, H. (1996) Reply to Fairclough: Discourse and interpretation: Conjecture and refutations. *Language and Literature* 5 (1), 57–70.

Widdowson, H. (1997) EIL, ESL, EFL: Global issues and local interests. *World Englishes* 16 (1), 135–146.

Wierzbicka, A. (1991a) *Cross-Cultural Pragmatics. The Semantics of Human Interaction.* Berlin: Mouton de Gruyter.

Wierzbicka, A. (1991b) Japanese key words and core cultural values. *Language in Society* 20 (3), 333–386.

Wilkins, J. (1968 [1668]) *Essay towards a Real Character and a Philosophical Language.* London: Thoemmes Continuum.

Williams, J.M. (1989) *Style: Ten Lessons in Clarity and Grace.* Glenview, IL: Scott.

Yoo, I. (2008) English for Korean postgraduate engineering students in the Global Academic Community: Perceptions of the importance of English, skills-based needs and sociocultural behaviours. Unpublished PhD thesis, Faculty of Culture and Pedagogy Institute of Education, University of London.

Young, L. (1994) *Crosstalk and Culture in Sino-American Communication.* Cambridge: Cambridge University Press.

Young, R. (1990) *White Mythologies. Writing History and the West.* London: Routledge.

Young, R. (1996) *Intercultural Communication Pragmatics, Genealogy, Deconstruction.* Clevedon: Multilingual Matters.

Yum, J.O. (1994) The impact of Confucianism on interpersonal relationships and communication patterns in East Asia. In L. Samovar and R.E. Porter (eds) *Intercultural Communication: A Reader.* Belmont, CA: Wadsworth.

Zamel, V. (1997) Toward a model of transculturation. *TESOL Quarterly* 31 (2), 341–353 (The Forum).

Zamel, V. and Spack, R. (eds) (1998) *Negotiating Academic Literacies. Teaching and Learning across Languages and Cultures.* Mahwah, NJ: Lawrence Erlbaum Associates.

Zylinska, J. (2005) *The Ethics of Cultural Studies.* London: Continuum.